K-Pop

K-Pop

POPULAR MUSIC, CULTURAL AMNESIA, AND
ECONOMIC INNOVATION IN SOUTH KOREA

John Lie

UNIVERSITY OF CALIFORNIA PRESS

University of California Press, one of the most distinguished university presses in the United States, enriches lives around the world by advancing scholarship in the humanities, social sciences, and natural sciences. Its activities are supported by the UC Press Foundation and by philanthropic contributions from individuals and institutions. For more information, visit www.ucpress.edu.

University of California Press
Oakland, California

Library of Congress Cataloging-in-Publication Data

Lie, John, author.
    K-pop : popular music, cultural amnesia, and economic innovation in South Korea / John Lie.
        pages   cm
    Includes bibliographical references and index.
    ISBN 978-0-520-28311-4 (cloth : alk. paper)
    ISBN 978-0-520-28312-1 (pbk. : alk. paper)
    ISBN 978-0-520-95894-4 (ebook)
    1. Popular music—Korea (South)—History and criticism.   2. Popular music—Economic aspects—Korea (South).   3. Popular music—Social aspects—Korea (South).   4. Music and globalization—Korea (South). I. Title.
    ML3502.K6L54   2015
    781.63095195—dc23   2014023191

24   23   22   21   20   19   18   17   16   15
10   9   8   7   6   5   4   3   2   1

CONTENTS

PRELUDE

In the spring of 2012, a sabbatical year that I was spending primarily in Paris, I found myself on a long trudge through a windswept Berlin suburb, with pedestrians few and far between and my sense of solitude accentuated by the unusually cold, dark day. I sought respite in a Vietnamese restaurant—empty, I saw upon entering—and ordered. As I began to eat, the young waitress continually eyed me, her only customer. After a few minutes, she reapproached my table and started firing questions at me. The point of this battery was to ascertain my national origins.

Reticent though I am, I let out that I am of Korean ancestry, and this revelation appeared to delight her. She erupted in an extended colloquy on her love for South Korean popular culture in general, and for that country's contemporary popular music known as K-pop, in particular. She told me that her friends gathered regularly to perform contemporary K-pop songs. Then she asked my opinion of how precise and authentic (*echt*) her K-pop dance step was.

Given what was then my own scant exposure to K-pop, all I could do was offer a halfhearted smile of approval for her vigorous routine and then turn back to my no longer solitary repast. But the intraprandial entertainment had also presented much food for thought. At the time, all I could think of was a transposition of Samuel Johnson's sexist jibe: South Korean popular music sung outside South Korea is like "a dog's walking on his hinder legs. It is not done well; but you are surprised to find it done at all."[1]

When I returned to Paris, an acquaintance invited me to a K-pop concert, supposedly featuring some of the genre's biggest stars. I would have preferred to protect my declining aural faculty, but the fleeting memory of the impromptu performance in Berlin piqued my interest. I was expecting the venue to be replete with ethnic or expatriate Koreans, and so I was dumb-founded to see that the vast majority of the youthful audience was white. There were some black concertgoers, but not many were Asian French or Asian citizens of other parts of Europe.[2] The MCs intoned their introductions, as did the K-pop stars their greetings, in Korean, a language that surely very few in the audience understood. But these young Europeans didn't seem to mind. They were every bit as ecstatic as the audiences I recalled from my time at rock and punk concerts in Boston and elsewhere during the century just past. As earworm-inducing refrains, catchy melodic lines, and propulsive rhythms adjoined precise choreography, professional sheen, attractive stars, and trendy costumes, the parade of K-pop acts was interrupted by fans who bestrode the stage to cover their favorite song-and-dance routines, lip-synching and swinging their hips to the delight of everyone present. On the metro ride home, dazed and confused, I dodged drunks and sought to make sense of the spectacle.

A few days later I went to Tokyo and was greeted by billboards announcing a new album by the South Korean group Girls' Generation (Sonyŏ Sidae in Korean; Shōjo Jidai in Japanese). I walked by a small shop and looked inside to see the middle-aged proprietor swaying her behind to a TV broadcast of the "hip dance" propagated by the South Korean pop group KARA. I also discovered that three South Korean groups had participated in the previous year's *Kōhaku Utagassen* (the annual "red-white singing contest," broadcast on New Year's Eve), a telecast that continues to capture a large audience and features many of the most popular singers in Japan.

From Tokyo I caught a flight to South Korea, where I was scheduled to deliver several lectures. My companions on the flight were a throng of middle-aged Japanese women whose topics of conversation included not just their planned shopping spree in Seoul, and their upcoming pilgrimage to iconic sites of South Korean television dramas, but also K-pop. I gave my lectures in Seoul, and by now I was no longer surprised by the large number of non-Korean students, not just from neighboring Asian countries but also from Europe and Latin America, who expressed enthusiasm for South Korean popular music.

I saw that K-pop had become a global phenomenon. But a scan of the media, print as well as social, soon revealed that my discovery was far from exclusive. Jon Caramanica, writing in the *New York Times* after attending a K-pop concert at Madison Square Garden, said that "any American reality-TV talent show or major-label A&R department worth its salt would be thrilled to have discovered" any of the K-pop acts he had seen, and he described the K-pop environment as one "of relentless newness, both in participants and in style."[3] Indeed, reports of K-pop fandom flooded my laptop screen from all over the world, from Germany and France, from Thailand and Peru, suggesting the possibility of a global K-pop in particular and of a globalized (as opposed to an Americanized or Anglo-Americanized) popular music in general.[4] The first decade of the twenty-first century had brought the Korean Wave, an inundation of South Korean soap opera that covered much of Asia. Now K-pop (some dubbed it Korean Wave 2.0) was the visible foam and froth of South Korean popular culture, washing ashore across Asia, the Pacific, and beyond.[5]

Meanwhile, in South Korea itself, governmental bureaucrats and serious scholars, spurred by external enchantment with the country's popular culture, expressed their appreciation by showering financial support and academic attention on the nation's newfangled soft power. The conservative Lee Myung-bak regime, without desisting from its orgy of censorship, couldn't muster enough encomia when it came to K-pop. President Lee addressed the nation by radio after a trip to Turkey, gushing that K-pop was "loved by young Turkish people" and citing such South Korean stars as the K-pop group JYJ as "a major asset to the future of [South] Korean culture."[6] At an academic seminar, a distinguished historian argued passionately that the reason K-pop is often performed not by individuals but by groups has something to do with Korean tradition, or "national essence" (*kuksu*), a term popular in pre–World War II Japanese fascist (organicist) thought. And in 2012, as the song and video "Gangnam Style" reverberated around the world, the mayor of Gangnam, a swank area south of the Han River in Seoul, was moved to speak. "Psy," the mayor declared, referring to the song's performer, "appeared right when we were ready to take Gangnam global. . . . We already believe we are on par with Manhattan or Beverly Hills in every way."[7]

All bluster and hyperbole aside, descriptions and explanations of K-pop do tend to rely disproportionately on the ready-made vocabulary of Korean tradition, Confucian culture, and other mythemes of contemporary South Korea. And I don't think that's right—which is the point of this book.

But *caveat lector:* the book is not a glorified fanzine for readers who would like to know more about their favorite K-pop stars and songs; the imprimatur of a university press should be enough to dispel such a notion.[8] Neither is it a treatise on musicology, poetics, or aesthetics; I regret that I did not include musical examples, but, as the sensible Roger Sessions has said, "I can imagine no duller, and certainly no more laborious, reading than someone else's technical analysis of a piece of music."[9] I have also eschewed extended analyses of lyrics: the words of popular songs do function at times as something of a poetry of everyday life, but it would be misleading to regard them as the main attraction of popular music. Although I touch on various topics and disciplines—including sartorial, corporeal, and televisual presentations—my main intention is to raise and answer three questions (addressed in chapter 1, the interlude, and chapter 2, respectively).

First, where did K-pop come from? This question takes us onto the terrain of the past—traditional Korean music, colonial and postcolonial Japanese influence, and the immediate and growing impact of US popular music. I argue that K-pop constitutes a break not just with the traditional Korean music of the past but also with earlier Korean popular music (indeed, the very history of Korean popular music is constituted by a series of such rifts).

Second, what does K-pop say about South Korea? Just as one might endeavor to see a world in a grain of sand, the phenomenon of K-pop invites insights into contemporary South Korea itself. Given the topic, perhaps it would be more appropriate to use an auditory metaphor, and to say that listening to K-pop is a way of auscultating the South Korean body politic. I stress in particular the etiology and symptoms of cultural amnesia.

Third, how did K-pop become popular? In addition to K-pop's aesthetic appeal, I analyze the rise of K-pop—the confluence of social change, economic culture, and industrial transformation that sustains the export imperative—and its production and consumption inside and outside South Korea.

There is something mildly scandalous about an aging academic—one who is, moreover, something of a *passéiste*—studying youth culture. After all, my previous publication on music was on György Ligeti's *Le Grand Macabre*. Between potential accusations that I am suffering from Peter Pan syndrome, if not from the Lolita complex, my intergenerational gaze across the Pacific may also be found a bit too nasty, brutish, and short. So let me forestall the usual academic prejudice by invoking Gershom Scholem. Accused of wasting his erudition on a bit of nonsense called the kabbalah (itself recently made famous by one of its adherents, the aging rock star Madonna), Scholem is reported to have replied that nonsense may be nonsense, but the study of nonsense is still scholarship.[10] More to the point, popular music—precisely because of its ephemerality, and even its ethnocentrism—is very good to think with. What better subject than popular music for a sustained meditation on the meaning of culture and globalization? To paraphrase Boethius, the surest path to knowledge is through the ear.

Perhaps the most appropriate way to analyze and comment on a particular genre is to practice and extend that genre, but how many people really want to see me perform in a music video? Another possibility may be (to riff on Walter Benjamin) that a compilation of music videos would constitute the ideal "book" on K-pop. Be that as it may, there is always a place for analysis and theory. Popular music is an essential experience of everyday life, susceptible to entropy as people forget its once pervasive and even subversive pleasures and, more bafflingly, lose all memory of its existence. Surely one role of writing about popular music is to rescue it from oblivion, and from unwitting repetition.[11] The proof of this proposition will be, presumably, in the reading of this book. In any case, because I have learned much of what little I know from books, it is appropriate for me to put what I have learned about this subject into yet another book.

A word about nontraditional sources. One of the great benefits of the digital age is that so many sources are available, openly and online. As a lifelong bibliophile, one whose intellectual instincts lean toward literal acceptance of Mallarmé's maxim that "the world is made to end in a beautiful book," I confess that my foray into extrabibliographical sources was punctuated by pangs of epistemic uncertainty and beset by methodological quagmires.[12] At the same time, and much as I remain wedded to print, I could not have written this book without the Internet in general and YouTube and its ilk in particular. As derided as YouTube and *Wikipedia* may be in some academic circles, I can only suggest that others would benefit as I have from these and other nontraditional sources of information. The paucity of documentation in the area of popular music makes conditions ripe for copycat fabrications in the manner of William Boyd's biography of Nat Tate, but the recent recovery of long-lost images and recordings makes for a marvelous experience of turning on and tuning in.[13] To give just one example, Han Myŏng-suk's explosive 1961 hit "Nooran shassŭ ŭi sanai" (The boy in the yellow shirt) was all but impossible to locate until recently. This song's implausibly infectious music and its indelible lyric refrain—*ŏtchŏnji*, signifying something between "somehow" and "of course," but in the context suggesting something like "I'm not sure why, but I seem to like him"—captivated a generation of South Korean as well as Japanese listeners in addition to fans from other countries. How many academic books have that sort of staying power? Yet national and university libraries have long disdained popular culture and its ephemera, and its viscera have been available only in rare repositories of collectors or in the marginal markets of secondhand dealers. (When Lee Myung-bak of South Korea was mayor of Seoul, his signal achievement was to excavate the buried Ch'ŏnggyech'ŏn River and transform it into an urban stream and stroll area, but in so doing he also wiped out the concatenation of used-book sellers and secondhand music dealers, apparently consigning yet another slice of Korean history to oblivion for the second and final time; the first time had been when he paved over the river and its embankment during the construction boom in the 1960s and 1970s.) Although many singers have covered "Nooran shassŭ ŭi sanai," among them the French chanteuse Yvette Giraud, I had never heard Han Myŏng-suk's original until the day I found it—there she was!—on YouTube.[14]

And a few final notes before I embark on the main movements of the book. I have used the McCune-Reischauer system of transcribing Korean characters into English, save for common words and names, such as Gangnam (rather than Kangnam) and Park Chung-hee (rather than Pak Chŏng-hŭi); and, as the Park/Pak example suggests, I have ordered East Asian names so that surnames come first. I have also eschewed the scientific style of citation because it perturbs narrative flow. When sources are cited in the notes, full bibliographical information is given for each work the first time it is cited in each section of the book, with short-form citations used thereafter; there is no separate bibliography (surely otiose in the age of digital databases). As for links to online sources, they were current and working as of December 2013. All translations are mine unless otherwise specified.

ONE

How Did We Get Here?

WHEN I WAS FOURTEEN, after a long absence from South Korea, I spent the summer in Seoul. It was 1974. Soon enough, I was bored out of my mind—I had rapidly read the books I had brought with me, and there wasn't much of interest on television or in movie theaters.[1] My maternal uncle took pity on me. He shepherded me through the hot spots of Myŏng-dong, at that time easily the most fashionable district in the country, the Gangnam of its day, when Gangnam itself was largely a swamp. But Myŏng-dong's narrow streets hardly screamed fashion or sophistication. The principal respite from dodging aggressive peddlers and ambling among uniformed students was a repast at some hole-in-the-wall eatery, or a visit to a depressingly dark tea-house that had dour servers to boot. I was momentarily amused by ice cream served on dry ice at the Savoy Hotel, but my smile lasted about as long as that artificial fog.

Somehow my uncle figured out that I was interested in music, and he took me to a variety of age-inappropriate shows. If miasmic memory serves, I saw Patti Kim, then the queen of South Korean popular music, and the crooner Kim Chŏng-ho, among others. We even went to the legendary venue C'est Si Bon. My uncle proudly pointed out that Patti Kim had performed in the United States.

Some of my relatives in Seoul lent me their recordings of the latest and best South Korean popular music. I recall listlessly attending to "P'yonji" (Letter) by the laid-back folk duo Ŏniŏnsŭ (Onions). It's not that these records were risible or otherwise objectionable, but I could only fidget my way through them. After all, I might as well have come from the dark side of the moon: having belatedly discovered *Led Zeppelin IV* (1971), I had been ascending that band's legendary stairway, often to the tunes of The Who and

Pink Floyd as well. The soft, slow South Korean serenades gave me hives, just as my kind of music gave my cousins tinnitus. (When I played my urbane uncle a cassette of the sort of music I claimed to like, he commented that he might appreciate it more with the right pharmaceutical accompaniment.)

Now, almost four decades later, nearly everything has changed, as a recent visit to South Korea confirmed. I saw that Myŏng-dong's massive face-lift had left behind very little of that district's fabled (some say sordid) past. The Savoy Hotel still stood, refurbished to be sure, but was no longer fancy or fashionable, its past glory having long since evaporated like so much dry ice. School uniforms and standard haircuts had been superseded by blue jeans and short skirts and a wide array of hairstyles and hair colors. Glowing cafés had replaced the district's dim teahouses—the servers smiled now—and fast-food chains jostled with upscale restaurants. But amidst this welter of change, itself a cliché of South Korean life, there were few things more striking than the transformation of the soundscape.[2] Upbeat tempi and bright timbres had silenced the melancholic melodies that used to waft, along with clouds of cigarette smoke, through Myŏng-dong's teahouses and watering holes. But the most vibrant difference was the sound of American-style popular music, once strange to South Korean ears and now dominating television shows and, it seemed, every other screen. And now it was no longer my uncle or my cousins but non-Koreans who apprised me of the ins and outs of South Korean popular music, showing me the latest music videos on their phones or tablets.

Forty years ago, an astute analyst might have anticipated the rise of South Korea as a manufacturing power, but I doubt that anyone would or could have had any inkling of the age of K-pop. Girls' Generation and Super Junior, SHINee and 2NE1, SISTAR and T-ara, 2PM and 2AM, BIGBANG and BEAST (B2ST)—these artists have become not just stars in South Korea but pan-Asian, even global sensations. The viral explosion of "Gangnam Style" in 2012 refuted the canard that South Korean popular music would never make it in the United States.[3] And if imitation is the sincerest gauge of popularity, then the proliferation of copycat videos suggests that something is indeed afoot.

So what happened? Nothing comes out of nowhere. A series of breaks does separate the past of Korean music from the K-pop present, and of course our biographies and histories are replete with shifts and changes. But K-pop represents something else—nothing short of a revolution, and by no means the only one in the shifting soundscape of the Korean peninsula.

The future, as we know, is notoriously difficult to envision. What may be even more challenging is to see the past, that proverbial foreign country, as it really was. In the following section, to make sense of the K-pop phenomenon, I explore the Korean musical past, not in order to endow K-pop with a proud genealogy but rather to reveal its birth as both belated and unrelated to the lineage of Korean music.

TRADITIONAL KOREAN MUSIC

The first and most consequential revolution in the modern Korean sound- ✓ scape is the decline of traditional Korean music.[4] "Traditional" is a category of convenience that inconveniently renders diversity into homogeneity, but I follow the dominant South Korean practice of labeling traditional Korean music as *kugak* (national music): the world of sound before the introduction of Western music toward the end of the Chosŏn dynasty (1392–1897).[5]

Inhabitants of the Korean peninsula crafted a distinctive musical universe in the course of the first millennium: *kayagŭm* and *kŏmun'go*, both zitherlike instruments, already appear in the oldest extant text, *Samguk sagi* (History of the three kingdoms, 1145).[6] Like archaeological accretions, disparate influences interacted to generate an interrelated ensemble of genres. The monarchy and the landed elite (*yangban*) employed music for state rituals and personal cultivation (and enjoyment).[7] Genre followed function; distinct musical styles existed for ancestral worship, banquets, military processions, and so on. *Chŏngak* (literally, "orthodox music") was the overarching category for Confucian, aristocratic music. Generations of the literati incorporated musical education as part of the essential *yangban* curriculum.[8] Art music was aristocratic music, which in turn was the sound of power. In contrast to the Apollonian virtues of *chŏngak* and elite music in general, Dionysian characteristics—expressive and emotional rather than formal and cerebral— dominated *minsok ŭmak* (people's music) or *nongak* (farmers' music).[9] Ritualized drumming and dancing marked seasonal festivals—most notably the Korean drumming music *p'ungmul*—and there were folk tunes (*minyo*).[10] *P'ansori*, which crystallized in the seventeenth century, featured a solo singer reciting an extended oral narrative accompanied by a drummer.[11] It gained respectability over time and presides as perhaps the exemplary traditional music in contemporary South Korea.[12] Itinerant troupes toured the peninsula presenting masques, acrobatics, and dance and musical performances.

Kwangdae (itinerant entertainers), as members of *paekchŏng* (the outcasts), were at the bottom of the Confucian social hierarchy, and the low regard in which they were held, not only for what they performed but also for who they were, would persist well into the post-Liberation period.[13]

It would be easy to exaggerate the distinction between the two main modalities of music. Whereas court musicians made refinements to musical instruments and developed elaborate notations (*chŏngganbo*), the nonelites played received instruments without any systematic musicological apparatus. From a musical standpoint, it is possible to suggest some tendencies and tentative generalizations: elite music featured slower tempi, longer tones, regular rhythms, and syllabic notes in contrast to the faster, shorter, irregular, melismatic characteristics of its populist counterparts. Yet these sharp contrasts obscure exception after exception. Furthermore, the binary distinction between elite and popular reduces the considerable complexity within each category as well as the interactions between them. *Kasa,* a genre of vocal music, was an interstitial form, and *p'ansori* encroached on the world of elite music. *Kisaeng* (courtesans) performed popular genres for the court and the literati.[14] Different religious and spiritual traditions, including Buddhist and shamanist, engaged in musical practices distinct from both *chŏngak* and *minyo* and traversed the social divides of Korean life.[15] Regional diversity remained stubbornly strong.[16] The distinctions between elite and people's music rested less on strictly musical divergences than on the social positions of listeners and performers, positions embedded in the rigid social hierarchy of Chosŏn Korea. Given our distance from the Chosŏn soundscape, it is easy to accentuate not only the correspondence between the social organization of status and that of sound but also the functional role of music in social life.[17] Yet the sociological emphasis, much as we wish to avoid the besetting sins of reductionism and determinism, would be far preferable to an emphasis on ethnocentric musicology.

The social organization of sound in Chosŏn Korea is incommensurable with that of European classical music.[18] In contrast to the European Romantic conception of autonomous or absolute music, traditional Korean music, whether music for state rituals or *nongak* for agrarian festivals, was inextricably intertwined with its sociocultural contexts.[19] The semisacred practice of listening to European classical music in silent contemplation, the performance of a musical composition without an accompanying narration or dance, the idea of autonomous music disembedded from context—all these practices and notions are alien to *kugak.*[20] Korean (and Asian) music is said to employ the pentatonic scale, but it is more accurate to speak of modes (*cho*), which incorporate not merely a set of pitches and intervals but also performance practices and melodic gestures.[21] *Changdan* (long-short) beats constitute the standard rhythm in traditional Korean music, although the idea of rhythm in *kugak* not only encompasses beats but also encapsulates tempi and dynamics in which rubato rules.[22] The philosophical valorization of harmony notwithstanding, the linear system is nonharmonic: variable pitch accompanies free transposition.[23] Hence, to those trained in European classical music, traditional Korean music appears unstructured. In spite of sophisticated musical notations, even elite music is improvisatory—born, paradoxically, of rote learning.[24] Even the very concept of music, at least as it crystallized in modern Europe, poorly captures Chosŏn Korean sound culture.[25]

For contemporary listeners, Korean or non-Korean, the commonalities of *kugak* are readily apparent: even those who have never consciously listened to a single note of traditional Korean music believe that they can identify it. The reason is that *kugak* is a strange and alien aural universe for most contemporary South Koreans. The introduction of the Western soundscape revealed the shared soundscape of Chosŏn Korea and in turn spawned the enormous condescension of the Westernized present, which reduces the considerable diversity of traditional Korean music to a simple and residual category called *kugak*. Symptomatic of this problem is the fact that the South Korean term for "music," *ŭmak,* is basically synonymous with the term *yangak,* "Western music."[26] Confucian ritual music and the Confucian social order faded together, just as *nongak* disappeared with the decline of agrarian life. Traditional Korean music represents a strange soundscape for contemporary South Koreans, for whom rhythm and blues (R & B) and reggae, bel canto opera and piano sonatas, are integral parts of South Korean life. In contrast, *kugak* is an imaginary museum, and one rarely visited at that. The desire to showcase traditional and distinctive Korean culture to the outside world generates the intermittent demand for *kugak,* though it is performed just about as rarely as the Olympic Games take place.[27] To be sure, there are recurrent reports of the revival of *kugak. Minsok ŭmak* had long been consigned to oblivion in South Korea, but the people's (*minjung*) movement, which fueled the anti-government, pro-democracy politics of the 1970s and 1980s, revived it—especially in the form of *samul nori,* a derivative and stylized genre of *nongak*—precisely when people's music had been almost completely expunged from the countryside.[28] It constitutes something of a revenge of the people that the most popular genres of *kugak,* such as *p'ansori* and *sanjo* (scattered melodies), stem from demotic roots. Yet almost inevitably these genres are modernized to render *kugak* palatable to the contemporary musical competence and tastes of South Koreans steeped in the Western soundscape.[29] In contrast to Japan, where a refined upbringing has entailed instruction (almost exclusively for daughters) in traditional Japanese instruments, such as the koto, similarly aspiring South Korean parents have rarely enjoined their daughters to take up traditional Korean instruments but instead have steered them toward Western piano and violin. For almost all South Koreans, comprehending the beauty of a *kugak* performance—its tonal colors, its melodic intensity, its raspy articulation, and much more—is as elusive as apprehending the aesthetics of Venda songs or Gregorian chant.

INTRADA CON INTREPIDEZZA

If the post–World War II generation of East Asia scholars exaggerated the impact of the West, by seeing modern East Asian history as a series of responses to Western challenges, that generation's intellectual descendants in the early twenty-first century may well be underplaying the West's impact. The shock of the new rattled the very foundations of East Asian polities, leaving few stones unturned, or at least untouched. It was not just a matter of Western technology but also of the Western way of life, from political-economic institutions and vocabularies to sartorial modes and spiritual molds. The apotheosis of this trend can now be seen across East Asia: whatever the accents of local idiosyncrasy may be, who would deny that the lingua franca is English, that vestments are European, and that the usual style of accoutrement, whether in bags or in phones, is Western in inspiration if not in production? When East Asian businesspeople gather, they speak English, wear European suits, carry Western tools (laptops and phones, not abacuses and brushes), and drink Western beverages. And I should add that they almost always listen to Western or Western-inspired music: what used to be the strange European soundscape, at once seductive and repulsive, has become natural, obvious, and inescapable.[30]

Who was the first ethnic Korean to experience European music? When was European music—the diatonic scale or the piano—first aired on the Korean peninsula? We cannot be sure, but elements of the European musical world entered via Christian missionaries and their hymns, enrolling ethnic Korean converts into European musical culture. Certainly by the time of the 1885 US Protestant mission, Christian music had definitively arrived on the Korean peninsula.[31]

The late Chosŏn regime was resistant to non-Chinese influences, and vast expanses of the countryside remained impervious to any undertone of a massive Western march. External encroachment rode roughshod over the levee that had been erected against barbarian incursion. The 1876 Treaty of Kanghwa was merely the first in a series of unequal agreements that would ultimately undermine Chosŏn Korea. Japan, rapidly Westernizing, was the primary power over the Korean peninsula after Japan's military victories over two competing regional powers, China (1894–1895) and Russia (1904–1905). Beginning in 1905, Japan ruled the Korean polity as a protectorate, annexing it outright in 1910. Henceforth, Japan controlled the major levers of politics, economics, and culture. The general trend of colonial rule was assimilation, at once expunging things Korean and implanting things Japanese, from language to personal names, and the world of music was no exception. The crucial caveat, however, is that it was not traditional Japan that Japanese colonial rule institutionalized; instead, it was modern Japan, an amalgam of influences, though these were preponderantly Western in form and content.

In the world of elite music, Japan did not impose *gagaku* (the Japanese rendition of classical Chinese–influenced court music) but rather European art music.[32] And the imposition was hardly unilateral: in 1900, Korean royals hired Franz Eckert, a German, to form the Imperial Military Band, and a year later—even before Western brass bands arrived in Japan—a brass band of just that kind performed in Seoul.[33] Eckert, the composer of the Japanese national anthem, or at least of its harmony, also composed the first Korean national anthem.[34] It may seem curious that the Japanese and Korean elites, in the absence of explicit external pressure, would independently capitulate on an ostensibly cultural matter, and this is especially the case for Korean royalty, which remained resistant to non-Chinese influences. But music, especially Western military and ceremonial music, was perceived as part and parcel of Western military and technological might.[35] That is, the Japanese and Korean elites considered music as belonging more to cultural technology than to traditional culture. Already by the 1870s, Japanese educational bureaucrats had introduced Western music education into the Japanese archipelago.[36] Western choral music was not only a mark of modernization—useful for catching up with and, ultimately, overtaking the West—but also a means of shaping ethical, loyal subjects.[37] The musical gulf between the elite and the masses would be bridged, it was believed, by Western notes and measures. And when Japan colonized Korea, Japan also brought its educational curriculum, including Western music education. Organ playing and choral singing now became essential elements of Korean schooling.[38] Western music instruction was supplemented by the dissemination of Western folk tunes and children's songs.[39] In brief, the Korean and Japanese elites were united in embracing the music of the West—that technologically and (in a more ambivalent sense) socially superior power—and in so doing they neglected, even castigated, their received music. *Kugak,* in response, adapted to the Western culture of music. In the 1900s, for example, *p'ansori,* although it remained a distinct genre, gave rise to *ch'anggŭk* (choral theater), and thus to musical theater or opera.[40] The expanding aural hegemony of the West is the basso ostinato of the twentieth-century Northeast Asian soundscape.

Nevertheless, it would be a gross exaggeration to say that the Western music education insisted on and imposed by Japanese (and Korean) educational bureaucrats transformed every Korean (or Japanese) citizen into an aficionado of European classical music. Far from it—Western-style formal education remained largely the province of the affluent. And for at least half a century, two distinct musical cultures reigned in Japan and Korea: top-down, government-imposed Western music, and bottom-up, traditional and diverse native music. European music, whether in its simple articulation as a military march or its elaborated development as a bel canto aria, struck most Northeast Asian listeners, at least initially, as repulsive and bizarre, though for some it was beguiling and bewitching.[41] In any case, a new generation was instructed in the European soundscape, and when that generation came of age—a development that, coincidentally, was coeval with urbanization and the other social changes that we usually summarize with the term "modernization"—one precondition of Western-inflected popular music was achieved: there were now people who were attuned to the new soundscape, people who were acquainted with and acquiring a new musical competence.[42] Western-inflected popular music would thereafter supersede not only elite European music but also native music. To repeat, it is *kugak* that would become marginal on the Korean peninsula, as strange as European music had been to Koreans in the early twentieth century. What became normative was popular music.

ENTR'ACTE: THE RISE OF POPULAR MUSIC

What is popular music? The term "popular" almost always signifies the less prestigious in a series of binary distinctions: elite, high, or refined against mass, low, or vulgar.[43] Sure enough, a common Korean term for popular music is *taejung ŭmak* (mass music), which connotes nonelite, nonclassical, nonart music. Even in Europe, the division became sharply etched only in the course of the nineteenth century: consider Mozart's eager embrace of listeners' adulation against Schoenberg's disdain for the audience's approval—or, more accurately, for the audience itself.[44] The rise of serious, autonomous, and absolute art music occurred in tandem with the spread of popular music, which retained its role as entertainment and accompaniment to conversation, festivity, and dance. The mere idea that D. H. Lawrence should characterize dancing as "just making love to music" seems vulgar and even sacrilegious.[45] The sacred solemnity of contemporary performances of classical music, where a stray cell-phone ring pierces the silence and breaks concentration, stands in stark contrast to the casual proliferation of popular music, from consumption-inducing beats in shopping malls to the thumping sounds produced at concerts, not to mention the semiprivate sonic world afforded by headphones and ear buds.[46] The wide audience for popular music seems proof of that music's simplicity, ephemerality, and inferiority. Similarly, when a classical composition is widely aired today, its popularity seems to pollute it, rendering it a member of the unfortunate hybrid category of "pop classical" (just as a pop song's exalted status may transform it into an instance of "classic pop," and sometimes the other way around). The cult of absolute music and the artist has relegated "classical music" to an ever-receding circle of connoisseurs and cognoscenti; everything else—that is, popular music—has become "music" pure and simple.[47]

The rise of popular music is also inextricably intertwined with the industrialization and commercialization of music. If the mass printing of sheet music was crucial for the spread of Tin Pan Alley tunes—a genre that solidified many of the conventions of the popular song, such as its normative length (about three minutes),[48] its short narrative structure, and its simple chord progression—then the modern shape of popular music cannot be understood apart from progressive modes of technological reproducibility (the phonograph, the radio, the mp3 player) and their social settings (cafés, dance halls, concert venues).[49] Popular music's mode of production comprises new social relations and institutions (professional producers and promoters of music; professional musicians and composers) and a decisive shift in the material reality of production (including, most critically, the new technology of sound amplification and reproduction). For nonelite listeners, the rapid evolution of technology greatly expanded access to music. Popular music—with its sustained march into the realm of the private, from the phonograph and the portable radio to the Walkman and the iPod—triumphed as the quintessential expression of consumer society: of individuality and identity, the facilitator and companion of privacy and solitude. It is now almost impossible to imagine life without a musical surround that can be summoned at will; until the twentieth century, however, music was a rare treat for the vast majority of people.[50] Who could listen to music on demand before the phonograph? Very few: only the wealthy and the powerful (who could command a standing musical ensemble) or those who could perform themselves.[51] The twentieth century, at least in affluent areas, has brought a steady expansion of access to music, primarily through commerce. The ubiquity of popular music was born of music's ready reproducibility and accessibility. "Progress" is a problematic word, laden with value presuppositions and wishful projections, but no word is better suited to characterize the improvements in affordability and portability (if not always in sonic fidelity) that have come about since the emergence of popular music.[52]

The infrastructure that created the possibility of popular music is coeval with modern economic and cultural life; it is also an urban phenomenon. The capacity to reach a large population relatively quickly has been enhanced by the growth of cities, including the colonization of the night and the expansion of leisure.[53] It is not for nothing that nightclubs and (nocturnal) bars along with theatrical revues and movie theaters—all dark places, as if to heighten the aural sense—have been major loci of popular music's performance.[54] By the late nineteenth century in the United States (that true superpower in the culture of commerce, and in the commerce of culture), public amusements had already developed highly commercial and urban forms, with vaudeville, dance halls, and cabarets in what was, precisely, the period of Tin Pan Alley's prime.[55] Together, popular music and movies—the medium in which popular music developed, even during the so-called silent era—became the shock troops of modernity.[56]

Modern urban life not only enhanced music's consumption but also accelerated changes in musical fashions.[57] Planned obsolescence and intentional oblivion, if not the music business's definitive raison d'être, are nevertheless at its heart. Some songs establish themselves as standards, but most are doomed to disappear as listeners tire of particular hits and stars and, most devastatingly, as a new generation comes of age. Especially critical in the accelerating cycle of hitmaking are younger listeners, who not only adopt particular songs or genres as badges of distinction and identity but also possess the discretionary income that will allow them to express their preferences.[58] Thus it was that youth not only came to embody a major life stage (as in, for example, the new category of "teenager") but also became a significant sector in the economy of music's consumption.[59] In addition, a meaningful moment was marked by the possibility of expecting and achieving autonomy in listening: a teenager of the 1950s dropped a coin into a jukebox, and young people today download songs onto their phones, but either way, the device (jukebox or phone) and the song (recorded on a disc or compressed in a digital file) combine to express both technological culture and youth culture. And so young people, equipped with the wherewithal of consumption, forge an identity from a brand of popular music that marks them as separate from their parents and from the previous generation. Again, the shift is not just about individual singers and songs but also about styles and genres as well as about new formats (from LPs to cassettes to CDs to digital files) and technology (from sheet music to portable record players to mp3 players). The dialectic of the parent-child relationship spirals around the still point of musical preference, producing generational misunderstandings not unlike those depicted in Nathalie Sarraute's haunting portrayal of giddy youths and indignant adults.[60] For elders, new music is often incomprehensible. Here, for example, is the usually incisive journalist Andrew Kopkind on disco:

> Rock was "our music" [which was] riding a historical tide.... Disco in the seventies is in revolt against rock in the sixties. It is the antithesis of the "natural" look.... Disco is "unreal," artificial and exaggerated.... [It] is contrived and controlled.... Disco is not a natural phenomenon in any sense. It is part of a sophisticated, commercial, manipulated culture that is rooted exclusively in an urban environment.... What all this means is that a sizable chunk of capital in the entertainment industry is now in the hands of the disco elite.[61]

Similar complaints are found throughout the literature of popular-music criticism. In this struggle, as Gustav Mahler reputedly declared, "the younger generation is always right."[62] The urge to seize the moment valorizes the present and the new, contributing in turn to the devaluation of the past and the traditional, which in any case is suspicious precisely because of its association with parents and elders.[63] The perpetual modernity of the popular-music canon goes hand in hand with a constant forgetting of the past.[64] Youth's discretionary spending power and the constant transition of the generations ensure that popular music beats on, borne ceaselessly into the future.

Certain conditions, then, pave the way for popular music. The industrial-technological revolution and the urban consumer revolution (or the expansion in the number of people who can consume music, either in performance or by means of its technological reproducibility) constitute the sine qua non of popular music. By the mid-1920s, the rudiments and many of the essential preconditions of popular music were already present in Korea. Therefore, despite the oft-rehearsed claim (heard most commonly among ethnic Koreans themselves) that Korea was behind the West and Japan, at least in the realm of popular music that time lag was truncated.

THE COLONIAL PERIOD

Japanese colonial rule brought the backdrops and accoutrements, as well as the blessings and curses, of Western life. The late Chosŏn era was not without trickles and infusions of Western influence, often via Chinese and Japanese intermediaries, but the rising tide became irreversible in some parts of Seoul during the colonial period. From telegraphy and railways to clothing and cuisine, Western technology and culture arrived as a compressed package. At least in urban settings, popular culture and popular music unzipped at a furious pace, defining the experience of the new.[65]

Educated Koreans, whether schooled in Confucian academies or trained in Western-style universities in Japan or elsewhere, largely reproduced the received status hierarchy and its prejudices during the colonial period. Folk songs were nothing more than vulgar peasant songs; the itinerant entertainers known as *kwangdae* were coterminous with beggars and streetwalkers. As much as Confucius lauded music, the Confucius-drenched *yangban* performed or listened to a particular style of formal and refined music, dismissing as almost inhuman the wailings and noises of unrefined peasants (no matter how much the *yangban* themselves may have enjoyed the same vulgar music, although performed in a more refined manner and in sophisticated settings, in the company of courtesans). Therefore, as Japanese rule entrenched itself, the *yangban* increasingly listened to what the educated Japanese professed to like.

Nonelite folk music and farmers' music were stubbornly rooted not only in the countryside but also in particular villages; local variations and regional diversity rendered them not so much a music of solidarity as a music of differentiation.[66] The canonical form of folk song, transposed to a modern musical idiom, occludes regional diversity. The indisputable national folk song of South (and North) Korea is "Arirang," but there were and are numerous regional variants.[67] In fact, "Arirang" was originally regarded as a relatively new song, and it achieved national status only after its adoption as a theme song in the popular 1926 film *Arirang;* thereafter, it was canonized and disseminated in European musical notations, and it was usually performed with European instruments.[68] Paradoxically, from the contemporary nationalist perspective, it was not the Korean elite but the Japanese colonial government that promoted the collection of Korean folktales and folk songs.[69] But Korean folk music was already in decline by the time Japanese and Korean scholars began to scurry in search of it.[70] The massive rural exodus that convulsed the peninsula for the entirety of the twentieth century dispersed ethnic Koreans not just across the Korean peninsula but well beyond it.

The sound of city life was a jumble, but the new Western-inflected soundscape soon surfaced above the din. European art music, although widely taught in schools and performed for official occasions, occupied a delimited temporal and spatial niche: it was the sound of power, the music of authority. The spread of Christianity also expanded the ambit of Western music on the Korean peninsula. Missionaries taught Koreans—especially girls, since many early missionary schools were for girls—to sing in ensemble and in Western harmony. By the turn of the century, the nascent world of popular music was far more resonant, especially in Pyongyang and Seoul. *Ch'angga* (choral song) was an amalgamation of American hymns, European anthems, Western folk tunes, and Japanese choral music (*shōka,* the Japanese term, uses the same Chinese characters as *ch'angga*).[71] The English translation of *ch'angga* is misleading, however, insofar as *ch'angga* was a composite genre, its principal characteristic being that it was nontraditional. For example, whereas most Americans would distinguish folk tunes from choral songs, "My Darling Clementine" was an extremely popular example of *ch'angga* in Korea. And the song's music may have been Western, but its lyrics were Korean, with a striking narrative departure from the original: the Korean version of "My Darling Clementine" is about a father-daughter relationship. *Ch'angga* was a new universe of sound among educated urbanites—among, that is, precisely those who had been exposed to the new soundscape in schools (by 1945, about a third of school-age children attended primary school). It is possible to locate the origins of *ch'angga* in the 1880s, but only around the turn of the twentieth century did it become recognizably audible as the music of Christians, modernizing nationalists, and other Western-inflected urbanites.[72] In other words, *ch'angga* not only was new and distinct from the traditional Korean soundscape but also was embraced by the educated elite, whose orientation was toward two powerful groups: Christian missionaries (the West) and the Japanese authorities. Over time, *ch'angga* spread to the countryside via traveling salesmen who peddled *ch'angga* books by playing the fiddle.[73]

The Korean elite's embrace of *ch'angga* transformed it, paradoxically, into resistance music. *Ch'angga* was the music of the educated, but it was this same demographic that led the independence movement in early colonial Korea, and the association between anti-Japanese, pro-independence politics and *ch'angga* remained an enduring motif in modern Korea. Already by the 1900s, the very idea of political or movement music (*undongga*) was inextricable from *ch'angga*.[74] Sentiments critical of Japanese rule were often articulated in *ch'angga,* not in Korean folk tunes (perhaps not surprisingly, since educated Koreans were likely to denigrate peasant music). The current South Korean national anthem was set to the music of "Auld Lang Syne" in 1896, partly because the song's pentatonic scale made the music more accessible to those who had been steeped in the traditional soundscape.[75] Thus began the pattern of setting Korean lyrics to an appropriated Western melody. Most lyrics were set to extant tunes, but, beginning with Kim In-sik in 1905, Koreans composed new pieces.[76] An Ik-t'ae (Eak Tai Ahn), perhaps the Korean musician best known to the West before Liberation, later undertook to compose new music for the national anthem, given the incongruity its being set to the tune of a Scottish folk song. Only after 1948 did South Koreans uniformly sing the national anthem to An's tune.[77] Not surprisingly, the Japanese authorities banned what were considered to be delinquent *ch'angga* (*furyō shōka*) as early as 1908; they also burned scores and closed some schools in 1911. Japanese censorship of Korean music persisted throughout the colonial period.[78] In place of the banned music, the colonial authorities promoted politically correct choral songs.[79] One consequence of the Japanese suppression was that most *ch'angga* taught and sung by ethnic Koreans after the 1910s were composed in the Japanese pentatonic scale rather than in the diatonic scale more common in European art music.

Western vocal music also entrenched itself as *kagok* (lieder), usually sung solo rather than by an ensemble, as was the intention with *ch'angga*. By the 1920s, modern Western-style *kagok* had supplanted traditional Korean *kagok* (which is why the mention of *kagok* prompts contemporary South Koreans to think of Western songs).[80] Particularly noteworthy is the 1920 song "Pongsŏnhwa" (Impatiens), composed by Hong Yong-hu (better known as Hong Nan-p'a).[81] Hong composed many pieces of enduring popularity, such as "Kohyang ŭi pom" (Hometown in spring), which was considered to be a *tongyo* (children's song), another genre fashionable at the time. With the publication of Pang Chŏng-hwan's "Sarang ŭi sŏnmul" (The gift of love) in 1921, and with the debut of the influential journal *Ŏrini* (Children) in 1923, children's literature reached a readership well beyond its age-appropriate audience.[82] Yun Kŭk-yŏng's 1924 song "Pandal" (Half moon), often regarded as the first *tongyo*, remains in circulation today. Yun studied European art music in Tokyo, and though the song is altogether European in appearance, it employs the pentatonic scale and is performed in 6/8 time, easily in the comfort zone of those steeped in the Chosŏn soundscape. It helped usher in the golden age of *tongyo* in the 1930s.[83] Kim Tong-jin, another influential composer, synthesized Brahms and the bel canto aria to produce several songs that were sung well into the post-Liberation period, such as "Kagop'a" (I long to go), "Nae maŭm" (My heart), and "Chindallae kkot" (Azalea flower); the latter takes its lyrics from Kim So-wŏl's famous poem. *Kagok* and *tongyo*, like *ch'angga*, remained primarily the province of educated urbanites with pro-independence politics, and these genres persisted in the post-Liberation period as part of the culture of the college-educated.[84] It is therefore ironic that almost all the composers who pioneered *kagok, tongyo*, and allied new music had been trained in Japan in European art music, and that they adopted musical conventions then prevalent in Japan.[85]

Popular music entered everyday life in urban Korea in the mid-1920s as *yuhaengga* (*ryūkōka* in Japanese; literally, "songs in fashion," or popular songs), sometimes called *sin kayo* (new song). *Yuhaengga* was not a spontaneous cultural irruption; rather, it was a business or an industry, if not quite a big business or the culture industry of its time.[86] Its proximate source was the 1916 Japanese song "Kachūsha no uta" (Song of Kachūsha), from the *shingeki* play *Fukkatsu (Resurrection).*[87] By the 1920s, colonial Koreans were attending the theater, watching movies, and frequenting the types of cafés that had appeared in Japan some two decades earlier, and popular music was featured in all these venues.[88] As in Japan, where *mobo* (the modern boy) and *moga* (the modern girl) were inescapable urban presences, *sin yŏja* (the new woman), *ch'ŏngnyŏn* (youth), and other new breeds of Koreans now appeared in Seoul.[89] The poet Yi Sŏk-hun rhapsodized in 1932, "Modern girls wander the pavement / Wondering how to be like Greta Garbo."[90] And *yuhaengga*— which had sources in the theater as well as in (silent) movies (the songs were usually performed by actresses during intermission), and which had become a topic of discussion in magazines and tearooms (*tabang*)—was a crucial element of the "new" or "modern" (*modŏn*).[91] As these new loci of urban entertainment spread music, they spawned fans and groupies.[92]

The exoticism of the new media meshed well with the enchantment of the new soundscape. A new breed of entrepreneurs sprang up, one that rubbed elbows with the illicit and the disreputable. Ethnic Japanese *yakuza* (gangsters or racketeers), working in concert with their ethnic Korean counterparts, ran a significant segment of the entertainment industry.[93] This entanglement of semilegitimate businesspeople with the popular culture industry was far from unique to colonial Korea, since itinerant musicians had often moonlighted as sex workers, both before and during the Japanese occupation.[94] The common association of popular music with (paying for) sex, (dealing) drugs, and even (hanging out with) mobsters and thugs was not necessarily a figment of overprotective parents' imaginations. In any case, popular music remained a pecuniary pursuit of lower-status, less educated people.

Furthermore, the mechanical means of sound reproduction, incipient and limited though they were (involving sound amplification and, later on, *sorip'an,* or "sound discs," as records were initially called in Korea), disseminated the new music, although largely to the relatively affluent urban population.[95] The first Korean-language recording by the *p'ansori* master Yi Tongbaek had been sold as early as 1907, but SP (short play) records, which were readily reproducible, proliferated only in the late 1920s, when Japanese record companies put down roots in colonial Korea.[96] The companies themselves operated in the prevailing Japanese manner, each one functioning as a studio system with its own house lyricists, composers, musicians, and singers. The gramophone and the projector were the avant-garde of the new urban culture, threatening to wipe away the traditional and the rural.[97] With the introduction of radio broadcasting in 1927, the technological preconditions for *yuhaengga* were established.[98] Soon thereafter, the new soundscape—so distinctive from the melody and timbre of court or religious music, and worlds apart from the rhythms and registers of rural Korea—filled the city air of central Seoul. It was most likely around this time that urbanites began to hum and sing popular songs.[99]

Yuhaengga was a universe of sound that was at once Korean, Japanese, and Western. What gave this mélange its coherence was that it appealed to a new, urban audience. Singers, composers, and producers, in addition to listeners, readily traversed distinct types of music over time.[100] The category of mass music at that time included not only the new *kagok* and *tongyo* but also genres that would be differentiated today, such as hymns, *ch'angga,* and *p'ansori.*

Yi Kyŏng-suk, who performed the song "Arirang" for the 1926 film of the same title, sang children's music as well as the 1927 hit "Nakhwayusu" (Falling flower, flowing water), also known as "Kangnam tal" (The moon of Kangnam), the first record produced in Korea.[101] Yi's expansive repertoire encompassed distinct genres of folk music, children's songs, and popular music, a range that suggests the superficiality of genre distinctions. In 1935, Okeh Records, the first Korean-managed label in colonial Korea, put out an advertisement for *taejung ŭmak* that included European art music (for example, "Ave Maria"), children's songs (*tongyo*), and new folk songs (*sin minyo*).[102] Contemporary classifications cannot do justice to the universe of popular music in colonial Korea.

In spite of considerable resistance to Japanese rule, the influence of Japan had become inescapable by the 1920s, whether because of the sheer might of the Japanese empire, the cultural prestige and political dominance of Japan, or the unlikelihood of Korean independence. Diglossia had marked Korean discursive communities and ethnic soundscapes before, but the two modes of expression had never been so closely intertwined as they were in the latter half of the colonial period. In the realm of urban popular music, Japan and Korea converged to constitute a shared, if not identical, soundscape.[103] The Japanese influence was preponderant in shaping the soundscape of *ryūkōka / yuhaengga;* many early *yuhaengga* were Japanese songs that had been translated into Korean, or sometimes direct imports. There is a poignant anecdote about a third-generation diasporic Korean in Uzbekistan who sings a "Korean" song that turns out to be a Japanese-language *ryūkōka*.[104] Yet it would be a mistake to hear in this soundscape a Japanese monophony. Korean contributions were substantial, as were those from other spheres of Japanese influence, such as China. Most famously, the preeminent Japanese popular-music composer Koga Masao, who had grown up in colonial Korea, incorporated such Korean elements as the use of three beats to establish his Korea-influenced "Koga melody."[105] In particular, ethnic Korean composers and singers achieved prominence in the Japanese archipelago, even though they did so by employing Japanese pseudonyms and passing as ethnic Japanese.[106] By 1932, for example, Ch'oe Kyu-yŏp (known in Japan as Hasegawa Ichirō) was already a star in Japan.[107] Indeed, the very existence of stars is a defining feature of popular culture, including popular music.[108]

Whereas *ch'angga* or *kagok* remained largely restricted to the educated urban population, *yuhaengga* appealed to a larger audience and overshadowed other genres. To put this idea simply, *yuhaengga* had much wider appeal because it adapted itself to the traditional Korean soundscape. Two songs underscore this shift.

The first of the two—the 1926 song "Sa ŭi ch'anmi" (Hymn to death), by Yun Sim-dŏk (Yun, with her short hair, was an iconic *sin yŏja,* or "new woman")—is often considered to have been the first hit in Korea.[109] The record almost singlehandedly advanced the new industry, thanks in part to a scandal: after Yun recorded the song, she and her married lover caused a media sensation by committing double suicide.[110] The music of "Sa ŭi ch'anmi" is uncompromisingly Western; the melody is lifted from Iosif Ivanovici's "Waves of the Danube" (1880). The morbid theme is in the province of *ch'angga* and *kagok,* which often expressed, to a Western tune, nostalgia for a lost homeland (and thus functioned as a subterranean call for Korean independence). Yun had been reluctant to record a "popular" song, and she sings it in the *kagok* or lied style, as would have befitted the opera singer she fancied herself to be.[111] Although the original melody is in three beats (it was a waltz), Yun sings it in the received four beats of *ch'angga* or *kagok.* In short, the song is distinctly outside what was, at the time, the traditional Korean soundscape.

By contrast with "Sa ŭi ch'anmi," the 1932 song "Hwangsŏng yett'ŏ" (Remains of Hwangsŏng castle), by Yi Aerisu (Alice Lee; Yi Po-jŏn; Ri Arisu), was the first successful song in Korea to combine Korean lyrics with a Korean composition.[112] The record's spectacular success—it sold fifty thousand copies—augured a music that could reach well beyond educated urbanites. There were some similarities and continuities between Yi and Yun. Both singers made their reputations by performing entr'actes at theatrical performances.[113] In addition, both Yun and Yi were drawn to suicide, not only because their lovers were married but also because the men they loved belonged to the landlord class, at a time when interstatus marriage was all but proscribed.[114] These similarities belie a critical element of change, however. Yi Aerisu's song employs the pentatonic scale and is in three beats. That familiar connection to the traditional Korean soundscape facilitated the reception of Yi's song beyond the narrow circle of Westernizing, educated urbanites. That is, *yuhaengga,* rather than inhabiting the new universe of Western music, accomplished a rapprochement, if not quite a reversion, to Korean listeners' comfort zone. Although *yuhaengga* was radically distinct from traditional Korean songs, Yi and her followers bridged the shifting soundscapes of colonial Korea.

Thus the expansion of the domestic market beyond educated urbanites, and the greater interaction with Japanese popular music (as well as greater access to the Japanese market), gave rise to *yuhaengga,* which would have organic links to the world of popular music in the post-Liberation period. The contemporary South Korean view tends to equate colonial-era *yuhaengga* with the postcolonial-period genre called "trot" (*t'ŭrot'ŭ*), which takes its name from the ballroom dance known as the fox-trot.[115] But before musical styles become formulaic, they exhibit family resemblances as well as distinct differences. For example, we listen today to Beethoven piano sonatas, but the sonata form itself solidified only in the 1840s, long after the composer's death. Similarly, contemporary listeners readily identify elements of trot in 1930s songs, but the genre itself crystallized only after the post-Liberation period, when it was also called *ppongtchak,* an onomatopoeic Korean term that sought to capture the distinctive two-beat (or four-beat) rhythm in contradistinction to the traditional three beats.[116] Indeed, *ppong* prevails as the predominant rhythm of post-Liberation South Korean popular music.[117] The *yuhaengga* of the 1930s, almost always composed in the Japanese pentatonic *yonanuki* scale, also featured a wide array of unmistakable visual and aural cues.[118] Singers and musicians often wore Western clothing, still uncommon in the colonial period, and were backed up by Western musical instruments. And beyond the spectacle, usually staged in a Western-style room or building, there was the strange soundscape, so distinct from the traditional singing of *kagok* or *p'ansori.* The singers crooned about new sentiments and themes, ranging from faraway exotic places and nightlife to nostalgia about hometowns and the vicissitudes of love.[119] Even when songs spoke of tears and farewells, the longing for the past or for the countryside was indisputably expressed from the standpoint of the urban present. The tunes were often catchy, with hummable, likable melodies. They fit in well with the new loci of musical enjoyment, the teahouses and bars, and we should not forget that they were often dance music as well. The allure of *yuhaengga,* which offered solace in times of sorrow, and pleasure against pain, was intoxicating to self-styled urbanites.

Two songs that even today remain staples of *noraebang*—those venues for karaoke singing that are inescapable in contemporary South Korea—are emblematic of the new genre. Yi Nan-yŏng's 1935 song "Mokp'o ŭi nunmul" (Tears of Mokp'o) is widely regarded as the paradigmatic trot song, though it was initially marketed as *chibang sin minyo* (rural new folk song). The Mokp'o of the song's title is a port town, a place of departure and farewell in a country undergoing constant displacement and diaspora; and the tears—as much about the past ("three hundred years" of *han,* or ressentiment) as about the present departure from a new wife—openly express the modern sentiment of romantic love.[120] Even in comparison to "Hwangsŏng yett'ŏ," a song from just three years before, "Mokp'o ŭi nunmul" sounds modern; in turn, the three-beat rhythm of "Hwangsŏng yett'ŏ" makes that song distinct from the four-beat rhythm of "Mokp'o ŭi nunmul." The superior recording technology used for "Mokp'o ŭi nunmul" also accentuates that song's brighter timbre. The lyrics of both songs are equally elegiac, but the Western instrumentation is much more pronounced in "Mokp'o ŭi nunmul." Yi Nan-yŏng's singing style retains some semblances of classical European vocalization—syllabic singing, clear phrasing, head resonance—but she literally brings the song down to the demotic sphere with her lower pitch and unaffected articulation. Her almost parlando style of singing replaces the liedlike singing used in *ch'angga* or *kagok*. Similarly, Nam In-su—he was later dubbed "the Emperor" because of his popularity—sings in 1938 of tears and sorrow in "Aesu ŭi sŏyakkok" (Serenade of sorrow), but the song is all about love: gazing at stars, sighing, closing the eyes to lament the passing of love. The title's invocation of a serenade, not to mention the plucking of a guitar, places it as a modern song, unmistakably distant in sentiment and sound from the world of *p'ansori* or even *kagok*. These songs were widely sung in the post-Liberation period for a compelling reason: their lyrics as well as their melodies had a ready continuity with the period that preceded the end of Japanese rule and with the period that followed.

Yuhaengga was not altogether devoid of the anti-colonial sentiments that marked *ch'angga*. Although *yuhaengga* was ostensibly about private, senti-mental issues of lost love and other nonpolitical themes, many listeners, whatever the intentions of the lyricists and singers may have been, perceived an anti-Japanese strain in what was even then considered to be a Japanese musical genre. For example, Chang Se-jŏng's 1937 song "Yŏllaksŏn ŭn ttŏnaganda" (The ferry is leaving) is about the line for the Pusan–Shimonoseki ferry (also known as the infernal ship that had carried many ethnic Koreans to the main Japanese islands), and listeners transposed the song's theme of personal separation to the exodus of exploited Korean work-ers. Not surprisingly, the Japanese authorities questioned the anti-Japanese connotations of the song's lyrics, as they also had done with respect to other songs featuring tears shed over bodies of water, such as Yi's "Mokp'o ŭi nun-mul" and Kim Chŏng-gu's "Nunmul chŏjŭn Tuman'gang" (Tear-drenched Tumen River).[121] Those songs, capturing the contemporary zeitgeist, reso-nated with many urban Koreans, who in turn resonated with the songs' subterranean anti-colonial sentiments.

There were also efforts, sometimes by singers who were retooled *kisaeng* (courtesans), to adapt and revitalize traditional Korean music, including *p'ansori* and *minyo*. Particularly significant was the genre of *sin minyo*, or *chibang sin minyo*, which arose in the 1930s as a conscious effort to bridge traditional *minyo* and *yuhaengga*.[122] By the mid-1930s, as record sales routinely reached forty to fifty thousand copies, record companies were eager to cultivate new audiences—new both to urban life and to popular music. There was considerable diversity in the songs that called themselves *sin minyo*, but their source of unity was their link to the countryside. Two songs from 1938, Yi Hwa-ja's "Kkolmangt'ae mokdong" (Feedbag cowboy) and Kim's "Nunmul chŏjŭn Tuman'gang," are classified as *sin minyo*, but both are more properly considered specimens of *yuhaengga* or *sin kayo*.[123] What made them "folk" music was their nostalgic and agrarian elements (such as the mooing of a cow in Yi's song, sung to the traditional three beats). Some scholars stress *sin minyo* as the first indigenous form of popular music, but the genre was deeply affected by Western and Japanese music, relied almost exclusively on European instruments, and was basically similar to other *yuhaengga* of the time.[124]

The world of *yuhaengga* was far from monolithic. The mix of influences—Korean, Japanese, American, and more—that percolated in colonial Korea created, for instance, Pak Hwang-rim's 1938 hit "Oppa nŭn p'unggakchaengi" (My brother is a busker).[125] In her nasal, jazzy singing style, and backed by not quite cacophonic but certainly loud instrumentation, Pak complains about her meddling and drunk street-musician brother. The lyrics, deeply untraditional, are faintly shocking even to some contemporary South Korean ears. At least one photo from that time shows the singer in a spaghetti-strap dress.[126] The song embodies an anarchic and anomic urban nightlife, far removed from the contemporary South Korean memory of that period as a time of unremitting oppression and cultural (and female) subjugation. When the song is juxtaposed with the smooth, melismatic trot songs of the 1960s, it should be readily apparent that the world of colonial Korean popular music was in no way monochromatic and surely not all prim or Confucian. Furthermore, a variety of new genres appeared during that period. Jazz made its debut in Seoul in 1930, though the genre encompassed not only American jazz but also French chanson and Latin music.[127] As in the United States and elsewhere, the term "jazz" was often used pejoratively, to denote an alien music that was questionably music at all but was unquestionably noisy.[128] In the 1930s, even the staid genre of children's music acquired an upbeat tone.

By the mid-1930s, popular-music culture was established in Seoul. I have already discussed the sale of records and the creation of stars as well as the spread of popular music from new outlets, such as theaters, movie houses, cafés, and bars. Urbanites readily embraced *yuhaengga;* it was fashionable precisely because of its evanescent but enjoyable songs and singers. The first concert of popular music in Korea was held in 1933, after Ch'oe/Hasegawa returned to Seoul from his triumphant Japanese tour. In 1935, there was even a poll for the most popular singer (Ch'oe was the winner).[129] Also in 1935, the remarkable impresario Yi Ch'öl, who managed Okeh Records, assembled singers for a series of concerts. His salesmanship enhanced the spread of popular music; his innovations included contests for new singers.[130] At the same time—the second half of the colonial period—ethnic Korean musicians were following the orbit of the Japanese empire and dispersing to China, Manchuria, and elsewhere to constitute the first wave of Korean music exports.[131] Most features of the South Korean popular-music scene today could already be found in Seoul by the mid-1930s, at least in some form, however inchoate.

With the intensification of the Japanese war effort, the Japanese state sought to mobilize its subjects by any means necessary. As a result, the colonial power not only imposed extreme measures of Japanization—the ban on the use of the Korean language in schools in 1937, and the enforced adoption of Japanese names for all Koreans in 1940—but also tightened control over and increasingly censored potentially subversive expression in the realm of popular songs.[132] The government's campaign was not exclusively negative, however. From the late 1930s on, the Japanese authorities promoted *kokumin kayō* (national songs), which employed the music of *yuhaengga* to convey positive messages about Japanese rule, both in the main Japanese islands as well as in the Japanese colonies, including Korea.[133] One example was "Fukuchi manri" (Thousands of miles of abundant land), the theme song of the eponymous 1941 movie about the emigration of ethnic Koreans to Manchuria. By the late 1930s, the national had transmogrified into the martial, with the rise of *gunkoku kayō* (martial national songs).[134] Needless to say, Japanese patriotic songs failed to be as popular as the 1930s *yuhaengga*. Nevertheless, many *yuhaengga* singers, such as Kim Yŏng-gil, took part in singing *kokumin* and *gunkoku kayō*.[135] The extensive collaboration of ethnic Korean singers in pro-Japanese activities remains an underexplored but inescapable aspect of popular music in the colonial period.

In short, then, the urban world of *yuhaengga* marked a significant break with the Chosŏn Korean soundscape, whether elite or popular, urban or rural. European instruments, clothes, décor, and styles projected an entirely new feel—the new, the Western, the modern—as well as a radically distinct aural experience. Few would prove able to resist the allure of the new musical universe or the new lifestyle it encapsulated. Yet the break was not quite total; the Chosŏn soundscape survived in Westernized garb. Korean songs, as already noted, were often composed in the pentatonic scale (and even though *kugak* was not composed in the Western scale, many of its pieces can be transposed readily to the pentatonic scale), and they retained something of the three beats of *changdan* (and were usually performed in 6/8 time). To be sure, however, *yuhaengga* was almost indistinguishable from Japanese *ryūkōka,* both of them adapting to and articulated in the Western soundscape.

THE POST-LIBERATION PERIOD

In 1945, the Japanese defeat in World War II liberated Korea, only to leave the Korean peninsula divided.[136] After Liberation, postcolonial South Korea experienced another revolution: the end of Japanese musical dominance, and the beginning of American musical hegemony.

Periodization generally suggests radical shifts, but reality is perforce more complex: individuals traverse distinct periods, and those who survive and thrive are often the ones who adapt to new styles and new paymasters. Yi Nan-yŏng's turbulent career is symptomatic of the larger changes and complexities. Born into poverty in Mokp'o in 1916, she began as an entr'acte singer at a movie theater during the first wave of *yuhaengga.*[137] After attaining fame with "Mokp'o ŭi nunmul," she released a series of hits, including duets with "Emperor" Nam In-su, and her repertoire encompassed everything from blues to light pop. In 1936, she began performing as Oka Ranko and achieved renown in Japan; by the 1940s, she was participating in the Japanese war effort. After Liberation, along with her husband (Kim Hae-song) and the aforementioned Chang Se-jŏng, she was a member of K. P. K. Akdan (K. P. K. Musical Group), which performed primarily "jazz" (American popular music) for US troops; that is, Yi made yet another shift in her soundscape, and in her audience.[138] During the Korean War, her husband was apprehended by North Korea, and K. P. K. Akdan was disbanded. In the confusion of the postwar years, Yi trained her children as musicians, forming the Kim Sisters and later the Kim Brothers. The Kim Sisters would make a splash among GIs in South

Korea, a success that led to shows in Las Vegas (*The China Doll Revue* at the Thunderbird Hotel from 1959 on) and to twenty-five appearances on *The Ed Sullivan Show,* the defining variety show of the 1960s in the United States (for context, Connie Francis appeared twenty-six times; Patti Page and Louis Armstrong, eighteen times each).[139] Yi also restarted her own singing career, performing with Nam (with whom she also became romantically involved) until his death, in 1962. Her career was ended by the 1961 South Korean legislation that banned music by defectors—a status generously defined to include not only those who, like Yi's husband, had gone unwillingly to North Korea but also their immediate relatives. Despondent, Yi died in 1965 at the age of forty-nine.

Although South Koreans sought to emulate the democratic United States, the long-standing status bifurcation of musical tastes persisted. The elite, having lost its traditional source of wealth and power in the land reform of the early 1950s, turned decisively toward education as a means of class reproduction. A critical element of this shift was the espousal of American (and Western) culture and the simultaneous repudiation of traditional Korean, Chinese, and Japanese culture. Traditional Korean music, in a long diminuendo, ceased to have anything to do with refinement, civilization, or class.[140] In its stead, European art music reigned. By the 1970s, the enthusiasm of the South Korean elite had churned out some superstar performers, such as the violinist Kyung-wha Chung and her brother, the conductor Myung-whun Chung. This development bespoke, rather than rupture, a continuity with the colonial period, when many aspiring ethnic Koreans had gone to Japan for training in European classical music. After all, world-class composers like Isang Yun and Unsuk Chin did not emerge from nowhere, and it is no coincidence that other prominent diasporic Koreans, such as Nam June Paik, cut their artistic teeth on classical European music.[141] As traditional elite culture crumbled along with the received social structure, European art music provided a rare continuous note, one that remains resonant in the twenty-first century.[142]

European classical music radiated prestige and power, refinement and sophistication. Its impact reached far beyond the educated elite. Few children of the South Korean middle class, and few children whose parents envisioned a grandiose future for them (in other words, very few children at all), escaped a brush with the dreaded piano or violin lessons. South Korean educational bureaucrats, following their Japanese predecessors, installed European classical music in the schools as the basis of music education. In the nineteenth century, few Koreans would have been able to identify even the most common European musical instruments, such as the piano; by the late twentieth century, one would have had to look long and hard for such a display of ignorance. From musical notation to the titles of masterpieces and the names of their composers, the world of European classical music became part of South Korean common knowledge. Another Western influence, Christianity, also exposed many South Koreans more intensively to the Western soundscape as new adherents of the faith sang their weekly hymns or listened to Christian music. In time, most South Koreans would walk down the aisle to the tune of Mendelssohn's wedding march or Wagner's bridal chorus. In addition, the US armed forces instilled the rhythm of the Western military march (along with addiction to alcohol and nicotine).

Even more than European art music, American music—its signature instruments (such as the saxophone and the trombone), its brighter timbre, and its upbeat lyrics—colonized South Korea immediately and totally in the restricted but vast networks of US military bases and the camp towns that sprouted up around them after 1945 (the term *kijich'on* means, literally, "camp village"). The end of colonial rule unleashed an exodus of the Japanese-dominated music industry, and thereafter Japanese music was all but banned from South (and North) Korea.[143] The destruction wrought by the Korean War (1950–1953) and the ensuing impoverishment of the country left Americans as the chief consumers of popular music in 1950s South Korea. Many young American soldiers who found themselves in South Korea on a hardship tour avidly embraced formal and informal offerings of rest and relaxation, from sexual services to musical entertainment.[144] The sheer economic might of the US military, not to mention the prestige it had gained when it liberated the country from Japanese rule, ensured that South Korean musicians, young and old, would eagerly perform whatever American GIs wanted to hear.[145] In the late 1950s, revenues from performances for US GIs probably exceeded the total export earnings of South Korea.[146] Yongsan and It'aewŏn, in what was then southern Seoul, where the Eighth United States Army was stationed, were ground zero of the American popular-music invasion (hence the Korean nickname *P'alkun*, meaning "Eighth Army," as the common synecdoche for the US military). In addition, the United Service Organizations (USO) arranged live shows, which provided the template for the first South Korean music show, *Sho Sho Sho*, broadcast by the government-owned TV station, KBS.[147] Another conduit of US popular music was the US military's communication networks, at first radio (beginning in 1950) and later television (1957). At a time when South Korea had few radios or television sets, the Armed Forces Korean Network (AFKN) was transmitting a steady barrage of Americana, including American popular music.

At officers' clubs, in dance halls, and at other venues, numerous South Korean musicians immersed themselves in the musical universe of American soldiers. These musicians included those who had previously performed in European classical music orchestras and those who had sung *yuhaengga* or even performed jazz in the colonial period. From quasi-orchestral renditions of big-band and swing music to the more accessible and imitable crooner songs—again, frequently just called "jazz"—South Koreans learned to perform for American GIs and, over time, for their own fellow nationals.[148] They also dressed and comported themselves in line with American expectations.[149] Eventually, just as their predecessors had spanned the Japanese empire, South Koreans would perform in the American zone of influence, not only in the United States, as we have seen, but also across its informal empire—Japan, Vietnam (especially during the war in the 1960s), and beyond.[150] In the immediate post-Liberation years, however, most acts were outright imitations, and the imitation began with the names of these acts. A string of South Korean sister acts emerged to emulate the Andrews Sisters, then at their apogee in the United States; these acts included not just the Kim Sisters but also the Arirang Sisters, the Lee Sisters, the Pearl Sisters, and others. Few South Koreans would have known much about American popular music before 1945—with the outbreak of the Pacific War, Japan had effectively sealed its territories off from American cultural influence—but by 1960 many urban South Koreans had at least passing familiarity with such popular American singers as Pat Boone and Patti Page, Doris Day and Nat King Cole. Some South Korean youths fell in love with the glittering world of American popular music, swinging with big-band jazz or swaying to heartrending ballads. For example, in the immediate post-Liberation years, my father envisioned himself as a jazz trombonist despite his upright rural background, and my paternal grandfather, reportedly for the first and last time, squelched that anti-*yangban* yearning with an exhibition of unrestrained fury. Quite clearly, though, *yangban* hegemony, its days already numbered, was unable to withstand a force even more powerful than Japanese colonial rule, and even more subversive of traditional Korean social order.

An important qualifier with respect to US music's dominance is that the music remained largely restricted to the camp towns, which few South Koreans ever entered.[151] Difficult though it is to recall a time before music was readily reproducible, music in 1950s South Korea was far from quotidian or ubiquitous. As noted earlier, the end of colonial rule had brought the departure of the Japanese music industry, and South Korea's poverty stunted the development of indigenous record companies and production facilities.[152] Record imports were restricted, a fact that did not prevent the circulation of illegal and pirated copies, but we should also recall that few South Koreans in the 1950s had the means to own a phonograph (and those who did tended to be the cultural elite, who preferred European classical music and *au courant* American musical genres). Certainly the sound of music was absent from my paternal grandfather's rural home in the 1960s, in clear contrast to the state of affairs in my urban-based maternal grandparents' home, where it was common enough to hear singing and humming of popular music, if only old-fashioned *ch'angga* and *kagok*.

The temptation with any backward glance, especially a cursory one, is to see periodic shifts in which genres and styles rise and fall and disappear, but we should not sweep older genres into history's dustbin, since many of them survived and even thrived in the post-Liberation period. Pre-Japanese forms of people's music, such as *p'ansori* and *nongak*, remained a significant presence in the South Korean countryside of the 1950s and 1960s. Itinerant troupes, often featuring *p'ansori* performances, provided an important source of entertainment when much of South Korea remained without electricity and thus with little access to radio and no access to television. Seasonal rituals as well as quotidian songs continued among farmers and fishermen, washerwomen and grandparents. In this context, it is not surprising that *sin minyo* and *tongyo* continued to attract listeners in the post-Liberation period. If the golden age of *tongyo* was the 1930s, the 1950s are considered by some to have been the heyday (*chŏnsŏnggi*) of children's songs.[153] *Kagok* and *tongyo* remained stubbornly Western, but without the newfound appeal of American popular music. *Sin minyo,* with its rural resonances, gradually lost its fan base, pressured on one side by a more obstinately rural, traditional agrarian music and on the other by more urban, up-tempo styles of music. In any case, most older and rural South Koreans found American music loud and alien. After all, anything new is potentially suspect, and most South Koreans, the vast majority of whom remained in the countryside in the 1950s, still inhabited a Chosŏn Korean or Japanese-influenced Korean soundscape. The blaring of trumpets and the shimmering of violin strings were alien to ears attuned to indigenous wooden flutes and gutted string instruments, which, moreover, were played in a completely distinct scale and rhythm. If those who first heard Debussy's *japonisme* compositions found his orientalist notes strange, it was the rest of his oeuvre that would have sounded exotic to most South Koreans in the decade after Liberation.[154]

In the immediate post-Liberation, pre–Korean War years, before the US presence became pronounced, 1930s-style *yuhaengga* underwent a revival, although in openly and proudly Korean guise. Nam In-su's "Kagŏra samp'alsŏn" (Go away, 38th parallel), originally released in 1945 and later to become a major hit, after its rerelease in 1948; Chang Se-jŏng's 1948 hit "Urŏra ŭnbangŭl" (Ring, silver bell), with its line about the fluttering national flag on a silver-and-gold horse-drawn coach bearing love through the streets of Seoul; the 1949 song "Kwiguksŏn" (Repatriating ship), sung by various people but most closely associated with Yi In-gwŏn—all three are patently patriotic, and all three address the concerns of their era.[155] To be sure, not all popular songs were nationalist—there was Hyŏn In's 1949 "Silla ŭi talpam" (Moonlit night in Shilla)—but political color overwhelmed domestic popular music during the Korean War, when songs about refugees, war widows, and soldiers proliferated.[156] In 1950, for example, "Sŭngni ŭi norae" (The song of victory) and "Chŏnuya chal chagŏra" (Sleep well, comrade-in-arms) were widely disseminated (the latter became a massive hit in 1951, when Hyŏn In recorded it). Many of these songs have more than a vague resemblance to 1940s *gunkoku kayō*—not surprisingly, since many of their composers, lyricists, and singers were involved in the Japanese war effort. What remained after three years of utter devastation, however, was not a repertoire of upbeat martial tunes but rather songs of travail and trauma. Yi Hae-yŏn's "Tanjang ŭi Miari Kogae" (The heartbreak of Miari Pass), though released in 1956, is exemplary. The song recalls "Arirang" as Yi sings of tears and farewells, presumably involving a husband "turning around to look and turning around again/barefoot and tottering/pulled over the Pass." Thus, in the mid-1950s, popular songs could still echo the genre of the national folk song and could tell of public and personal tragedy.

Nevertheless, the impact of the US occupation, which would continue after the formal independence of South Korea, was profound, and it overpowered the world of post-Liberation *yuhaengga*. The Rhee Syngman regime (1948–1960) was pejoratively called "the translators' government." The material things that Americans brought were visible—jeeps, chocolate, Coca-Cola—and would soon reign as common objects of desire. No less significant were American cultural products, ranging from Hollywood movies to popular music.[157] South Korean musicians, whether listening to records or reading musical scores in the *American Hit-Kit of Popular Songs,* immersed themselves in the soundscape of the United States. Again, the geographical impact of that soundscape was initially limited, but it shaped popular-music culture in Seoul and other large cities, not just in terms of songs but in terms of a way of life. All it takes is a glance at some of what was popular in South Korea in the 1940s and 1950s—"Mujŏng purŭsŭ" (Heartless blues) in 1948, "San Francisco" in 1952, "Arizona Cowboy" in 1955, and "Taejŏn purŭsŭ" (Taejŏn blues) in 1956, not to mention song titles featuring the words "tango," "cha-cha-cha," "mambo," and "boogie"—to perceive the ineluctable influence of the United States on everything from song lyrics to fashionable dances.[158] Yet outside the immediate confines of the camp towns, the Japanese influence remained strong. Whether the task is to trace boogie-woogie's popularity in the late 1940s or the popularity of Latin beats in the mid-1950s, we see that South Korean fashion followed that of Japan, after a gap of a few years. But Japan's was the influence that dared not speak its name. Until 1952, Japan was also occupied by the United States, and Japanese musicians mediated American music for Koreans, often by way of colonial ties and postcolonial diasporic networks, which included the dissemination of Japanese-printed sheet music.[159]

The 1950s are something of a forgotten decade in South Korea. Most South Koreans, pressed to offer a description of that period, would mutter something about the destruction caused by the Korean War, the corruption of the Rhee regime, and the poverty of the country. And they would assume that trot music dominated in those years. Yet trot did not dominate, and the reality was not all doom and gloom. Indeed, even the most cursory look at popular-song jackets and lyrics, or at advertisements and magazine articles about popular music, reveals a much more vibrant scene, one buoyed by the unbounded optimism of American culture (which in turn rested on the arrogance of the so-called American Century), and the view from today is all the more remarkable for the unvarnished smiles of the women in less-than-Confucian garb who gaze back across more than half a century. Their colorful nylon clothes and exposed skin make those South Korean women a race apart from their almost completely covered counterparts of only twenty years later. To contemplate this situation from a different angle, Pak Chae-hong's 1955 hit "Mulbanga tonŭn naeryŏk" (The roundabout history of the water-wheel) openly satirizes worldly success and prestige and is clearly critical of the Rhee regime, whereas the repressive cultural policy of Park Chung-hee in the 1960s and 1970s stifled that earlier era's optimism and openness and consigned its outlook to oblivion. The famous 1961 composition of Son Sŏk-u

(Seog Woo Sohn/Sung Woo Sohn), "Nooran shassŭ ŭi sanai" (The boy in the yellow shirt), sung by Han Myŏng-suk, is catchy and upbeat, a song that could and in fact did have appeal outside South Korea.[160] Especially when it is performed in Han's syllabic, staccato singing style, it has, notwithstanding the obvious differences, a family resemblance to the chirpy American songs of the 1950s—for example, to Doris Day's 1956 hit "Whatever Will Be, Will Be" (with its grammatically incorrect subtitle, "Que Sera, Sera"), or to the 1959 song "Lipstick on Your Collar," by Connie Francis. And Han, like Doris Day and Connie Francis, but unlike most other South Korean women of her era, has a short hairstyle and even a short dress. What is even more striking, the song is suggestive of a romance between a South Korean woman and an African American GI—an encounter that, if made explicit in the lyrics, would have upset many upright South Koreans.[161] The enormous popularity of light music (*kyŏng ŭmak*) in urban South Korea, reflecting musical tastes not at all far from those of the American mainstream, should also be emphasized, no matter how marginal other US trends (such as the rise of rock music) remained in South Korea in the 1950s. As noted in the prelude, one symptom of the forgotten post–Korean War, pre-Park years is the fact that Han's record, one of the greatest hits in the history of South Korean music, was all but impossible to locate by the 1980s.[162]

This social dynamic is previewed in Han Hyŏng-mo's 1956 film *Chayu puin* (Madam Freedom).[163] The film's tradition-minded professor-husband is troubled by debt (which prompts his wife to work outside the home, a rather radical gesture for a middle-class housewife at the time) and by a neighbor who listens incessantly to popular music on his record player. Eventually the neighbor consorts with the scholar's wife, and we are given a tour of bars and dance halls in 1950s Seoul. At the end of the film, the would-be liberated housewife is cast out; a disgraced woman now, she is covered by faintly falling snow as her husband and their son stare at her from the warm comfort of their home. The emancipatory moment of South Korean popular music after the Korean War was expunged by military rule.

TROT

Which genre dominated South Korea during the long, increasingly splenetic rule of Park Chung-hee (1963–1979)? Most South Koreans would say that it was trot music.

For a musical genre currently considered at once extremely traditional and quintessentially Korean, trot was in fact a modern amalgam. It was European in inspiration and instrumentation: derived from *ch'angga* and *kagok,* trot was almost always accompanied by a Western orchestra. Its presentation was generally decidedly urban and modern: trot singers and musicians often wore Western clothing.[164] The typical musician was an ethnic Korean who had trained in European classical music in Japan or had performed jazz and other Western-inflected popular music during the colonial period (often in Japan or Manchuria) and had played for Americans in the post-Liberation period.[165] The proximate source of trot was the Japanese-influenced *yuhaengga*; trot songs are often composed in the Japanese pentatonic (*yonanuki*) minor scale, and in a two- or four-beat rhythm. Only the language of the lyrics would have provided a key point of differentiation (though translation easily bypassed the linguistic barrier, which didn't exist for people schooled during the colonial period). Trot was Korean because its singing style often mimicked the melismatic style of *p'ansori,* redolent of strong emotion. To be sure, there was a significant variety of singing styles, ranging from those that had roots in rural folk songs and *sin minyo* to those that were influenced by American genres, especially jazz and blues. (In Japan there was a separate style called *mūdo kayō,* or "mood songs"; this style was especially popular in the 1960s but was usually classified as trot in South Korea.) The melancholic music tugged at the proverbial heartstrings of South Koreans, but trot was far from traditional, and, in contrast to Japanese *enka,* was characterized by a brighter timbre, a higher pitch, and a more upbeat tempo. Light pop, rock, and other types of American popular music sound dry and impersonal to trot aficionados; to those who prefer the American styles, trot seems all wet.

The paradox of trot is that in spite of its indisputably urban and even cosmopolitan character, it served as a kind of soul music for South Koreans who were coming of age in the decades of rapid urbanization. That association stemmed in part from lyrics that articulated common experiences—tales of coming from the countryside to the alienating city, of lasting friendships and romances or of catastrophic breakups, of family romances and troubles—lyrics that articulated, in short, any of the all too familiar narratives of South Korean lives in the turbulent decades of the post–Korean War era. One need not be a devotee of the reflection thesis (the notion that music reflects and reproduces social reality) to note the human comedy and tragedy depicted in trot lyrics. The story narrated in a trot song is principally an urban story, predicated in turn on the narrator's recent exodus from the countryside. Very few trot songs are about rural life, and if the inevitably rural *kohyang* (hometown, or *Heimat*) is invoked, it is as a remembered object of nostalgia. The countryside was the repository of everything traditional, including music. Farmers had their agrarian tunes in the 1950s and 1960s; roaming *p'ansori* singers registered the declining Korean soundscape.[166] Yet the Seoul soundscape was too urban, too American, too alien—at once artificial and superficial. The new urbanites found respite not in recalling the rural but rather in finding something of a halfway house—not quite American or Western or even Japanese, but new and different enough to be interesting, old and familiar enough to be soothing. Trot was the secret garden of transplanted urbanites.

One unassailably modern dimension of trot is the fact that its ascent coincided with the dissemination of new technologies. When South Korea made the transition from 78 rpm SP discs to 33 rpm LPs, it was a change that liberated the listening experience.[167] Around the same time, radio ownership and radio transmission spread across the country. Although television had technically begun in South Korea in 1956, the first full-scale television broadcast took place in 1961. The new technological moment coincided with and contributed to the creation of a unified popular culture in South Korea in the mid-1960s. Popular music continued to be consumed primarily in the public sphere, that is, in movie theaters, teahouses, bars, and nightclubs. The growing national audience made trot the national popular music and made Yi Mi-ja the personification of the genre.[168] As Yi herself put it, "In 1964 'Tongbaek agassi' [Camellia girl, a movie theme song] was a great hit, selling more than one hundred thousand records for the first time in the history of Korean popular music.... One year I released more than ten albums. Especially in 1964 and 1965, the situation was such that only my records would sell."[169]

Trot captured some of the Korean soul, but it was also suspected of being an enemy alien: Japanese.[170] *Yuhaengga* was indisputably intertwined with Japanese imperial culture, and trot, as its successor, was indelibly marked by its origins. Producers, composers, singers, musicians, and, of course, the audience had been steeped in the influences of the Japanese period, and it would have been almost impossible to peel away every layer of Japaneseness from South Korean popular music, even after a decade-long immersion in American popular music. The aforementioned Hong Nan-p'a, widely regarded as the father of modern Korean music, and Nam In-su, among others, became targets of anti-Japanese attacks long after the colonial period, and even after the era of the Park dictatorship.[171] Yet, as noted in connection with the American influence of the 1950s, Japan had long served as a mediator of external influences and trends. Precisely because overt Japanese influence was elided, not so much by explicit legal proscriptions as by governmental campaigns and popular hostility, it was easy in the 1950s to emulate Japanese popular songs and even, at times, to plagiarize them. The first copyright law, enacted in 1957, had almost no effect when it came to expunging piracy of Japanese songs, or to acknowledging Japanese influence.[172]

Rhee Syngman, the first president of South Korea, spent much of his adult life in the United States and harbored visceral anti-Japanese sentiments. But Park Chung-hee, who came to power after the 1961 military coup and dominated South Korea until his violent death in 1979, found himself in a much more ambiguous and precarious position vis-à-vis Japan. Park had been trained in the Japanese military academy and is said to have regularly indulged his taste for Japanese popular culture until his assassination; indeed, he was reportedly indulging that taste at the very moment of his death.[173] Therefore, Park, unlike Rhee, needed his anti-Japanese bona fides, especially after he concluded the 1965 Normalization Treaty with Japan, an act that provoked a massive backlash. Park sought to enhance his nationalist credentials by enunciating anticommunist and anti-Japanese rhetoric and policy. In Park's brand of nationalism, the two main antagonists were precisely the two countries that were culturally closest to South Korea: North Korea and Japan.

Park's cultural policy—Spartan and puritanical, as befitted a military man—sought to extirpate the legacy of the Rhee regime. Anti-corruption campaigns targeted not only politics (electoral fraud) and business (cozy deals between political and business elites) but also the cultural and social decadence of the post–Korean War years, a degeneration whose manifestations ranged from the sex industry to the sartorial emancipation of Korean women. In spite of his regime's pro-American veneer, Park's attitude toward American popular music was less than enthusiastic, but the regime, to bolster its anti-Japanese credentials, repeatedly banned trot songs. Yi Mi-ja's spectacular 1964 hit "Tongbaek agassi" was deemed *waesaek* (Japanese in color or style), and the government prevented recordings of it from being sold the following year, lifting the ban only in 1987.[174] The definition of *waesaek* was never precisely specified in connection with the song; certainly Paek Yŏng-ho's composition utilized the Japanese pentatonic scale, but that would not have distinguished "Tongbaek agassi" from most other South Korean songs of this period. The musical rationale for the ban seemed to rest instead on the recording's melismatic, legato singing, which used chest (it is tempting to say "stomach") register. The belting, even bellowing, from the lower tessitura generated the wailing that was the signature style of some *enka* singers (that style, a form of melismatic singing, was called *kobushi*), but it was a style that also had a legitimate Korean antecedent in *p'ansori* singing.[175] Furthermore, this type of soulful, sometimes mournful singing seemed to express the same ubiquitous sentiment of *han*—that combustible mixture of anger, sorrow, regret, and resentment—conveyed by *waesaek* trot.[176] In effect, Yi Mi-ja's style of appoggiatura-filled syncopated singing approximated blues and soul music, whereas other, non-*waesaek* singers (Ha Ch'un-hwa and Song Tae-gwan, for example) escaped censure because they were closer to *sin minyo*, or to American pop and rock (as Cho Yong-p'il also was, a decade later). Accustomed as we are to reifying and essentializing trot music, we should also remember that its very popularity rested in part on its diversity, and hence on its ability to cater to different tastes. Yi Mi-ja's vocal technique was regarded by some as at once vulgar and non-Korean (though only the elite could sustain the opinion that she was not a good singer). The proto-trot singing style, as exemplified by Nam In-su and Yi Nan-yŏng, is much closer to *kagok* or lied singing practice, and it was probably this style that facilitated these two singers' transition to American-style pop singing later on.[177] Be that as it may, the government had a number of reasons for censoring music. A later hit by Yi, "Kirŏgi appa" (Goose father), was banned ostensibly because of its *waesaek* character, but the reason for the ban was more likely the song's alleged criticism of a governmental policy that was dispatching South Korean men to the war in Vietnam or to construction projects in the Middle East.[178] The unsurprising irony is that even as Park prohibited others from listening to Yi's songs, he invited Yi herself to the Blue House (the South Korean version of the White House) to sing for him and his coterie.[179] All told, twenty-seven songs by Yi were banned. The proscription against Japanese popular music would finally be loosened in the 1990s; only in 2004 would it be more or less completely rescinded.[180]

Park was not wrong to consider trot Japanese because it appealed to the Japanese audience. In the post–World War II period, most Japanese regarded Korea and Koreans with facile contempt. The sources of disrespect included a number of plain facts: that Korea had been a Japanese colony (and thus inferior, in spite of the ideology of imperial kinship); that South Korea remained an impoverished country, and one with a military dictator (in contradistinction to indisputably democratic Japan, which was also rapidly becoming affluent); that North Korea was a communist dictatorship (this criticism disregarded the enthusiasm for communism among some Japanese leftists); and that ethnic Koreans in Japan (known as Zainichi) were perceived as poor, rebellious, and inassimilable.[181] In spite of the prevailing anti-Korean sentiment, some Japanese listeners eagerly purchased records by South Korean singers. Chang Se-jŏng, for example, released "Ariran hatoba" (Arirang Harbor) in 1961, and in 1968 she rereleased her 1937 hit in Japanese, as "Renrakusen no uta" (The song of the ferry).[182] The first genuinely successful post–World War II Korean musical export was Yi Sŏng-ae's 1977 hit "Kasumapuge" ("Kasum ap'uge" [My heart aches] in Korean). It would initiate a boom in South Korean songs, capped by Cho Yong-p'il's runaway 1982 hit "Fuzankō e kaere" (Return to Pusan Harbor), called "Torawayo Pusanhang e" in Korean. Cho was the first openly Korean singer to compete in the "red-white singing contest," the *Kōhaku Utagassen* broadcast that takes place in Japan on New Year's Eve and was for a long time the most-viewed television show in that country.[183] In 1988, Kye Ŭn-suk (known in Japan as Kei Unsuku) also competed on *Kōhaku Utagassen,* three years after her Japanese debut. Thus a steady stream of South Korean trot singers made their mark in Japan in the last quarter of the twentieth century.

More striking still was the sheer preponderance of ethnic Korean singers in Japan. Given the existence of systematic employment discrimination, it was a commonsense notion among Zainichi in the immediate post–World War II decades that an ethnic Korean boy in Japan should become a baseball player (baseball was easily the most popular and lucrative sport) and that an ethnic Korean girl in Japan should become a singer.[184] In fact, however, boys as well as girls sought fame and fortune in the popular-music industry. Almost all of them sought to pass as ethnic Japanese and to occlude their Korean background. However, Miyako Harumi's classic 1965 *enka* song "Namida no renrakusen" (The ferry of tears) is reminiscent of 1930s Korean *yuhaengga* in the theme of its lyrics, and her signature raspy roar, recalling the sound of *p'ansori* singers, almost begs to be identified as Korean. Less visible than the singers were the mainly South Korean backup musicians, composers, and producers who shuttled back and forth between South Korea and Japan, sustaining the two countries' similar soundscape of popular songs. But similarity does not mean absolute sameness. The most remarkable example of this principle may be "Kasuba no onna" (The woman of the casbah). This 1955 composition by Son Mog-in, whose vast oeuvre includes the 1935 hit "Mokp'o ŭi nunmul," was released in a South Korean version in 1967 but faltered even though it was sung by the redoubtable Patti Kim (the record's jacket features her in a black dress with décolletage).[185] But the cover by Midorikawa Ako, also released in 1967, was a breakaway hit in Japan.[186] Exotic locales and incidental ethnic themes, such as those related to blues and tango, were long-standing features of Japanese songs, especially *mūdo kayō,* whereas South Korean trot songs tended to be about South Korea.[187]

The dominance of trot became entrenched in 1970s South Korea. In addition to Yi Mi-ja, two male singers—Nam Chin and Na Hu-na, who had debuted in 1967 and 1969, respectively—were superstars by the mid-1970s.[188] Even in the 1960s trot had been considered old people's music, but its fan base in the cities grew as newcomers from the villages continued to arrive in droves. These fans eschewed traditional Korean music, but they couldn't quite bring themselves to embrace American or American-inflected popular music. Thus trot was, in effect, a cultural integument of the new South Korea and its burgeoning national popular culture. Although movies had been the primary cultural genre to cut through the still powerful status divisions in South Korea, trot began to bridge the previously deep chasm between high and low.[189] The golden age of trot was the era not only of accelerating economic growth, rapid rural exodus, and national cultural integration but also of rapid dissemination of television sets. In 1970, just over 6 percent of South Korean households owned a TV, but that proportion had increased to more than 30 percent by 1975 and to nearly 98 percent five years later. And while in 1970, TV ownership was an overwhelmingly urban phenomenon, with a television set in 95 percent of households in the cities, by 1980 virtually every household in South Korea owned a TV.[190] As a result, trot, once it had become entrenched in the cities, proceeded to spread throughout the peninsula, thanks to television broadcasts. KBS's pioneering *Sho Sho Sho* featured more light pop and *kayo,* and later *kayo* programs would feature more trot singers as the television-watching audience expanded.[191] Movie houses, cafés, bars, and other loci of popular music's consumption remained important, but by the mid-1970s, television had become the principal medium.[192] It would not be an exaggeration to say that television was the fulcrum around which the South Korean nation came together—physically so, since the entire family frequently watched television together.[193] *Kayo* shows were very popular in the 1970s, and trot was the most popular genre. Thus trot was the background music of the Park era.

The story of trot's hegemony between Liberation and the rise of K-pop obscures the considerable vitality and diversity of South Korean popular music from the 1950s to the 1990s. Cho Yong-p'il of "Fuzankō e kaere" fame has been a superstar since 1975, but he had a previous life as an electric guitarist in a rock band. The original South Korean version of his 1982 Japanese hit was in fact nouveau trot; some contemporaries called it *t'ŭrot'ŭ ko-ko* ("trot gō-gō," the second part of this phrase being a Japanese term for rock music) or *rokku ppong* ("rock *ppongtchak*," the second part of this phrase being an alternative term for trot), a label that suggests a rock-infused type of music.[194] In the context of the usual two- or four-beat rhythm of trot, Cho's use of a rock-influenced eight-beat rhythm is not unlike the shift from a bicycle to a motorcycle. Cho's enormously successful career constitutes something of a pentimento, with the occluded rock-music core of his work surfacing over time.[195] It would be a misleading oversimplification to equate the South Korean popular music of the 1960s and 1970s with trot music, just as it would be to assume that trot was simple and static.

As trot's popularity extended to the countryside in the 1970s, urbanites, especially youths, lent their ears to other forms of popular music. A 1967 television special on the year's top twelve hits is suggestive.[196] It began with Ch'oe Hŭi-jun's *sin minyo* song, followed by two trot songs, but the next six were light pop songs (*kyŏng ŭmak*). Already by the 1960s, trot seemed old-fashioned to young urbanites—not surprisingly, since its broad contours had been shaped in the colonial period. AFKN radio and later television disseminated, in addition to the overflow of camp-town musicians, American-style popular music. The terms *kayo* and trot are often regarded as synonymous, but *kayo* usually denotes light music. Popular American tunes sung in Korean by Hyŏn Mi, such as "Tennessee Waltz," or by Pak Chae-ran, such as "Pearly Shells," found appreciative South Korean listeners. These easy-listening or lounge songs, with their associations of urbanity and sophistication, would soon be classified as Muzak by the rock generation, but for the time being they filled the air of modern establishments—that is, establishments that were not Korean but also not quite American, such as hotel lobbies and lounges, teashops, and bars.[197] Along with Han Myŏng-suk's infectious song, other joyful jingles filled the urban soundscape, such as Ch'oe Hŭi-jun's 1961 song "Nae sarang Churian" (My love Julian) and Cho Ae-hŭi's 1964 song "Nae irŭm ŭn sonyŏ" (My name is girl). As suggested by the case of Ch'oe, who later sang *sin minyo* in the 1967 television special, singers often covered distinct genres over time.

Apart from the background impact of American music, subterranean imports of post–World War II Japanese popular music (also influenced by American music) should not be overlooked.[198] In spite of the anti-Japanese political atmosphere, the South Korean music scene, especially in Seoul, closely tracked developments in Japan. In particular, colonial-era ties and postcolonial interactions ensured a steady flow of Japanese popular music to South Korea. That is, South Korean businessmen (in the 1960s, businesspeople were almost exclusively men), students, and musicians brought back Japanese records and songs. Myŏng-dong was full of supposedly banned Japanese publications and records. In contrast to the melismatic practices that characterized trot singing, *kayo* singing tended to be much more syllabic. Ironically, the staccato singing style was then alien enough to be considered a mark of low vocal talent. In taste and temperament, however, urban South Koreans were not so far from their counterparts in Japan. Domesticated (or Japanese-influenced) pop music, often composed and performed by ethnic Koreans, created a regional music soundscape, a hybrid of European instruments and techniques and the signature Japanese pentatonic scale.[199]

The Eighth Army remained a center of musical performance, linked to the largest and most influential music market in the world. Given the plethora of musicians, some ventured outside the American zone to perform for their co-nationals. Patti Kim is an exemplary figure in this regard. After debuting in 1959 as a singer for the Eighth Army, she became phenomenally popular, performing in Las Vegas, Tokyo, and Southeast Asia.[200] She was initially promoted by Benny Kim, the outstanding impresario for the Eighth Army, and later she worked with and married Ch'oe Chi-jŏng (also called Yoshiya Jun), a well-known jazz musician in Japan and a major figure in South Korean popular music.[201] With a repertoire that ranged from light pop to lounge music, Patti Kim, like the Kim Sisters, appealed to those who preferred what came to be pejoratively classified as easy-listening music. Although she appeared on television, her mainstay was live performances in concerts and nightclubs, venues that appealed to more affluent, older listeners. Another export from this era was the Korean Kittens, who spent the mid-1960s touring abroad and made an appearance in 1964 on the BBC show *Tonight*, singing the Beatles' "Can't Buy Me Love" in a mixture of Korean and English.[202] The central figure of the group, Yun Pok-hŭi (Yoon Bok Hee), would go on to have a successful career in musicals but became an overnight sensation in

1967 when she was photographed upon her return to Gimpo Airport in Seoul wearing a miniskirt.[203]

By the 1960s, rock was ascendant in the United States and elsewhere, and some South Koreans eagerly embraced the latest trends. There was a British invasion of South Korea, though it was heavily mediated by the United States and Japan, and it led to the first flowering of rock, called "group sounds" (the term is Japanese in origin).[204] The indisputable dynamo of this movement was Sin Chung-hyŏn (Jacky Shin).[205] Having honed his guitar-playing chops in the camp towns, Sin composed, produced, and sponsored singers who would not have been out of place in the US music scene of the 1960s. His 1964 debut album, *Pitsok ŭi yŏin* (The woman in the rain), features a four-some—three guitarists and a percussionist (the group was called Edŭ p'o, meaning "Add 4")—singing a style of light rock reminiscent of the early Beatles. The instruments were the same as those of the Beatles, and the lyrics, though in Korean, were sung in a fast, upbeat pitch and tempo. The music was loud (for the time), with pronounced percussive beats and bass lines. In a sharp departure from the traditional norms of Korean music, the scale, rhythms, and style were clearly Western. Sin's achievements richly deserve the retrospective respect and honor he has garnered. Particularly noteworthy is his 1974 song "Miin" (Beautiful woman), a singular hybrid that combines the soul of *nongak* with the stylings of Eric Clapton: as a solo electric guitar plays in the pentatonic scale, the listener almost hears the dynamic jangle of agrarian Korean music.

Perhaps even more innovative, and indisputably more popular, were the light pop songs with dance routines that Sin championed. Beginning with the Pearl Sisters and their 1968 hit "Nima" (Darling), Sin shaped a series of acts and composed songs for them, including, most prominently, such women soloists as Kim Ch'u-ja and Kim Chŏng-mi.[206] Sin's burst of creativity in the late 1960s and early 1970s introduced progressive American music to South Korea, from light pop and mournful ballads to rock with psychedelic, funk, and acid-rock undertones. In "Kŏjitmaliya" (Lies), Kim Ch'u-ja's 1971 classic, the opening guitar solo, the forceful rock beats, and the catchy, haunting refrain encapsulate a musical moment distinct from trot or light pop (not to mention from *sin minyo* and *p'ansori*) and announce the arrival of a new soundscape. Even the album jackets, whether for Kim Ch'u-ja's 1971 *Kŏjitmaliya* or Kim Chŏng-mi's 1973 *NOW*, feature innovative, funky typefaces and color schemes reminiscent of the art of Anglo-American rock, as exemplified by the jacket of the Beatles' 1965 album *Rubber Soul*. And fashions are decidedly un-Confucian: we see the miniskirts and hot pants that were emblematic of the late 1960s and early 1970s in the West. The Pearl Sisters, preceding Girls' Generation by more than three decades, made their exposed legs something of a trademark. As their 1968 song "K'ŏp'i hanjan" (A cup of coffee) suggests, the Pearl Sisters and their colleagues exemplified a new urban consumer culture, one that included coffee.[207] The extent of the deviance from Korean musical traditions—dancing accompanied by singing, wildly swinging arms and bodies—can be gauged by the rumor that Kim Ch'u-ja was sending secret signals to North Korea.[208] Yet as we view her energetic performance in the 1971 film *Naeil ŭi p'aldogangsan* (The Korean peninsula of tomorrow), we also see an upscale audience dancing in what was still the comparatively tame style of early rock. By the end of the 1960s, the young and the curious, flocking to new musical venues in the Myŏng-dong district of central Seoul—places like New World, C'est Si Bon, and Die Schöne—constituted what came to be known as the *Myŏngdongjok* (the Myŏng-dong tribe).[209] At the precipice of Park's rapid turn to autocratic rule, the spirit of Americanization—which had accelerated during the post–Korean War 1950s, with intimations of political, cultural, and sexual freedom—was far from having been snuffed out.

If trot was too Japanese, rock was too American and therefore, paradoxically, even more suspect. Its assumed associations with sex, drugs, and politics (that is, with the student movement and the specter of communism) prompted the Park regime to place Sin and his associates under heavy surveillance. Rock in South Korea experienced a brief period of efflorescence in 1973 and 1974, and the paranoid are not always wrong: the country's early rock musicians, with their ties to the music scene of the military camp towns, did pioneer a lifestyle that valorized sex and drugs.[210] (However, it was not as if the elders themselves, given their leanings toward the proverbial wine, women, and song, were innocent of physical and pharmaceutical transgressions.) The crescendo of the government's crackdown—the ban on long hair in 1970, and on miniskirts in 1973—climaxed in 1975 with Presidential Emergency Decree Number 9. The 1975 edict banned 222 South Korean records and 261 foreign songs, on the grounds of everything from "negative influences on national security" to "pessimistic content." Later that year, in December, Sin was imprisoned in connection with a sensational marijuana scandal.[211] Thereafter, and until the mid-1980s, rock music was silenced in the South Korean soundscape, along with the nascent culture of rock music, including sexy clothing. Thus the Park regime, which had been intent a decade earlier on expunging Japaneseness from trot, unintentionally strengthened trot's place in South Korean popular music from the mid-1970s to the end of that decade.

But it would be simplistic to blame governmental repression for South Korean rock's demise in the mid-1970s. Outside the circle of urban youth, the sort of music performed by Sin and his associates was derisively called *ttanttara* (jangling, or loud noise), though in this regard the adjective "jangling" was something of a cultural universal for the music of that reputedly rebellious generation. Even among young, curious, countercultural urbanites, however, rock remained less than a majority taste, and the culture of rock music, or at least of the 1960s youth culture that had spread across the West, did not thrive in South Korea.[212] The standard living arrangements provided little privacy for listening to loud music, and few could gain access to the instruments or the space needed to create or absorb *ttanttara*. Even radio was relatively rare—as late as 1970, only one in ten South Koreans owned a radio set—and so radio failed to play the important role it had played in popularizing the new, youth-oriented music in the United States, Japan, and elsewhere.[213] The Baby Boomers who would constitute the rock generation in the West and Japan (though not in South Korea, where the Korean War had interrupted and skewed that demographic pattern) found their anthems elsewhere.[214] The 1960s, and rock music, largely bypassed South Korea.

If American progressive rock foundered in South Korea on the twin shoals of governmental repression and popular indifference, folk music (or folk-rock music) emerged as an alternative genre around which anti-government urban youths coalesced in the 1970s. In South Korea, folk music was often called *t'ong kit'a* (literally, "barrel guitar"), a reference to a barrel to sit on while playing the inevitable and ubiquitous musical instrument.[215] Like the activists of the US student movement, South Korean university students turned to folk as the preferred music of politicized youth. South Korea has a self-conscious and legendary tradition of student movements: the ouster of Rhee is usually called the April Student Revolution, and the long reign of Park embroiled many students in spiraling, strident, anti-government rhetoric and actions, which provoked even more violent anti-student rhetoric and reactions from the Park regime. As the dialectic of opposition and repression escalated throughout the late 1960s and 1970s, contemporary folk songs, owing more to Bob Dylan than to "Arirang," found a following.

Modern folk music was not just the music of the new generation globally; it was almost the very sound of simplicity and authenticity. Unlike commercialized popular music, with its extensive divisions of labor, folk music embodied the ideal of wholeness and integrity in the character of the singer-songwriter. The accessible melodies were usually sung plainly, if not plaintively, and the singing was accompanied only by a guitar or two; by contrast with rock music, the means of performance were relatively inexpensive. In the course of the 1970s, folk music, constituting the counterculture or the underground, became inextricable from the student anti-government movement in South Korea. Not only did the music remain mellow, the extra-musical dimension was mellow, too; the drugs of choice were nicotine and alcohol, not the psychoactive substances often favored in the United States and elsewhere. In 1969, the pioneering folk performer in South Korea was probably T'ŭwin P'orio (Twin Folio), but the most eminent folk performer was Kim Min-gi, and the most emblematic folk song was his 1971 "Achi'm isŭl" (Morning dew). Even though the song was released before the 1972 promulgation of the authoritarian Yusin Constitution, Kim was chastened for his anti-government message, and the song was banned, only to become the anthem of the anti-government movement.[216] The 1974 song "Haengbok ŭi nara ro" (To the country of happiness), by Han Tae-su (Han Dae Soo), is more properly understood as an anthem of youth and the new generation. The song—reminiscent of early Dylan, with its bright timbre and youthful lyrics—was a ray of light in the dark, dismal years of Yusin rule.[217] Folk music maintained its elective affinity with the anti-government student movement into the 1980s. Unlike Han, however, Yang Hŭi-ŭn, Kim Kwang-sŏk, and other notable performers sang simple, slow melodies, their singing style converging, in this regard, with the style of contemporary balladeers.

By the time of Park's death, South Korean popular music had undergone nearly two decades of heightening repression. The marks of state surveillance and discipline were everywhere, and the nightly curfew was only the most egregious strike against liberal, leisure society: young people could wear neither long hair (for men) nor miniskirts (for women), and before the screening of a film, or during the blaring of the national anthem at six o'clock each evening, everyone was obliged to stop everything, stand erect, and salute the flag. In this and other ways, the authoritarian face of South Korea mirrored that of North Korea.[218] Trot was too Japanese, Japanese songs were imperialist, rock was sex-addled and drug-infused, and folk songs were anti-government; even composers of classical music, such as Isang Yun, came under fire for their political views. In a move reminiscent of colonial-era (and possibly North Korean) cultural policy, the government, after suppressing so many "unhealthy" songs, attempted to gain the upper hand over the unruly world of popular music by promoting *kŏnjŏn kayo* (healthy popular music).[219] "Saemaŭl ŭi norae" (The song of the new village), perhaps the most representative of the so-called healthy songs, was said to have been written and composed by President Park himself—in the Japanese pentatonic scale, which should come as no surprise. Mercifully, however, it was performed by professional singers.[220] Another of Park's supposed pieces was "Na ŭi Choguk" (My homeland), a revival of colonial-era, wartime *gunkoku kayō*. The government-sanctioned healthy songs had cheerful lyrics and melodies—the most popular one was an unabashed celebration of the Republic of Korea—and at least one of these songs had to be included on every LP.[221] (Imagine listening to a Bob Dylan record and finding a Pat Boone song at the end!) South Korea in the late 1970s was, to say the least, an openly authoritarian society with an active culture of censorship.

Governmental suppression never completely standardized or squelched individual tastes in music, however. Even though some *kŏnjŏn kayo* attracted genuine fans—for example, Chŏng Su-ra's 1984 pop paean to the country, "A! Taehanmin'guk" (Ah! The Republic of Korea)—most people listened to a variety of genres. Certainly the inroads made by radio and by recorded, reproducible music had greatly expanded the listening possibilities. As I have emphasized, a retrospective glance at the 1970s runs the risk of exaggerating trot's popularity, and even in the mid-1970s, at the height of Park's repressive rule, Japanese music could still be found in teahouses and individual homes. Rock and anti-government music, too, although muted in public, could still be heard, not only in the camp towns but also in various urban quarters.

Toward the end of Park's repressive rule, a new, national, post-trot popular music emerged. It was the era not only of the presidential emergency decrees but also of the romantic scandals that tarnished the reputations of Nam Chin and Na Hu-na, the two giants of trot. Two other singers made their dramatic entrées around this time. I have already discussed the first of them: Cho Yong-p'il, who became a superstar with his rock-influenced trot (but Cho, like Sin Chung-hyŏn in 1975, was arrested for marijuana use in 1977 and was banned from performing for three years).[222] The other new singer was Hye Ŭn-i. Hye's 1976 debut song, "Tangsin ŭn morŭsilkkŏya" (You wouldn't know), and the following year's "Tangsinman ŭl saranghae" (I will only love you), catapulted her to the summit of stardom.[223] Although she sang a few trot songs, it would be a category mistake to call her a trot singer; the two songs just mentioned, which were composed and promoted by the jazz musician Ch'oe/Yoshiya, are pop ballads.[224] Hye had started out as a poorly paid nightclub singer, but she managed to project an uncanny sense of freshness. In fact, the singer and her songs were a volatile mix of contradictory impulses: she seemed innocent and almost virginal but also worldly, perhaps too much so; her lyrics were melancholic, even tragic, but her singing and her appearance were ineffably cheerful; her songs sounded like slow ballads, but they featured jazzed-up instrumentation (there is a bluesy feel to the saxophone that introduces "Tangsinman ŭl saranghae"); Hye's stage presence was effete and effeminate but also charismatic and dynamic; and although she purported to be a nationally iconic singer of the trot era, she was in fact closer to the age of folk or even disco, as in her 1980 mega hit "Che 3 Han'ganggyo" (Han River Bridge number 3).[225] It was fortunate for Hye that she was attractive: although popular music has always valorized physical appearance, television elevated the significance of a singer's looks, and over the course of the next two decades, with the advent of the age of universal television ownership, the visual element of a musical performance became almost as important as the aural.

In short, Park's repressive rule effaced the blossoming of American pop and curbed the enthusiasm for trot in 1960s South Korea, and thwarted the rise of rock in the early 1970s. Trot dominated during the period of accelerated exodus from the countryside to the cities; the new *kayo* became hegemonic precisely when South Korean social and cultural integration were more or less complete. Trot and *kayo* were both hybrid genres that had sustained some links to the older Korean soundscape. From our current perspective, Cho and Hye may seem to be all about trot, but it would be an act of enormous historical condescension to ignore the fact that in their day they were seen as refreshing and forward-looking, and to forget the very reasons for their popularity, which included not only their considerable vocal prowess but also their absorption of other motifs that were current in South Korean popular music, elements ranging from the American to the Japanese, and from rock to jazz. It would not be an exaggeration to say that a distinctive South Korean *kayo* was born precisely when an integrated national audience came into being.

THE INTERREGNUM: NATIONAL POPULAR MUSIC IN THE 1980S

Park's death unleashed the pent-up demand for democratic participation, as amply demonstrated during the Seoul Spring of 1980. The rump regime promulgated martial law in May of that year and suppressed demonstrators in Kwangju some days later. The Fifth Republic under Chun Doo-hwan almost immediately tightened governmental control over the mass media and by the end of the year had dissolved forty-four of the sixty-four extant media companies.[226] Yet Chun was no Park; and, more important, South Korea had undergone an irrevocable transformation. The Chun regime, unable to sustain its rule by force, pursued what has come to be known as the 3S policy of promoting screens, sex, and sports. I have already noted that television ownership was nearly universal by 1980. Color television broad-casting began in 1981. The following year, the nocturnal curfew was lifted when *Aema puin* (Madame Aema), widely remembered as the first erotic South Korean film, became all the rage (and eventually spawned at least ten sequels). And the year after that, the government lifted its repressive restrictions on the clothing and hair of middle and high school pupils, thus ending the tyranny of drab couture and "rice bowl" coiffure. Popular entertainment was encouraged, with less stringent restrictions (in the depiction of romantic relations, for example). Popular music was now government-sanctioned mass entertainment; even the government-promoted healthy music was peppy, upbeat, and difficult to distinguish from mainstream pop. Professional base-ball was launched in 1982. In short, the Fifth Republic followed a neo-Marxist prescription regarding the depoliticizing effect of popular culture.

South Korea in the mid-1980s was a morass of change and contradiction. Affluence and poverty, starkly juxtaposed, coexisted with a military rule that seemed permanently engaged in surveillance and discipline. Students and workers demonstrated; riot police beat them into submission. Popular music was part and parcel of the entrenched struggles.[227] Yet on the surface South Korea was a place of repose, and the world of popular music in the 1980s seemed static. This impression stems from the sheer dominance of television. Television stations, having dethroned movie theaters as the principal loci of entertainment in South Korea, aired staid and certainly depoliticized pro-grams, music included. Because television sought to reach the entire nation, its content tended toward the least common denominator, which extended to the choice of songs. Anything out of the ordinary would have resulted in rapid censure by the government, a job made easier by the fact that there were effectively only two stations, and one of them was government-owned. (A third station was nominally out of the censors' reach, but the US military's Armed Forces Korean Network was not known for inciting popular discontent.)

The post–Yusin Constitution regime of repression was successful in generating outward and sometimes inward conformity. There was a general preference for slow, virtuosic singing of music composed in the pentatonic scale. That is, faint echoes of colonial-period *yuhaengga* reverberated in South Korea in the 1980s. A good example of this phenomenon is provided by the disgraced Cho Yong-p'il, who bounced back in 1980 with a megahit, "Ch'ang pakküi yŏja" (The woman outside the window). Gone is the eight-beat rock rhythm; in this song, the chastened Cho sings slowly, claiming to have spent three years in exile learning *p'ansori* in the mountains so that he can connect to "the blood of the Korean people."[228] Humbug aside, a superstar like Cho does not remain a superstar by ignoring which way the wind blows.

Organic continuity or even reversal does not imply homogeneity or lack of change. Just as Hye's music marked a shift from trot, the balladeers of the 1980s were distinct from Hye. They incorporated folk music's simplicity and colloquialism into post-trot music, which resembled the Japanese ballads of the 1970s and 1980s. And this is no surprise, not only because of the transnational movements and influences of ethnic Korean musicians but also because of the common regional soundscape born of long colonial rule and postcolonial American influence. The government continued to censor undesirable music, a category that included almost the entire range of popular music in South Korea. However, even in the staid world of trot, there were fresh faces and styles. One superstar who emerged in the early 1980s, Chu Hyŏn-mi, was an ethnic Chinese woman who had grown up in South Korea. Like Hye, Chu was an outstanding vocalist who also benefited from her attractive appearance.

For younger listeners who rejected trot, however reinvigorated that genre may have been, the ballad was the music of choice. Starting in 1978, Yi Mun-se released a string of songs that were well received, especially the 1981 hit "Nanŭn haengbokhan saram" (I am a happy man), and he reached the height of his popularity with 1988's "Kwanghwamun yŏn'ga" (Kwanghwamun sonata) and 1991's "Yetsarang" (Old love). The latter two were sweet or bittersweet love songs, but Yi incorporated elements of folk, rock, and other genres. Another male singer of ballads, Kim Hyŏn-sik, distinguished himself with songs of his own composition. A representative song from 1986, "Nae sarang, nae kyŏt e" (My love, my side), shows him as both more powerful and more melancholic than Yi Mun-se. Kim's raspy voice could have issued from a *p'ansori* singer but was indisputably infused with pop sensibilities, and so it sounded modern.

A singer popular across all age groups was Yi Sŏn-hŭi, who catapulted to stardom with her 1984 hit "J ege" (To J). In the era when she emerged, listeners yearned for romance, appreciated vocal prowess, and were still able to overlook the requirement for conventional beauty as a major criterion of pop-music stardom—and Yi, bespectacled and unisex in presentation, seized the moment. She often wore suits, projecting both conservatism (by covering her body) and a progressive outlook (by a display of a sartorial androgyny that challenged male dominance in an era when most women wore skirts). Even more than Yi Mun-se, she ranged widely in her music, singing trot, folk, and even rock songs with great dexterity and emotion. Precisely when television was both ubiquitous and the universal form of entertainment, Yi Sŏn-hŭi managed to place herself front and center and was seemingly beloved by everyone from preteens to grandmothers. Her magic was in appearing to be the essential, homogeneous Korean who just happened to be a great singer and could also navigate the hybrid soundscapes of 1980s South Korea. There were different tastes and genres, but there was only one television set, and Yi Sŏn-hŭi was the perfect compromise.[229]

But if we turn our gaze away from the TV (and turn the sound off), we can clearly perceive the conflicts and contradictions of 1980s South Korea, as expressed in popular music. When *ch'angga* and *kagok* began to lose their hold on educated South Koreans—the population of college students began to grow rapidly in the 1980s—ensemble singers turned to people's music, an amalgam of folk and popular songs expressing protest against the authoritarian regime and its social backdrop.[230] Singing groups sprouted up on college campuses that were embroiled in anti-government activities, first at the elite colleges and then more widely: this was the *norae undong* (song movement), part of the *minjung* (people's) movement.[231] Not surprisingly, the genre of music performed by these groups is sometimes known as *minjung kayo* (people's song).[232] By the late 1980s, some of these ensembles, such as Shinch'on Blues and Tongmulwŏn (Zoo), had turned professional, incorporating folk-rock elements. Needless to say, not all these singers evinced a stridently anti-government ideology, either personally or musically, and few were explicitly countercultural in appearance or lifestyle. The television station MBC had launched Taehak Kayoje, its annual university song festival, in 1977, marking the significance of this demographic as a musical force.[233] As a result, many of the performers in this generation infiltrated South Korean popular music and influenced mainstream tastes.

Beyond college campuses, some young listeners yearned for sounds other than the gentle melodies of folk music or the melismatic smoothness of pop ballads. Ever since the sensational 1975 drug scandal involving Sin Chung-hyŏn, governmental and school authorities, in league with parents and other elders, had been united in the attempt to extirpate *ttanttara* and its cultural manifestations. But this repression on the part of the older generation failed to squelch rock completely; there were always radio broadcasts (over short-wave radio, if necessary) and LPs for savoring the latest from the West. The "group sounds" that emerged in the 1970s came largely out of the camp-town music scene. The new generation of soft-rock groups, which proliferated after the suspension of the older generation of rockers, usually consisted of college-based bands, such as Sand Pebbles (Saendŭp'ebŭljŭ), winner of the first grand prix in the competition attached to the annual university song festival. "Na ŏttokhae" (What can I do), a song from 1977, lacks the power and charisma of Sin's music, not to mention that music's amplitude and bass, and is not far removed from a mainstream pop ballad except for the use of electric guitar.[234] These characteristics also apply broadly to other self-proclaimed rock bands of the late 1970s, such as Sanŭlim (Sanwoolim/Mountain Echo) and Songgolmae (Songolmae/Peregrine Falcon). Only in the mid-1980s did rock defiantly reassert itself. Tŭlgukhwa's 1985 song "Haengjin" (Forward) and a 1986 song by Sinawi (Sinawe), aptly titled "K'ŭge radio rŭl k'yŏgo" (Turn up the radio), with the subtitle "heavy metal," heralded the universe of deafening sound that had eluded these groups' predecessors.

A closer and deeper look into the mid-1980s suggests that a number of music venues in Seoul would not have been out of place in New York or Los Angeles. Some of the avant-garde discotheques and bars in central Seoul, It'aewŏn, and Gangnam, along with establishments in the camp towns, were playing the same music that was then being aired in the United States: disco, postdisco, and dance pop, plus smooth jazz and R & B, and even techno and New Wave. And a glance at the listeners and dancers in those venues reveals new constituencies: affluent youths (hitherto shut out of these establishments, whether by parental dictate or prevailing norms), diasporic Koreans (returning most noticeably from the United States but also from Japan and elsewhere), and trickles of nonmilitary and nonmissionary foreigners. These music venues also imported American popular music, including its most prized recent innovation: music videos. The soundscape in Seoul was once again transforming, as if in concert with the city's skyline: during the reign of trot, colonial-period architecture and a few fresh neotraditional buildings dominated; with the rise of Hye and the new *kayo,* mass-produced, indistinguishable apartment complexes came to constitute Seoul's built environment, and the old structures were mercilessly pulverized as high-rises contin-ued to go up. But this new *kayo,* like so many old buildings, would soon be eclipsed by another genre altogether.

The agent of change was youth, which arose as a distinct social category, and one with discretionary spending power. The social gravity of popular music had long been a moot issue for South Korean adolescents and youth in general because they did not have the technological, sociological, or financial means to consume popular music. As I have said, almost every household owned a television set by 1980, but few households had more than one, and watching TV on that single set was a collective activity. Given the prevailing gerontocratic climate, the preferences of young people were far from influen-tial. Beyond the private sphere, cafés and bars catering to American GIs and South Korean businessmen had long been the dominant players when it came to popular music's paying audience. Concerts were few and far between. But the most decisive factor was that few young people before the 1980s had pos-sessed the wherewithal to purchase records, much less phonographs. The new mode of youth-led consumption emerged only in that decade, with the enrichment of South Korea and the greater spending power of young people.

South Korean youth had constituted a salient social category before the mid-1980s, but young people collectively had been far from inclined to pur-sue rock music or tunes for teenyboppers. And the powerful student move-ment, rather than generating a counterculture of emancipation, had accentu-ated the cult of seriousness and struck a blow against the potentially decadent culture of sex, drugs, and rock 'n' roll. Given the ham-fisted nature of mili-tary rule, the most notable cleavage in South Korean politics as well as in South Korean popular music was between the pro-government and anti-government factions, but the two factions converged in their hypernational-ism. The dance between the autocratic government and the student move-ment came to a standstill: a national stasis of unsmiling Confucianism, performed to music played in the Japanese-inflected pentatonic scale. In other words, musically as well as extramusically (in terms of dress and demeanor), sincerity and seriousness reigned as consensus values and virtues—a situation rather unpromising for any flowering of popular music. When photographs and video clips of popular musicians from the late 1950s are compared with photos and clips of popular musicians from the late 1970s, the disappearance of smiles and of bared shoulders cannot be denied; in that span of twenty years, fun became mere frivolity, and sexiness became scandalous. Popular songs and singers, whether pro-government or anti-government, came to be subsumed within the narrow ambit of the culture of seriousness and sincerity. Nevertheless, despite the persistence of the puritanical and the sanctimonious, a new breed of less serious, more fun-loving South Korean youth emerged in the 1980s.

By the mid-1980s, we begin to see the precursors of K-pop, of performers who bear a family resemblance to contemporary South Korean popular musicians. The crucial backdrop is the fusion of music and dance that occurred in the United States in the late 1970s and early 1980s. Music and dance are of course inextricably intertwined in many ritual and leisure contexts, but R & B and disco seem, in retrospect, merely to have set the stage for the pop revolution in dance. Here, the soft and the hard intertwine. Michael Jackson's 1979 album *Off the Wall* featured motion-inducing music, but his superb skills as a dancer were rarely seen outside concert venues and the occasional television appearance. But MTV, which was launched in 1981, integrated the two most powerful currents in popular culture—music and movies—when it made listening to music and watching a video a pair of simultaneous, synergistic experiences. Music videos that fused singing with dancing (or at least with some sort of visual narrative) constituted a pop *Gesamtkunstwerk* that quickly assumed a commanding presence in US popular culture.[235] The genre that K-pop would inhabit was exemplified by Michael Jackson and MTV. Probably the key work of this new mixed genre was the video of "Billie Jean," a song from Jackson's 1982 album *Thriller* that became a huge hit. The video had a major effect on virtually all of popular music.[236]

Kim Wan-sŏn, who debuted in 1986, was a trailblazer, with her peppy songs accompanied by dynamic dancing. Called the Madonna of South Korea (the inevitable comparison to an American star underscores the importance of American popular music), Kim reigned briefly as a superstar. But Kim's wild swaying—which differentiated her from the vast majority of other singers of this era, who stood erect and usually motionless—came under suspicion among governmental authorities, and she was repeatedly warned to tone her act down.[237] Not since the Pearl Sisters and Kim Ch'u-ja, in the early 1970s, had South Koreans seen a co-national sing and move so vigorously. Kim's immense success led to the release of a single in Japan and launched her brief but successful career as a Taiwanese star. As a young star molded largely by her manager, she enjoyed an ascent that anticipated the modus operandi of K-pop.[238] And if there was a South Korean Madonna, then there had to be a South Korean Michael Jackson, too. That was Pak

Nam-jung, who became known for his deft dance moves. A sense of cool was clearly entering South Korean youth culture. At the same time, the so-called idol groups—young and attractive boys and girls singing and dancing to a music that was clearly differentiated from their parents' music—made their first appearance in 1987 with the single "Ŏjetpam iyagi" (Last night's story), by Sobangch'a (the group's name means "fire truck").[239] Sobangch'a, far from the perfectionism of contemporary K-pop performers, was virtually a circus act: the members wore gaudy, glittering clothes, sang meaningless lyrics with gusto, and ran and jumped energetically around the stage, enacting an almost literal fire drill. But even though Sobangch'a was widely derided as silly and effeminate, the group attracted throngs of adoring fans—and offered a taste of things to come.

THE SŎ T'AE-JI REVOLUTION

The massive political protests and mobilization of 1987 brought out not only the usual suspects, such as university students and factory workers, but also white-collar professionals and middle-class housewives, and led to the formal transition to political democracy in South Korea, symbolically and visibly cemented by the 1988 Seoul Olympics. In a way, everything I have written so far is history, in the colloquial American sense of that term. Change, unlike its presentation in the before-and-after photos common to advertisements for plastic surgery, is almost never discontinuous, because it feels gradual and practically imperceptible to people living in real time. Nevertheless, a revolution in popular music came seemingly out of nowhere in 1992. In other words, in the history of South Korean popular music, we can point to the period before and the period after Sŏ T'ae-ji wa Aidŭl (Seo Taiji and the Boys).[240]

This revolution was televised. Sŏ T'ae-ji wa Aidŭl's first major national exposure came on a nationally broadcast program, which featured several talking heads who commented on new songs; it was basically *The X Factor,* but without the voting. The middle-aged commentators were, to put it mildly, uncomprehending, uncomfortable, and uncharitable about the trio's debut song, "Nan arayo" (I know).[241] They dismissed the performers' skill and *sforzando* as inferiority and immaturity and gave Sŏ T'ae-ji wa Aidŭl the lowest score. If this had indeed been *The X Factor,* the trio would have been booted off the very first episode. But the judges themselves were invalidated by the judgment of history, so to speak: the song sold an astonishing 1.7 million copies (at the time, the total population of the country was about 40 million people), and it remained South Korea's top-selling song for seventeen consecutive weeks. Sŏ T'ae-ji wa Aidŭl's performance featured rapping and break dancing, and it was, in retrospect, very much a period piece, like Sŏ's clothing and the spectacle of his singing and dancing. But what is astonishing is how much South Korea's top hit of 1992 sounded like contemporaneous American popular music; in the early 1980s, when Michael Jackson and Madonna dominated popular music almost everywhere outside the Korean peninsula, South Koreans would have named three trot performers—Yi Mi-ja, Cho Yong-p'il, and Na Hu-na—as iconic national singers.[242]

Like many things minatory in the cultural realm, Sŏ T'ae-ji wa Aidŭl proved to be vatic, annihilating all that had been made of South Korean popular music. Sŏ's group announced the arrival of youth as popular music's primary audience in South Korea. Musically, Sŏ T'ae-ji wa Aidŭl not only legitimated rap and hip-hop in South Korea but also narrowed, or even erased, the temporal gap between South Korean and American popular music. Sŏ himself listened widely to the anglophone popular music of the 1980s and 1990s, ranging from the Clash and Sonic Youth to the Red Hot Chili Peppers and Rage Against the Machine.[243] In the post-Liberation period, South Koreans were still used to talking about the general state of their nation in terms of how many years, or even decades, the country lagged behind Japan or the United States. Much the same discourse dominated some sectors of popular music, too, even though it was often impossible to compare South Korean popular music with popular music in Japan or the United States. As the singing star SE7EN, who would make his debut in 2003, says of his formative influences, the impact of Sŏ's trio was paramount: "Oh, this is it. . . . I couldn't believe that this style of music existed in the world."[244] The younger generation in democratic South Korea embraced the new and, in so doing, not only asserted the centrality of youth to popular music but also rendered moot the question of the country's musical backwardness.

Sŏ T'ae-ji wa Aidŭl challenged and ultimately destroyed many conventions of South Korean popular music. Trot songs as well as a surprising number of ballads and folk songs employed the Japanese pentatonic scale, but after the explosive impact of Sŏ T'ae-ji wa Aidŭl, use of the pentatonic scale would steadily decline. The long chapter of Japan's deep influence on Korean popular music was coming to a close.[245] It was the new and dominant

American soundscape that made much pre-1990s South Korean popular music sound like trot, or old people's music. For an ear attuned to the post-Sŏ period, Yi Sŏn-hŭi or Yi Mun-se might as well have been trot singers, worthy of consignment to the prehistory of K-pop. And the same disjunction appeared as the standard singing style changed from legato to staccato, from melismatic to syllabic, from crooning to spitting. Lyrics, no longer voiced in plaintive vibrato, were now articulated as parlando, as rapping. Even when sung in Korean, they sounded as though they were in English. The neo-Confucian ethos of seriousness and sincerity, along with conservative attire and a demure posture, gave way to a new urbanity and pizzazz. The sartorial semiotic turned away from diligent, obedient businesspeople and toward urban youths (presumably unemployed or underemployed) with attitude. Sŏ T'ae-ji became the face of hip-hop's aesthetic of bling and baggy clothes. Sŏ also marked something of a turning point in the male aesthetic: the agrarian ideal of a moon-shaped face and a stocky, robust body was supplanted by the androgynous, urban look of a longer, pretty face and a tall, thin frame. In any case, girls and young women found Sŏ dashing, to the bafflement of their male counterparts and their elders. Until Sŏ exploded onto the scene, the normal presentation of self in a performer had meant standing up straight and virtually motionless, but the new norm soon came to embrace gesticulation and dance as essential elements of performance. And the group did not merely sway or move in the way that most South Koreans then thought of as dancing (fox-trot, go-go, hustle); the group engaged in the acrobatics of break dancing.[246] In 1996, Sŏ T'ae-ji wa Aidŭl also successfully challenged governmental censorship. Although the government's formal and informal interventions never completely ceased, governmental oversight faded in its fervor and frequency, a change facilitated by the successive progressive presidential reigns of Kim Dae-jung and Roh Moo-hyon. Finally, Sŏ T'ae-ji wa Aidŭl was a rare instance of the self-produced and self-promoted group. Its musical innovations and political independence were underscored by its commercial autonomy. Even though the trio sought to capture the mainstream market and appeared frequently on national television, the group also represented the avant-garde of indie music in South Korea.

Needless to say, Sŏ T'ae-ji wa Aidŭl did not have this transformational impact in a vacuum. Without South Korea's economic enrichment and political democratization, and without the emergence of South Korean youth who had access to discretionary income, the group would have disappeared, just as the television judges had wished. The diminishing influence of Japan and the growing impact of the United States were belated developments as well as foregone conclusions. By the early 1990s, few South Koreans had any sustained personal experience of the colonial period; postcolonial Korean-Japanese discourse was no longer conducted in Japanese but in English. Moreover, the convergence between South Korean and US musical sensibilities and tastes reflected the profound intercultural contact between the two countries. I have already mentioned the systematic introduction to US popular culture that came with the US military presence. For much of the post-Liberation period, the United States was the country most admired in South Korea, and many South Koreans looked up, however ambivalently at times, to the American way of life. The liberalization of study abroad in the early 1980s also dispatched many eager young South Koreans to the United States. Even more numerous were members of the South Korean diaspora. Korean Americans and South Koreans abroad, many in New York and Los Angeles, witnessed and participated in the very birth of popular-music genres and dances and brought them back to South Korea. Lee Soo-man (Yi Su-man), the founder of the influential company SM Entertainment, was one such witness, and one of his first stars, Hyŏn Chin-yŏng, was Korean American. Especially in the 1990s, a steady stream of Korean Americans, including Kang Su-ji (Kang Soo Jee), SOLID, Yu Sŭng-jun (Yoo Seungjun/Steve Yoo), Lena Park (Pak Chŏng-hyŏn), and many more, began returning to South Korea so they could perform in the country. In every facet of the US popular music industry there were well-trained South Koreans or Korean Americans, from composers to choreographers, from fashion designers to videographers.[247]

To cite an age-old formula of fame and success, Sŏ T'ae-ji wa Aidŭl was in the right place at the right time. After democracy came to South Korea, the country was ripe for a new generation of music fans to jettison their parents' and elder siblings' music in favor of the new. Young people now had the money to spend on music and the technology for its consumption (including their own TV sets). Democratic, affluent South Korea was set to shed some of its past musical proclivities—or, as it turned out, almost all of them. Certainly the flash of social change was flooding South Koreans with new musical influences from around the world. But hip-hop, in fact, had been introduced earlier. Not only does the aforementioned Hyŏn Chin-yŏng's 1990 work "Sŭlp'ŭn manek'ing" (Sad young model) incorporate the rhythms of hip-hop, Hyŏn himself performs the Roger Rabbit dance steps as if he were Bobby Brown, who was then enjoying his own long fifteen minutes.[248] Deux (Tyusŭ), who debuted in 1993, and Turbo (T'ŏbo), who debuted in 1995, entrenched hip-hop music and dance in South Korean popular-music culture while Roo'ra (Rulla), Cool (K'ul), and especially Koyote (K'oyot'ae), whose respective debuts took place in 1994, 1994, and 1999, established postdisco hip-hop–influenced dance pop as a vibrant genre. Rap also entered the mainstream by way of Ri Ssang (Leessang) and Yu Sŭng-jun. It was just a matter of someone's assembling a successful package of rap and hip-hop, music and dance, for a new generation that sought something novel and exciting.

The early 1990s were a time of considerable ferment in Seoul. Democratization and the people's movement had swept through the city, and innovative, idiosyncratic performers proliferated. Beyond American music, South Korean performers often covered J-pop songs.[249] As noted earlier, even though the long-standing Japanese influence was fading, a new generation still followed popular tunes from the Japanese archipelago, music that, as J-pop, had entered a period of innovation in the late 1980s. We cannot understand the emergence of K-pop idol groups without considering the example and influence of Japanese idol singers and groups, but in the 1990s groups like Anzen Chitai and the Southern All-Stars demonstrated deft ways of articulating the latest American sounds. Unfortunately, there was also considerable piracy of J-pop by South Korean musicians.[250]

The 1990s also brought efforts to incorporate traditional Korean sounds into contemporary popular music. In the realm of European classical music, Isang Yun had alluded to Korean melodies and used Korean instruments, but it was only in this turbulent political-cultural period that the rock guitarist Kim Su-ch'ŏl (Kim Soo-chul) and the folk musician Yi Sang-ŭn (also known as Lee Tzsche) explored the rich realm of traditional Korean music.[251] In particular, Yi Sang-ŭn's eponymous 1993 album brings together *sanjo* and jazz improvisation to create a distinct musical world. Nevertheless, that road remains seldom traveled.

A much more popular path is represented by the invention of indie music and its introduction into South Korea. In this regard, rock was the dominant genre, as exemplified by the soft rockers Yun To-hyŏn and Deli Spice, noted for having brought contemporary Western rock (à la U2) to South Korea. Starting in the mid-1990s, postrock music genres emerged in rapid succession, including punk (Crying Nut, whose debut was in 1995, and No Brain, who debuted in 1996), grunge (Ppippi Band, 1995), postmodern rock (Nemesis, 1997), and acid jazz (Roller Coaster, 1999).[252] Ppippi Band is sometimes considered to have been the first indie band in South Korea; it was indisputably the first "weird" band, featuring a lead singer who didn't, or couldn't, carry a tune but who dressed and danced with splendid nonconformity. Another noteworthy trait of that time is covert, and sometimes overt, social and political criticism, as exemplified by Panic's 1996 album *Mit* (Bottom). In the mid-1990s, the Hongdae area (that is, the area around Hong'ik University) surfaced as the capital of the South Korean indie music scene. In 1997, Jaurim (or Chaurim, which means, literally, "purple rain forest") released its first record; the band had been a pioneering presence and remains exemplary in the genre of indie rock music.

Interesting and intriguing though indie music is, it remains a marginal phenomenon in South Korea. The post–Sŏ T'ae-ji universe is more readily apparent in South Korean popular music's mainstreaming of R & B. The Japanese radio disc jockey Furuya Masayuki recalls the vibrant music scene in Seoul in the late 1990s and waxes enthusiastic about R & B, which he called K-pop.[253] Kim Kŏn-mo, who debuted the same year as Sŏ's trio, far outsold Sŏ T'ae-ji wa Aidŭl: Kim's third album, released in 1995, sold close to 3 million copies. In spite of his limited vocal range, Kim managed to integrate new influences seamlessly into both an R & B-infused music and pop ballads. His 1992 song "Cham mot tŭnŭn pam pinŭn naerigo" (Sleepless, rainy night) opens with rap, and his 1993 blockbuster "P'inggye" (Excuse) reveals a clear reggae influence. Kim's 1996 hit "Chalmottoen mannam" (Wrongful encounter) brought rave music to South Korea. His adroit mixing of styles pointed to a new articulation of South Korean popular music. Given the South Korean penchant for identifying a local parallel to a key American figure, Kim came to be known as the Stevie Wonder of South Korea. Beyond Kim, the groups SOLID and BROWN EYES firmly established the place of R & B in South Korean life. The point here is that R & B was virtually nonexistent before 1992 in South Korea; afterward, it came to constitute something close to the mainstream in the new urban, youth-centered music.

Sŏ T'ae-ji wa Aidŭl did not cause the invention of indie music or the popularity of R & B or hip-hop in South Korea. The group's success was merely indicative of what was to come, though its explosive popularity did pave the way for many new styles of music. It is possible to see the Madonna of South Korea (Kim Wan-sŏn), or perhaps the Pearl Sisters, as having initiated dance music in South Korea; we shouldn't forget that *yuhaengga* and trot were often music to dance to. But Sŏ's group made dance music the new normal. And much the same can be said when it comes to the infusion of urban American black music in the form of R & B, rap, or hip-hop.

From the standpoint of K-pop, the most consequential effect of the Sŏ Tae-ji revolution was that it spawned idol groups. The defining moment arrived in 1996, with the breakout success of H.O.T. (High Five of Teenagers). H.O.T.'s debut single, "Chŏnsa ŭi huye" (Descendants of warriors), expressed a viewpoint, widespread among young students, that was critical of school-yard violence and unsympathetic parents and teachers. But H.O.T.'s "Candy" is more characteristic of the group. The music video for the song is set in Lotte World, a Disneyesque amusement park; the performers wear clownish outfits and oversize sweatshirts, innocently and cheerfully sing nonsense lyrics, and happily bounce around, though these antics are punctuated by dance routines.[254] It is fair to say that there is absolutely no edge to be found in H.O.T.'s music; the group incinerated anything that would be out of place in a Disney movie. And even the most sympathetic viewer of the "Candy" video would be hard pressed to find much musical merit in it. The group displays a certain resemblance to the pioneering boy band Sobangch'a, and to the sort of anodyne singing ensembles that the Japanese production agency Johnny's Jimusho was churning out at the time. Although H.O.T. is replete with marks of Americana, including occasional allusions to US musical culture, the group's sonic world could be comfortably contained in the middle-class apartment that was becoming the standard habitat in Seoul. The mindless melody of bubblegum pop (which seems immortal) presented a softer, kinder, gentler rendition of what Sŏ T'ae-ji wa Aidŭl had proposed four years earlier. H.O.T. tamed the edges off the Sŏ T'ae-ji revolution. The group also signaled the decline of Park's authoritarian culture and its inevitable emphasis on seriousness.

H.O.T. created a social sensation. Screaming girls thronged the group's concerts. Young men adopted the group's "H.O.T. cut" hairstyle (long in front, short in back) and B-boy style (oversize shirts and slacks). Merchandise affiliated with the group ranged from candy to perfume, and it sold well. One fan even committed suicide when the group disbanded.[255] By 1997, hot on the heels of the group's success, the emergence of new boy bands and girl bands was already almost relentless, as demonstrated by the appearance of Sechs Kies (Cheksŭ K'isŭ), NRG, Baby V.O.X., S.E.S., Fin.K.L (P'ingk'ŭl), and on and on. What was new about the phenomenon was that these groups' bright-timbred, tinny-sounding, upbeat songs, with their cheerful, mindless melodies, would challenge and eventually sweep over the melancholic trot songs and more heartfelt ballads of previous generations. In terms of exports, these groups were still far from the success that K-pop groups would enjoy some ten years later, but they were making their mark in the late 1990s, and that level of success included the first whiffs of foreign fandom.

Songs, stars, and styles fade away slowly, as I have emphasized throughout this chapter, and it is not as if trot, folk music, or ballads totally disappeared. In the rapid *tour d'horizon* that this chapter has been, the narrative stress has necessarily fallen on the new and unusual. Consequently, the chapter is presentist, in the sense of emphasizing links to the future. But a narrative focused on what will endure and go on to influence others will miss not only the fact that older people continued to listen to the favorite songs and genres of their youth but also the reality that the mainstream audience remained stubbornly conservative. The rumors of trot's demise are greatly exaggerated. A remarkable number of singers—some of whom were active in the 1970s, such as T'ae Chin-a (Tae Jin Ah), and some of whom are new sensations, such as Chang Yun-jŏng (Jang Yoon Jung)—still appear on South Korean television shows to peddle nostalgia. All the same, contemporary revivals and new trot songs are usually presented in up-to-date arrangements, much louder and faster than the *ttanttara* of the 1970s; the immortal words of the composer Morton Feldman, though uttered in a different context, might not be out of place in a description of this newer trot music: "It's too fuckin' loud, and it's too fuckin' fast."[256] In the 1990s, probably the single most popular style of song remained the love ballad, with its links to the 1980s and even earlier eras. It is likely that the balladeer Sin Sŭng-hun (Shin Seung Hun) sold more records than any other South Korean performer in the 1990s. The media crowned him the emperor of love ballads, and for many South Koreans this meant that Sin's soft, slow, sweet, soporific love songs, from 1990's "Miso sok e pich'in kŭdae" (Your smile in reflection) to 2001's "I Believe," represented the pinnacle of popular music. And not far behind Sin Sŭng-hun was Yi Sŭng-hwan. The tradition of South Korean ballads has continued into the twenty-first century, with such standout performers as Cho Sŏng-mo (Jo Sung Mo), Paek Chi-yŏng (Baek Ji-young), and the singer-songwriter Kim Tong-ryul (Kim Dong-ryool). Their popularity can be gauged by their ubiquity: it is hard to watch a South Korean soap opera without being serenaded by one of these singers' love songs.

That probably explains why H.O.T.'s 1996 sensation "Candy," in spite of all the brouhaha, only reached fourth place among that year's best-selling CDs. Sin Sŭng-hun and Kim Kŏn-mo sold many more records. Yet it would have been difficult to deny—and, from the twenty-twenty hindsight of the early 2010s, it would have been all but obvious—which way the wind was blowing. The most rapidly expanding segment of the music-purchasing public was the previously penurious demographic of teenagers. This was a generational shift better gauged by the volume of screaming fans than by the number of record sales.

FERMATA

I have sought in this chapter to distill the long and rich history of Korean music. However compressed and truncated my account has been, the emphasis has been on discontinuities, beginning with the rift that separates traditional Korean music from the Western soundscape that has dominated the twentieth century and beyond. The Sŏ T'ae-ji revolution marks the most recent of Korean popular music's breaks with the past, and K-pop was born of post-Sŏ trends. Chapter 2 elaborates on the age of K-pop, and it delves into K-pop's production and exportation, but the following section—the interlude—considers the larger significance for South Korea of the historical transformation that has been outlined in this chapter.

Interlude

SEVERAL YEARS AGO, an eminent social scientist arrived in black *hanbok* (Korean clothing) for a lecture I was delivering in Seoul. Because it is so rare now to clothe oneself in *hanbok,* I asked her why she was dressed up. She said that she had just come from a funeral.

Baffled, I asked her, "Since when do Koreans wear black to a funeral?" Not only have people living on the Korean peninsula worn white at funeral ceremonies for as long as we can make out, the choice of white for funerals is also common across Asia.[1] In any case, black has been uncommon in the traditional Korean repertoire of sartorial dyes.[2] What is even more significant is that this woman is a distinguished student of Korean rituals and folkways. That a highly cultivated woman, someone who had spent much of her adult life studying Korean culture, should apparently have forgotten that white was once the traditional color of mourning may have been a sign of creeping senility, but it seems much more likely that it was a symptom of South Korea's tremendous transformation and the attendant cultural amnesia. For every stentorian pronouncement about South Korean nationalism, an element of traditional Korean culture seems to evaporate from South Korea. Even as South Korean soap operas endlessly replay scenes from the Chosŏn dynasty, contemporary South Korean life has squelched substantial and organic ties to traditional Korea. The end of the traditional Korean soundscape and the emergence of K-pop exemplify South Korean cultural transformation and amnesia.

This interlude serves as something of a cadenza. It is not about K-pop; rather, it is a meditation on what K-pop says about contemporary South Korea, and so it may be more akin to pizzicato or, to be perhaps more accurate, to *col legno battuto,* a plucked or percussive discussion: a polemic.

THE CHOSŎN DYNASTY AND THE CONFUCIAN
MIRAGE

Ask almost any contemporary South Korean about Korean tradition, and she is likely to say something about the Chosŏn dynasty and the Confucian legacy. She would be largely correct: much of what contemporary South Koreans regard as Korean culture and tradition does date to that long-lasting dynasty. Although some antecedents can be traced back even further, much of what contemporary South Koreans identify as "Korean" has its roots in the seventeenth century or the period shortly thereafter.[3]

The contemporary discourse about the Confucian legacy is almost always misleading, however. What is most disturbing, the Chosŏn-Confucian literati were in no doubt about their genealogy (having traced the sources of Korean civilization to China), or about their own place: squarely in the Sinocentric world order. A protonational territorial identity undoubtedly coexisted with the embrace of the Confucian worldview, but it would be an exaggeration to ascribe a strong Korean identity to those Sinophilic, Confucian officials and landlords. The dominant principle of the world order was *sadaejuŭi,* a tribute system in which one enshrined the rule of the great— namely, Chinese civilization. The increasing assertion of Korean distinctiveness stems from the fall of the Ming dynasty and the rise of the Qing. The presence and activities of the barbaric Qing, like those of the Japanese to the east, accentuated the self-conception of the Chosŏn elite as keepers of the veritable Confucian-Chinese tradition.[4]

Confucianism as the ruling ideology not only vitiated the Koreanness of the ruling elite—the monarchy, the aristocracy, and the landlord class (usually called *yangban*)—but also placed the elite against and above the people we would call ordinary Koreans. The very foundation of Chosŏn Korea was a series of status divisions. It may be too simplistic to say that the country was characterized by a dual social organization of elite and male Confucianism against demotic and female shamanism, but such a characterization would correctly highlight the fundamental disunity of Chosŏn Korea.[5] In a country where at times nearly a third of the population existed as *chŏnmin*—outcasts who were beneath the status of *yangmin* (good or ordinary people), a category that was itself subdivided into *yangban, chung'in* (middle people), and *sangmin* (ordinary people)—the idea of a common Korean identity was inchoate at best.[6] In any case, Confucian rule was largely nominal, since the central government had few officials and almost no infrastructural capacity to discipline the population at large.[7] Chosŏn Korea, lacking a strong integrative force, exhibited great regional diversity. Not only was the majority of the population illiterate, most people also lived outside the system of the Confucian principles and ethos, subscribing instead to the folk traditions of shamanism and other non-Confucian beliefs and practices. In the course of the long Chosŏn dynasty, Confucian principles and practices spread, as agrarian households aspired to the beliefs and ritual system of the prestigious and powerful elite, but it would be misleading to impose, in retrospect, the elite Confucian matrix on the agrarian majority, or to presume an isomorphic identity between the elite and the nonelite.[8]

The mirage of the past as a unified cultural entity sustains the illusion of the present perfect continuous. The past, however, has passed—mercifully, in many ways. Chosŏn-period Confucianism was a ruling ideology that valorized cultural cultivation for the elite literati and consigned the masses—non-Confucian, and therefore questionably Korean—to toil in ignorance. Yet it is commonly believed that Confucianism undergirds everything in contemporary South Korea, from the everyday ethos of diligence and punctuality to family values and low crime rates. In this way of thinking, a straight line connects the dynastic examination system (which applied only to select Chosŏn-period government officials) with the contemporary "diploma disease" and the maniacal emphasis on succeeding in examinations and getting into university, obsessions that in turn have spawned "cram schools" (*hagwŏn*), which trap young pupils into studying well into the night. But this contemporary projection ignores past reality: education was only for the landed elite and aspiring government officials.[9] And the legacy of that reality is clear: at the end of colonial rule, more than 75 percent of the population was illiterate, and as late as 1960 the literacy rate in South Korea was no higher than it was in Thailand or the Philippines.[10] To the extent that a system of universal elementary education was instituted in colonial Korea and South Korea, the motivating force was external, coming from the Japanese colonial government before 1945 and from the occupying US military after 1945. It is indisputable that the population has been seriously engaged in academic competition since the 1960s, but this is a modern trend born of a culture of ambition and the possibility of upward mobility. That is, democratizing and demotic South Korea, not the traditional Confucian country, is what plunged the populace into the morass of "diploma disease" and created a *hagwŏn* heaven.[11]

It would be equally misleading to limn a straight line from the Chosŏn-Confucian ethos to the contemporary South Korean work ethic. The very point of Confucian life was to create and sustain a form of leisure society for the elite. As late as the mid-twentieth century, an American anthropologist could report of a South Korean village: "The [*yangban*] did no work, wore horse hair hats, and lived off the labor of their tenants or each other. Their local power was great and sometimes absolute and operated a system of nepotism which was classic in its proportions."[12] Although there are hints of the capitalist work ethic in the late nineteenth century, along with nascent signs of capitalist industrialization, economic traditionalism reigned in pre-colonial Korea.[13] The roots of the contemporary South Korean work ethic lie not in the Chosŏn-Confucian ethos but in the incentives of capitalist industrialization, in the often untrammeled power of the state and of management, in the new culture of upward mobility, in the military and its regimentation, and in other forces that are found squarely within modern Korean life.

The recent revalorization of Confucianism in South Korea is actually a symptom of the unbridgeable distance between the non-Confucian present and the Confucian past. When Confucianism was a more salient presence, Koreans waxed eloquent about its desuetude and dysfunctions. Certainly this was the case even at the height of the Chosŏn era, as can be observed in such stirring critiques as Hŏ Kyun's *Hong Kil-dong chŏn* (The legend of Hong Kil-dong) and Pak Chi-wŏn's *Yangbanjŏn* (The tale of yangban).[14] In general, twentieth-century Koreans have identified Confucianism as the principal source of Korean ills (such as the fact of Korea's having fallen behind Japan and become its colony); for instance, Sin Ch'ae-ho's 1908 work "Toksa sillon" (New theory of history) accused Confucianism of "sowing confusion and chaos and instilling inferiority."[15] The post-Liberation efflorescence of philo-Americanism has also derided tradition and Confucianism in favor of such Western ideals as democracy, science, and progress. Park Chung-hee repeatedly blamed Confucianism for South Korea's backwardness and sought to extirpate Confucianism's nefarious consequences, including the existence of the reactionary landlord class and the system of status hierarchy.[16]

One thing is certain: had Confucianism survived and thrived in South Korea, K-pop would not have been possible. In chapter 1, I touched on political censorship and cultural taboos, but K-pop violates almost all the Confucian precepts. Needless to say, K-pop songs do not belong in the Confucian soundscape or in the musical culture of *kugak*. The singers would be held in low esteem and would be seen as outcasts, on a par with streetwalkers. They would also be expected to dress and dance properly (rather than exposing their bodies and making sexually suggestive moves) and not to tamper with their parentally endowed faces and bodies (hence no plastic surgery).[17] Romantic love, one of the major themes of K-pop songs, is also antithetical to Confucian morality, and when post-traditional Koreans talk about love, it is in precise contradiction to the strictures of Confucian tradition.[18] In a sense, K-pop songs and dances recall—if they recall anything at all of traditional Korea—the wild gyrations and bestial wailings of shamanist dance that so exercised the Confucian literati.[19] In other words, the demise of Confucian culture is one of the preconditions for K-pop.

If I am right about the disappearance of Chosŏn-era Confucianism from contemporary South Korea, then why did so many South Koreans so readily adduce Confucianism as the explanation for one or another aspect of South Korean culture and society? The poverty of the sociological imagination is one compelling reason; beyond tradition (Confucianism) and nationalism, there isn't a rich discourse in South Korea to make sense of South Korean particularities. Confucianism is almost the only readily available *differentia specifica* for making sense of South (or North) Korea, the trouble here being that it is hard to locate the differential path between South and North in Confucian tradition. Decades of authoritarian rule and the examination-based educational system have impoverished South Korean self-understanding and self-reflection; generations of South Koreans have been forced to memorize and regurgitate names and dates rather than think seriously about Korean history, culture, and tradition, which in turn have been the province of politically correct anticommunist nationalist historiography. Some South Koreans, partly in reaction to the vibrant student and labor movements of the 1980s, sought to resuscitate the idea of Korean history and culture as Confucian.[20] For example, one business-school professor, after a lifetime of imbibing American and Western learning, undertook an extensive study of the Confucian classics so he could re-create harmony in the classroom and the workplace—but he forgot that the Confucian ethic, at least for the *yangban*, was intended to sustain a life of leisure, and was inimical to the prevailing contemporary capitalist ethos. Be that as it may, Confucianism, after being relentlessly denounced for nearly a century, has made a comeback as the ethos underlying South Korean tradition and culture. The evidence of this successful resuscitation can be seen in how readily Confucianism is offered, *faute de mieux,* as the rationale for everything from educational madness to K-pop.

No historical period is more contentious in South Korean historiography than the colonial period; a contemporary convention is to ascribe all the woes of modern Korea to Japan, and to admit no good as having come out of colonial rule. Although the West and its achievements entered the Korean peninsula before Japanese occupation, and post-Chosŏn Korea might well have forged its own distinct modernity or capitalist industrialization without Japan, what almost all Koreans took to be the Western (and the modern) came largely during the colonial period, via the filter of Japanese language and culture.[21] *Yuhaengga,* as we saw, was a Korean permutation of Japanese *ryūkōka*—not exactly the same thing, but the former was predicated on the latter.[22]

The shock of the new arrived most viscerally in the form of organizational and technological innovation. Mass schooling, the military and its destructive weaponry, the Western bureaucracy with its discourses and uniforms, capitalist factories and department stores—all these and much more entered Korea in a rapid and compressed manner in the first half of the colonial period. In turn, urban areas became the crucible of the new: foreign ideas, art forms, and lifestyles penetrated the peninsula, usually mediated by Japanese sources. New vocabularies and ideas, which captured the imagination and the passion of impressionable and idealistic youth, largely came from Japanese translations.[23] And the new Japanese-inflected soundscape of *ch'angga* and *yuhaengga* filled the city air. Thus what some call colonial modernity was a *translated* modernity and, in large part, an adaptation of Japanese modernity—which is not necessarily to deny Korean particularity and peculiarity.

In retrospect, it is not surprising that the colonized population, more often than not, grudgingly emulated and even embraced the colonial masters and their civilization. But what is striking about colonial Korea is the extent of capitulation to Japanese rule. Perhaps the most emblematic instance of this phenomenon is that Yi Kwang-su, the most influential writer of the time, advocated jettisoning the Korean language in favor of the Japanese.[24] In all colonial situations, the question of collaboration is inevitable; it is impossible to sustain colonial rule without a measure of cooperation from the colonized. Yet it is one thing to cooperate in political or economic decisions and their execution; it is another matter altogether to squelch the civilizational legacy and assimilate actively and wholeheartedly to the new, conquering power. The situation in Korea was all the more unusual because it was common in the nascent period of modern nation building for an author to assume the role of iconic national writer. Think of Goethe in Germany, Pushkin in Russia, or Natsume Sōseki in Japan—polyglots all, but it would strain credibility to read of Goethe's having advocated French as the lingua franca of Germany's cultural sphere, or of Pushkin's having endorsed German in Russia's, or of Natsume's having argued for English in Japan's.[25] None of these writers was under pressure from a colonial power, but Yi nevertheless promulgated a death warrant for Korean language and culture.[26]

Yi was far from alone in cultural capitulation. Much to the chagrin of South Korean nationalists, the erstwhile Confucian elite had all but collapsed when it came to protecting Korean civilization or advocating Korean political independence. As one symptom of this cultural defeat, the first great nationalist intellectual, Sŏ Chae-p'il, became a US citizen and died as Philip Jaisohn. To the extent that the scions of the erstwhile elite even participated in anti-colonial, pro-independence politics, they were overwhelmingly affected by foreign belief systems, such as Christianity and communism. After the March First Movement of 1919, overt resistance to Japanese rule ceased on the Korean peninsula. It is easy enough to credit Japanese effectiveness or cruelty, but the reality is that Japanese rule was hegemonic (and was thus perforce a mixture of assent and dissent, acculturation and repression). As a new generation of Koreans was schooled in the Japanese curriculum, its members learned about the modern—a singular entity, but in fact an admixture of the West and Japan—and the modern proved attractive, certainly much more so than the traditions of Confucian-Chosŏn civilization, which, so to speak, lost out to Western-Japanese modernity. Even the poet Kim So-un, who wrote pioneering books on Korean folklore, could not but support the Japanese imperial effort.[27]

The Korean elite embraced the Japanese modern and eschewed its own heritage: Confucian-Chosŏn civilization. True to the legendary fervor of the converted, an embarrassing number of the elite remained not so much silent as active accomplices in the Japanization of Korea.[28] In chapter 1, I noted that the colonial government, rather than ethnic Korean intellectuals, was instrumental in collecting and thus preserving Korean folktales and folk songs. Ethnic Japanese intellectuals, rather than their ethnic Korean counterparts, also pioneered studies of Korean history and anthropology.[29] The construction of Japanese orientalism—the study of the inferior Other—may have been an instance of knowledge as the will to power, but few ethnic Koreans were expending any effort to preserve or recover Korean manners and mores.

It is symptomatic that ethnic Koreans also abandoned Chinese classics in favor of Western and Japanese models. Yi Kwang-su, in the guise of nationalism, relentlessly blamed the incursion of Confucianism and Chinese culture for the destruction of Korean culture and literature.[30] But it was not just Yi, relying on Japanese sources and working in Japan to create a new Korean literature, who diluted the Korean cultural heritage.[31] Ceramics and other traditional crafts were famously championed by Yanagi Muneyoshi, but not by any eminent Koreans.[32] Likewise, some ethnic Japanese were praising the work of the dancer Ch'oe Sŭng-hŭi at a time when she herself was bemoaning her fellow Koreans' neglect of traditional Korean dance.[33] And in 1921 the Japanese musicologist Tanabe Hisao described traditional Korean music as an "international cultural treasure," but *kugak* and demotic folk music were rejected by educated ethnic Koreans during the colonial period.[34]

Needless to say, the Korean elite did not all become pro-Japanese, but nearly all the countercolonial, pro-independence struggles occurred outside the Korean peninsula. It is not altogether clear what communism meant for the Korean nation—political independence from Japanese imperial rule, to be sure, but also the withering away of the state and the nation?—but North Korean leaders could at least point to their putative heroism in having resisted Japanese rule in Manchuria and elsewhere.[35] The indelible association of communism with national independence would catapult Kim Il-sung and his comrades to popularity after Liberation.[36] In contrast, the newly independent South Korea lacked any obvious source of legitimacy. The traditional ruling elite was tainted by its close collaboration with the colonial ruling apparatus, so much so that almost no one was ready to govern when the war (and thus colonial rule) ended.[37] It is difficult to recapture the extent of Japanese hegemony in colonial Korea, but we should recall that the otherwise sane Yi Kwang-su gave up on the Korean language, and that some excessively idealistic Korean youths aspired to be kamikaze pilots.[38] It is no wonder that most South Koreans today see colonial rule as an era of unremitting darkness: cultural amnesia as contemporary convenience.

THE TRIUMPH OF THE AMERICAN CENTURY?

South Korea became independent in 1948. The new ruling elite in South Korea was led by Rhee Syngman (Yi Sŭng-man), an anticommunist nationalist who had spent more than thirty years away from the Korean peninsula.

His first cabinet was dominated by the very *yangban* class that had been, at best, quiescent during the colonial period. The notable exception was Kim Ku, who was soon assassinated. The Rhee regime, between exterminating its political and intellectual rivals and suppressing rural uprisings, justified the worst suspicions of its critics.[39] It is difficult to name a less beloved founder of a modern nation-state. Indeed, Rhee is no longer even infamous, merely forgotten.[40] After all, Rhee and the comrades who came to power with him did little to end colonial subjugation. The immovable geopolitical reality is that the United States and the Allied powers had defeated Japan. By the time of the "fall" of China, in 1949, the Cold War was the defining reality, and the division of the Korean peninsula was an inevitable corollary. In the new post–World War II reality, the insurgent communists replaced the defeated colonizers as the primary enemy. In other words, South Korea's archenemy— about whom South Koreans were not allowed to voice positive sentiments, and whom, for a long stretch, they were not even permitted to view in photographs—was none other than South Koreans' co-ethnics in North Korea.[41] That is, not just Japan but North Korea as well was effaced from or stereotyped in the South Korean imaginary, and the United States loomed as the alpha and omega of South Korean reality.

The South Korean elite's embrace of American culture was rapid and thorough. The specter of *sadaejuŭi* once again haunted South Korea, this time in mid-twentieth-century American garb. The grandparents of the elite had been steeped in Sinocentric culture, and the parents of the elite (like many of the elite themselves) had been steeped in Japanocentric culture, with its deep admiration for European and especially German civilization; now, at the apogee of the short American Century, the new movers and shakers, along with aspiring youths, were turning to the United States. Overnight, English displaced Japanese (which in turn had superseded Chinese) to become the foreign language of choice. The Rhee government translated and executed what the US military conceived.[42] The extent of Americanization can be gauged by the rapid spread of American first names among politicians and high-level bureaucrats. For example, the second leader of South Korea was no longer Chang Myŏn but John M. Chang. It was the fashion of the urban middle class to adopt the trappings of American life, not only in design, fashion, and architecture but also (if slowly at first) in food and entertainment. Given that the United States and especially its military were the font of power and wealth in South Korea, much of urban South Korea was oriented toward their whims, from food and clothing to entertainment, whether musical or sexual. Many South Koreans harbored the desire to live in the United States itself and thus to flee their impoverished and insecure homeland. Over half of the physicians who graduated from one of the top two medical schools in South Korea between 1952 and 1985 ended up in the United States.[43] This is a shocking proportion, given the privileged status of physicians in South Korea: better, in brief, to be an ordinary medical practitioner or even a shopkeeper in the United States than to be a member of the privileged elite in South Korea. This mind-set soon spread throughout South Korea, making that country a land of diasporic departures.

The reign of Rhee is remembered in contemporary South Korea as a time of stagnation and corruption. Rhee and his cronies engaged in outright electoral fraud, conspicuous corruption, and random violence.[44] It is for good reason that almost no one fetes the founding president of South Korea. To put it simply, Rhee preserved the content of *yangban* dominance but shifted its form to that of American-style democracy.[45] The effect was confusing and contradictory. Most educated Koreans (a group that was largely male) were more or less bilingual in Korean and Japanese by the end of colonial rule, and even for a long time after Liberation the primary conduit of information was Japanese-language books (usually translations of foreign volumes).[46] Yet Japan was an entity at once repressed and reviled. The Rhee regime would purge most of the high-level ethnic Korean officials who had staffed the Japanese colonial bureaucracy, but it would retain the Japanese institutional apparatus.[47] Certainly Rhee did his utmost to expunge Japan from South Korea, but it would take decades of anti-Japanese cultural campaigns and American influence for South Korea to shed Japan's profound influence. At the same time, people did not stop at learning conversational English or listening to American pop songs but also began to assimilate the ideological tenets of the American way of life—not only political democracy but, even more important, the belief in progress and mobility. Although the nascent student movement that triumphed in the April Student Revolution often had a Confucian and nationalist cast, we should not ignore the fact that the newly educated South Koreans saw themselves in the light of an ideal America where democracy was obviously superior, corruption was insistently rejected, radical claims of status equality and individual dignity were espoused, and the pursuit of wealth and happiness was legitimate.[48] That is, these South Koreans looked to an American future, not to the Confucian or Japanese past. The optative world of Hollywood movies and American pop songs—a world of both material plenty and casual egalitarianism, promising upward mobility and a better life—framed and colored the new South Korean worldview. As noted in passing in chapter 1, the sweetness and light of some South Korean popular music in the 1950s was a world away from the tears of departure and the tacit expressions of *han* that had marked the popular songs of the colonial period.

In short, the Rhee regime attempted to expunge the past (a generation of Japanese influence) and introduce the future (American culture), all the while seeking to sustain the social status of the *yangban* class. The American influence would eventually prevail over the Japanese, but the Korean War would more immediately foil the effort to continue elite rule.

THE KOREAN WAR

The Korean War, by its sheer destructiveness, blighted a generation in North and South Korea alike.[49] About a tenth of the population perished, and many others were injured or displaced; hardly anyone escaped undamaged from the war. There is nothing like fratricidal combat to foment emotional vituperation. The visceral anguish and anger fueled South Korean anticommunist nationalism—the same force would also sustain North Korean anti-imperialist nationalism—and lent urgency to the calculated logic of the superpower-sustained Cold War.

The emotional impact of war, though obvious to survivors, is difficult to convey to others; post-traumatic stress disorder is a condition that applies to individual combatants and victims, not to collective memory. Yet the sheer devastation is incontrovertible. Throughout the peninsula, few buildings and monuments survived the repeated bombardments. People who escaped death often lost loved ones, and the country was full of physically disabled and mentally disturbed Koreans. Less tangibly, cultural memory vanished—not only books and manuscripts but also photographs, correspondence, and diaries. Even the scions of the landed elite often had to choose between vacating their homes and facing a communist army bent on liquidating the bourgeoisie, and so they often left behind (and at times burned) the tokens and proofs of their privilege, and therefore of their memories. The individuals, families, and organizations of the post–Korean War years are shockingly ill documented.

The loss of memory and history in turn loosened people's moorings; the Korean War vitiated people's sense of homeland (*kohyang*). In part, the situation merely continued the colonial-era social transformation; peasants continued to be displaced from their villages and continued to seek their fortune in the cities. But the war destroyed any facile belief in the Korean nation as a united homeland; this had been a recent and nascent idea, but it was an ideal that still could have been a coagulant for the erstwhile colonized population. More tangibly, *kohyang* began to disappear from South Korean consciousness. Today many people confidently announce that they are from Seoul, a statement that suggests willful distortion or abysmal ignorance of family history. It is as if, at the end of the Korean War, the survivors found themselves at ground zero of their new lives. Half a century after the war's end, South Korea remains a land of displacement and departures, a fact that in turn contributes to South Koreans' embrace of a formalistic and formulaic nationalism.[50] With concrete localities incinerated or left behind, the abstract nation became the master object of nostalgia, longing, and hope.

The Korean War tolled the death knell of Chosŏn-Confucian Korea. The war was still another reminder of the irrelevance of neo-Confucian orthodoxy, which had valorized the literati over the warrior, the merchant, and the engineer. If Japanese rule hadn't underscored the need for a strong military, then the Korean War surely did so. The military gained prestige, and universal male conscription, which had begun under Japanese colonial rule in 1942, became a fact of South Korean life.[51] The American might that had saved South Korea was taken as yet another proof of the superiority of the American way of life, and of the irrelevance of Korean tradition. For the ruling class, however, the Korean War brought a form of collateral damage that was even more devastating than the ideological assault: land reform.[52] Landownership and primogeniture had formed the material basis of *yangban* patriarchy, but massive land redistribution ended both. It was no longer a mark of prestige and power to own land, and now landowners, rather than collecting rents from their land or plowing profit back into it, had to seek other means of maintaining or aggrandizing their wealth. In any case, the war had shown that when it came to land, you couldn't take it with you; a prestigious diploma would prove to be better than real estate. This change signaled a fundamental break between the "before" of Chosŏn Korea and the "after" of capitalist South Korea. The foundation of the agrarian elite, having remained largely intact during the transition from the Chosŏn dynasty to Japanese rule, had now been toppled.[53] And with the interrelated thrusts of capitalist industrialization and its attendant urbanization, the agrarian social order, along with the extended households and villages that were its two major institutional pillars, underwent a steady and inexorable decline.[54]

It may seem reductionist to relate the eclipse of tradition to the decline of the *yangban* elite and the agrarian order, but it is impossible to deny the correlation. The decline of *yangban* hegemony had surely begun before land reform, but it accelerated thereafter. Educated South Koreans stopped reading the *Analects* and other Confucian classics in favor of American management tracts; they professed Christianity, democracy, and Western creeds in general over Confucianism, shamanism, and other native spiritual and value systems; and, as chapter 1 shows, they gave up traditional music and took up European music. The South Korean elite stopped hoarding old books, Korean scrolls and screens, and even the celebrated ceramics and *hanji* (Korean paper). What is most shocking to a Western bibliophile, one for whom incunabula and even earlier manuscripts are within reach, is that in South Korea an antiquarian book is defined as any volume published before 1959.[55] This is, to be sure, a trend from the colonial period; eager Japanese and, later, American connoisseurs snapped up discarded *yangban* treasures for a pittance. Domestic enthusiasm for Korean antiquarian books and antique furniture remains surprisingly muted even today.[56] In the ostensibly irrelevant activity of collectors, in conspicuous consumption, we can clearly see the eclipse of the traditional legacy.

THE PARK REVOLUTION

The 1961 military coup ended the democratic interregnum that had followed the 1960 April Student Revolution. Whatever the true intentions of the young military officers behind the coup may have been—and there is no particular reason to believe that their motivations differed from those of other officers in so-called Third World countries where military coups are a garden-variety form of political change—these officers called for an end to corruption and for the inauguration of a more just society and a more dynamic economy. Park Chung-hee, who soon wrested power from his fellow plotters, repeatedly stressed, in the early speeches of his reign, personal morality and social order, purity and progress.[57]

The Park regime ended the long *yangban* political dominance. The regime's rise to power was not so much a singular revolution as a coup de grâce; the collapse of the Chosŏn dynasty, the period of Japanese colonial rule, the post-Liberation dominance of the United States, the Korean War, and land reform had all played their part. Yet the student revolutionaries and Chang Myŏn, who replaced Rhee, represented a certain continuity with the Chosŏn era in that the vast majority of the revolutionaries hailed from the *yangban*-class. In contrast, Park had come from a humble background.[58] One of Park's first acts was to arrest leaders of big business (*chaebŏl*) as well as high-ranking governmental officials and thus to curtail the influence of the traditional elite. More strikingly, he promoted younger technocrats from modest backgrounds to lead the new South Korean government.

Park's most significant act was to militarize South Korea. As mentioned earlier, the conventional Chosŏn-Confucian attitude had slighted the military, but the Park regime exalted it. The military came to serve as something of a finishing school for South Korean masculinity: South Korean men learned to obey orders, live by the clock, smoke and drink, and lead a homosocial existence. The military trained generations of South Korean men in its own image, stripping them of their rural roots and turning them into South Korean anticommunist nationalists and modern workers.[59] Park, whose outlook had been formed during his education at the Japanese military academy, promoted not only a prewar Japanese vision of political economy, with its emphasis on steel-and-concrete industrialism, but also the military as the normal and ideal form of organization, even as a way of life. When South Koreans think of organizational structure, they think of the military. Henceforth, military discipline—authoritarian, hierarchical, meritocratic, and efficient—would be institutionalized in South Korean life. (Even the production of K-pop, as we will see in chapter 2, is predicated on a militaristic training regime.) No phrase is more common in South Korean organizational life than *ppalli, ppalli* (fast, fast): the quintessentially un-Confucian and nonagrarian military ideal is one of Park's many indelible stamps on South Korea.

Park faced a persistent legitimation crisis, however. Lacking credentials as an anti-colonial independence hero—bona fides like those of his counterpart Kim Il-sung—the unsmiling Park, with his training by the Japanese military, was hardly charismatic or popular. Neither could he appeal to traditional sources of legitimacy, such as an elite social background or superb educational achievement. Thus he stressed anticommunist (that is, anti–North Korean) nationalism and the trickle-down benefits of economic growth. The former could yield only so much enthusiasm; it is difficult to generate loyalty from repression and torture.[60] Therefore, Park adopted economic growth as the raison d'être of his continuing rule. In so doing, he entrenched the counter-*yangban* ideology of economic success as the summum bonum of South Korean life. This cultural change manifested itself slowly. Wealth was not disdained as much as it had been by the Confucian literati during the Chosŏn period, nor were cultural achievements during the Park Chung-hee years as meaningless and superficial as they can seem from the hindsight of the twenty-first century. Yet there is no question that this-worldly material success surfaced as the primary good of South Korean life, as the South Korean dream. The ideal life of the Confucian past ran aground on the shoals of pecuniary pursuit.

Park's final blow against the Confucian elite was his institutionalization of capitalist principles. Despite the current fad of tracing connections between Confucian culture and capitalist success, historically Confucian polities denigrated commercial pursuits. The hierarchy of occupations is clear in the Confucian classics: a life of contemplation, not the pursuit of profit, is the way of the gentleman.[61] Confucian culture, if largely because of its agrarian base, remained inimical to a world that prioritized trade and production. Park relentlessly criticized Confucianism as the source of political-economic stagnation in Korea, though in this regard he was very much a mainstream thinker in the pro-American 1950s and 1960s.[62] Yet what was decisive here was less what he thought or said than what his regime did.

Park's elevation of export-oriented industrialization in the late 1960s transmogrified South Korea into a country singularly dedicated to exports and economic growth. At that time, the new master cultural logic of South Korea was still far from having been ordained.[63] South Korea's first five-year economic plan had advocated import-substitution industrialization; to the extent that exports were discussed, the discussion was about promoting agricultural exports, such as rice and laver. But Park's blow against the monopolistic power of *chaebŏl,* which coincided with the irrepressible demand for low-tech industrial products (a demand generated by the US involvement in Vietnam), showed one possible path for the South Korean economy: the export of industrial goods. Just as the Japanese post–World War II economic recovery owed much to expanded US demand during the Korean War, South Korea benefited immeasurably from the US deployment in Vietnam, and from the United States' seemingly insatiable appetite for uniforms, shoes, and other low-tech goods.[64]

Yet South Korea's economic growth was far from adequate. The country was deformed by the contradictions of economic growth—the simultaneous emergence of affluence and poverty, the exploitation of the labor force, regional inequality, the rapid rural exodus, and so on.[65] Economic growth also necessitated Park's dependence on his other ideological pillar, anticommunist nationalism. What the Korean War had begun, Park's rule completed. The vilification of the enemy was something of a national crusade: North Korea was invariably called Pukkoe (Northern puppet regime). The existence of an enemy nearby, and possibly within, justified all sorts of abuse, from censorship and surveillance to random arrests and physical torture to blackmailing and blacklisting, and South Korea was brought perilously close to a state of totalitarian rule. Censorship of and control over popular music were merely two elements of an authoritarian political rule that could not but color South Korea in dark hues, especially in the second half of Park's long reign.

Anticommunist nationalism also had the curious effect of sundering the unity of ethnic Koreans. The rhetoric of "one Korea" meant that South Korea was the true and only Korea. More than six decades of division have now weakened kinship ties and local attachments across the 38th parallel, as marked by linguistic drift and physiological differentiation.[66] North Korean refugees in South Korea are readily identifiable by their manner of speech, dress, and behavior. Even more striking is the difference in mean height between South Koreans and North Koreans, which may be upwards of seven inches. Ethnoracial homogeneity among the denizens of the two Koreas can no longer be assumed. Dubious though I am about the extent of cultural and national integration during the Chosŏn dynasty, Chosŏn Korea's political unity is undeniable. But decades of anticommunist nationalism, in conjunction with the failures of the North Korean state, seem to be severing the idealized unity of Korea.

Nationalism was not merely anticommunist but also revolutionary. It was not only Confucian garb that Park sought to peel away from South Korea but also the country's Japanese layer.[67] Although Park himself had been steeped in the prewar Japanese military culture, he intensified Rhee's visceral anti-Japanese rhetoric and policy. The attack of Park's regime on trot music was merely one manifestation. The impact of revolutionary nationalism was most evident in Park's disavowal of Chinese script, especially in the 1970 presidential decree that championed Korean script (han'gŭl).[68] Interestingly, the student and radical movement of the 1970s and 1980s would complete Park's project; the leftist daily Han'gyore sinmun initially went so far as to use Korean rather than Arabic numerals. Whatever the educational or cultural rationale for the shift to Korean script, the consequence was a significant break with the past of Korean civilization. To put this idea simply, much of the writing from the Korean past became inaccessible to the new *han'gŭl* generations after the 1980s. A typical work published by a scholar in South Korea in the 1960s would have been as legible to the scholar's eighteenth-century counterparts in Chosŏn Korea as to her contemporary colleagues in China or Japan. But the traditional unity of East Asian civilization withered as younger South Koreans were no longer able to access earlier texts—not only the Confucian classics and their Korean commentaries but also news-paper articles and serious novels from before the 1970s. In the name of nationalism, then, ties to tradition were loosened, if not severed.[69] Tradition, which should have been nationalism's handmaid, turned into its Other.

The ideology of nationalism, which should have valued tradition, in fact did so only formally and not substantively. Worse, this ideology turned into a modernizing belief and practice that looked principally to the future great-ness of South Korea (a prospective greatness that was largely American in inspiration). Precisely because the predicates of South Korean nationalism often contradicted common nationalist principles (for example, South Koreans' co-ethnics in the North became their principal enemy), what thrived was not the substance of nationalism but its form—the narrative structure of celebrating and glorifying what was South Korean and what South Koreans had achieved. Paradoxically, but predictably, the fact that the substance of the celebration had changed so rapidly did little to dampen the celebration's fervor. Nationalist discourse functioned as an empty signifier: South Korea was to be anti-Confucian in the 1960s and pro-Confucian in the 1990s. Ethnoracial purity was a principal predicate of Koreanness for a while, but with the promotion of globalization, multicultural Korea became the new norm.[70] In either case, South Korea was worthy of celebration and love. The fervor of hypernationalism went hand in hand with the emptiness of the traditional and the national.

EVISCERATION OF THE PAST AND EMBRACE OF THE NEW

Beyond any particular legislation or policy, what transformed the everyday life of South Koreans was the massive change wrought by capitalist industri-alization. The half century between the early 1960s and the early 2010s tracks a revolutionary shift in the manner and mode of South Korean livelihoods and lifestyles. Around the time of the 1960 April Student Revolution, observers could reasonably characterize South Korea as tradition-bound, agrarian and rural, and Confucian; no one could do so by the early 2010s, or probably even by the time of the 1988 Seoul Olympics.

Raw statistics tell the story.[71] At the beginning of Park's rule, in 1961, more than 70 percent of the population lived in rural areas, but by the end of his rule, in 1979, more than 60 percent resided in cities. As late as 1970, more than half the labor force was engaged in the primary sector, but that figure had sunk to 11 percent by 1995. The mean fertility rate was well over 6 children per woman as late as the early 1960s; the comparable figure in 2012 was barely above 1.2, one of the lowest mean fertility rates in the world. (There are demographers and family planners who began their careers by seeking ways to stem population growth but ended up studying ways to enhance fertility in South Korea.) In the early 1960s, hardly any South Koreans owned or had even seen a television set; by the early 2010s, one would have had to look far and wide to find a South Korean household without a broadband connection. The first university was founded in colonial Korea in 1924; by the early 2010s, more than 80 percent of college-age youths were enrolled in tertiary educational institutions. Per capita GNP in the early 1960s was barely above $100; it was above $20,000 in the early 2010s.

In other words, any and every facet of life could and did change. South Korean children in the 1950s routinely begged US GIs for chocolate and candies; their children worry about ways to improve the lives of impoverished people in the global South. Seoul south of the Han River used to be a vast swath of swamps and farms; present-day Gangnam, thanks to Psy's viral video, is widely recognized as one of the world's hot spots. Seoul streets in the 1960s—dirt roads that had more human- or ox-pulled carts than cars, and more beggars than foreign automobiles—were sites where the majority of women still wore *hanbok;* today, for affluent South Korean youth, the mere suggestion of an ox-pulled cart or a dirt road in central Seoul would be simply incredible. Before the 1960s, almost every Korean lived in a house (affluent people in Chinese-style houses with courtyards, poor peasants in shacks); by the 2010s, almost every urbanite—and the country was indisputably urban— lived in a high-rise apartment building. Some lived in sumptuous, spacious flats, whereas others lived in cramped and unkempt rooms, but bourgeois comforts that were rare in the 1960s—a separate kitchen with running water and electrical appliances; an indoor bathroom with a flush toilet (and, increasingly, a shower); Western furniture, such as sofas, tables and chairs, and desks; electronic goods like television sets and laptop computers—had become necessities by the 2010s. Whereas people had once squatted to use the outhouse, the idea of hunkering down on anything less than a warmed toilet seat now seems anathema to young urbanites. And not only was it the norm to live in a house in the 1960s, one also lived with many other people, including not just extended family members but also distant relatives, passing acquaintances, and rent-paying lodgers. By the 2010s, an apartment had usually become the nuclear family's castle. The family of half a century ago inevitably evoked one's lineage and a litany of one's blood relatives; now the family is a far narrower entity, rapidly approaching the Western norm of the nuclear familial unit. The concept of "housewife" was far from firmly established in the early 1960s; it was more of a bourgeois ideal, since many women worked on farms and in factories. By the 2010s, any aspiring middle-class household included a full-time mother whose primary occupation was to turn her children into winners in the educational examination contest. There were no "teenagers" in the 1960s, and there were few overt manifestations of generational conflict; today, the rise of popular culture has empowered the young and divided the generations. As recently as the early 1960s, South Korea was a predominantly agrarian country, its inhabitants sharing the material foundation of Chosŏn Korea. In the course of rapid industrialization, the country would experience perhaps the most rapid rural exodus in history: villages literally disappeared, and the countryside was vanquished. As a result, the rhythm of life was transformed from the daily and seasonal cycles of farming life to the clock time of factories and offices. Land itself, as noted earlier, became devalued; the countryside in turn became nothing but an instrumental entity to be sold or destroyed for cold cash, its primacy reasserted only in the frenzy of real-estate speculation.

Export-oriented industrialization transformed the country into one gargantuan marketplace. If South Korea was poorly endowed in terms of natural resources—tungsten, laver, and ginseng are uninspiring in the modern capitalist world economy—South Koreans would turn themselves into commodities. People with formal-sector jobs, whether in factories or offices, were the fortunate ones, but by the late 1980s South Korea had the dubious distinction of being the world leader in adverse labor conditions among industrializing societies, with perhaps the lowest wage level and the highest rate of industrial accidents.[72] Massive exploitation of a generation of South Korean workers made possible the rapid economic growth of the 1970s and 1980s.

The only thing worse than being exploited was not being exploited. The informal sector thrived as the rural exodus disgorged countless ex-farmers into the cities. They scrambled to earn their livelihoods as street vendors, shoeshine boys, housemaids, and prostitutes. Girls and women cut their hair—hair was consistently one of the top five exports in the 1960s—and sold it for a pittance to supplement their household finances. Most dramatically, sex work came to constitute the largest occupational field for young women, serving the desires of cash-rich American soldiers, Japanese tourists, and South Korean businessmen. It is not that sex work had not existed in Chosŏn Korea, but prostitution became a major industry in South Korea, where commercial rather than Confucian principles now dominated.[73]

In short, South Korean ways of life today, in the early 2010s, would be almost unrecognizable to the South Koreans of half a century ago. Change is experienced incrementally and quantitatively, but its net effect is qualitative transformation. Perhaps the best way to understand the massive changes in South Korea is to consider them in relation to the North Korean refugees who are living in South Korea. Although South Korea has been under separate rule since 1948, only in the early 1970s did South Korea begin to outperform North Korea on most economic indicators.[74] Yet it has taken only the last forty years to render most North Korean refugees in the South incapable of adapting to the lifestyle of their putative co-nationals. I have already mentioned the sheer difference in mean height, but that gap also extends from the work ethos and social relations to the manipulation of the marketplace and media technology. In these areas, South Koreans have deviated from the long-standing norms of the Korean peninsula.

Capitalism, consumerism, and popular culture superseded Confucianism, agrarian life, and folk culture. At the time of the 1960 April Student Revolution and the 1961 military coup, even as the elite idolized American might and values, the dominant ideology in South Korea was still colored by Confucianism. Beyond the sacralization of ancestor worship, age-based hierarchy, and gender inequality there was the indisputable system of status hierarchy, born of concentrated ownership and unequal education. In a quasi-caste society, one's status identity, especially if one belonged to the *yangban* and the landowning class, was the master signifier that shaped one's marriage choices, work trajectories, and social standing. The power elite of South Korea in the 1950s was almost inevitably of *yangban* background; almost every member of the Rhee cabinet came from this stratum, as did *chaebŏl* owners. As I have argued, the Korean War–era land reform, effected in part to counter the appeal of North Korea and communism, expunged the centuries-long source of wealth and prestige almost overnight. The 1961 military coup can be understood in part as a revolt from below, led by lower-status military cadets and founded on the value, as much Japanese as American, of meritocracy. The final blow was capitalist industrialization, which decisively shifted the source of power, prestige, and status in South Korea. Already by the mid-1980s, parents with marriageable daughters had begun to concern themselves less with a potential groom's hereditary status than with his educational credentials and potential income and wealth. This grand shift, from a focus on traditional status to a focus on economic standing and educational attainment, manifested itself in the decline of Confucian ideology: if the summum bonum was no longer a life of leisurely contemplation, then the culture of getting and spending entailed a wholesale revaluation, one that led people to seek modern living and follow a modern lifestyle. Another crucial element of the South Korean dream, apart from the trajectory that led from educational credentials to prestigious employment, had to do with the quality and texture of life—with not just material plenty but with enjoyment and entertainment as well. What became critical here was economic enrichment. As recently as the latter years of the 1960s, more than 50 percent of the average household's earnings still went to food, but by the late 1980s that percentage had dropped to about 30 percent.[75] The 1980s were also the decade when the South Korean middle class embraced leisure and its pursuits. This was the decade that witnessed the beginning of the golf craze, the desire for car ownership on the part of middle-class people, their wish to experience travel and tourism (these were liberalized only in 1982), and their growing enthusiasm for what was most accessible: popular entertainment, which meant not just movies and television but also music and, increasingly, popular music, as elite disdain and rural indifference waned.[76]

Another major break in South Korean collective consciousness deserves emphasis: the shock of the 1997 IMF crisis (in South Korea, it is common to refer in this way to the effects of the International Monetary Fund's intervention in what has elsewhere simply been called the Asian financial crisis). External observers since around the time of the 1988 Seoul Olympics have been tempted to see everything in South Korea in terms of an ever-upward narrative: economic dynamism, political democracy, and cultural efflorescence. And by the mid-1990s, most South Koreans did believe in the progressive narrative. With the emergence of a generation of youth that had grown up in affluence under a democratic political system—the sort of young people who embraced Sŏ T'ae-ji wa Aidŭl—memories of underdevelopment, whether economic or political, were fading. As a sign of the country's having arrived as an economic powerhouse, South Korea joined the OECD in 1996. The following year, Kim Dae-jung was elected president; Kim, a former dissenter, at one time had been sentenced to death, and his elevation solidified the claim that South Korea had become a genuine political democracy. Yet the easy celebration of economic affluence, political democracy, and continuous progress faced the recalcitrant reality of the 1996 Asian currency crisis, which hit South Korea in 1997. One long-enduring consequence of the crisis, beyond its challenge to *chaebŏl* dominance, has been a pervasive sense of uncertainty. By contrast with Japan, however, where the bursting of the real-estate bubble in 1991 left the country introspective and involuted, the general trend in South Korea has been to stress the need for exports and globalization. Paradoxically, then, the IMF crisis deepened South Korea's penchant for growth and innovation, its dependence on exports, and its external orientation. In other words, South Korea in the aftermath of the IMF crisis, instead of turning toward the past, memory, and tradition, appears to have accentuated its drive toward the future, toward creative destruction, and toward cultural amnesia.

Not everything traditional has disappeared. The family remains important, and children still profess respect for their parents, teachers, and elders (though I am not sure that any culture has truly obliterated the salience of the family, or of age-based hierarchy). Yet who will deny that the regnant ideology in the forging of a marriage has to do not with the salience of parents and property relations but with romantic love? In chapter 1, we saw that female singing stars of the colonial period faced status-related prejudice and opposition from their families when they sought to marry men from the landlord class. As late as the 1980s, the practice of conducting a serious inquiry into a prospective spouse's family and hierarchical status was de rigueur; now, in the twenty-first century, that traditional practice has all but disappeared. To the extent that family background does come up for discussion, the conversation centers primarily on the parents' financial resources and secondarily on their educational attainment; an inquiry into the hierarchical status of a prospective spouse's family would mark one as terribly old-fashioned. Virginity until marriage was widely the norm in the 1980s; in the 2010s, few speak of it.[77] Divorce is increasingly common and accepted. The earlier widespread modesty in dress has all but disappeared. If Yun Pok-hŭi (Yoon Bok Hee) caused a scandal with her miniskirt in the 1960s, she would hardly raise an eyebrow in the streets of Seoul today. Even upright men, who wore dark suits, white shirts, and somber ties as late as the 1990s, now sport a rainbow of colors.[78] Christianity has superseded Confucianism.[79] It is no longer Confucian morality and past economic practices but American-style capitalism and commerce that dominate South Korea today.

Thus South Koreans, bereft of tradition, ride each new wave of fashion. Indeed, much of contemporary South Korea's particularity and peculiarity resides in the recent commercial innovations that comprise everyday life. In 1980, for example, when the Japanese manager of Lotte Department Store in Seoul waged a campaign to sell chocolate for Valentine's Day, few South Koreans were aware of that romantic holiday, celebrated on 14 February in countries all over the world.[80] Soon, however, 14 March became White Day in South Korea, with Black Day following on 14 April, Rose Day on 14 May, Kiss Day on 14 June, and Silver Day on 14 July. Young South Koreans proudly point to these newfangled rituals as expressing something deep about Korean culture. It is within this cultural mind-set that K-pop reigns, blissfully free from the soundscapes of the past but loved as *Korean* music. In other words, consumer culture *is* South Korean culture, experienced in the perpetual present tense.

HEROES AND MONUMENTS

My narrative of Korean/South Korean history has stressed discontinuity and the expunction of tradition. As I have repeatedly said, people conceptualize biography and history as continuous, and thus my interpretation may seem idiosyncratic, even perverse. If so, another way to consider my argument is to observe a curious feature of contemporary South Korea: the absence of modern heroes and monuments.

Nationalist discourse often purports to begin from time immemorial, but most modern nation-states are relatively new. The United States is widely regarded as a young country, but in fact it is "the first new nation" and one of the oldest nation-states.[81] Germany as a cultural and linguistic sphere may have existed for millennia, but Germany as a unified political entity emerged only in 1871. As culturally and linguistically unified entities, most European nation-states—when they are in fact culturally or linguistically unified at all—postdate the industrial and democratic revolutions. Given the modernity of nation-states, they celebrate not only their protonational heroes but also those heroes' modern counterparts. Thus France may teach its children about the Gauls, but the firm foundation of modern France is the French Revolution. In a similar spirit, as I have suggested, most nation-states have had literary lions who exemplify, as the basis of imaginative literature, the modern vernacular and therefore also the modern national language. In a more direct sense, countries celebrate the political heroes who founded the modern nation-state: George Washington and the Founding Fathers in the United States, Mao Zedong and his comrades in China, Gandhi and Nehru in India. Typically, these heroes have statues and buildings named after them in the capital and other cities; their portraits are engraved on the national currency and postage stamps, and everyone in the country acknowledges their significance, sometimes with sacred awe.

But South Korea is different. The founding president, as noted earlier, is almost universally dismissed as corrupt and ineffective. In 1956, a bronze statue of Rhee Syngman eighty feet tall (one foot to celebrate each one of his eighty years) was erected in Namsan, in central Seoul, but it was toppled four years later in the April Student Revolution.[82] Today no major statue of any president graces any public space in South Korea. As for North Korea, the three-dimensional likeness of Kim Il-sung is inescapable; there are reportedly more than five hundred major statues of him.[83] In contrast, the name "Chang Myŏn" is the answer to a question dealing with historical trivia. The importance of Park Chung-hee is difficult to deny, but the country is split deeply and passionately over Park himself. For every person who lauds him as the architect and engineer of the contemporary South Korean political economy, at least one or two more remember him as a ruthless despot. Chun Doo-hwan, Roh Tae-woo, Kim Young-sam, Kim Dae-jung, Roh Moo-hyun, Lee Myung-bak, and Park Geun-hye all have their followings, but it is fair to say that they have as many detractors as fans. At least at this moment, in the early 2010s, it is difficult to project who, if anyone at all, will emerge half a century from now as a true national hero. In literature, South Korea's great modern writer, Yi Kwang-su, was a traitor, as we have seen, and he remains a national embarrassment. The traditional crafts—ceramics, papermaking, and so on—have been so systematically devalued, along with the traditional arts of painting, music, and dance, that almost no practitioner has achieved anything close to national recognition. Although there are some spectacularly successful modern South Korean artists who bask in global renown—the performance artist Nam June Paik, for example, or the classical composer Isang Yun—they have been tainted by their anti-government pronouncements. On the fiftieth anniversary of the founding of South Korea, the influential journal *Wolgan Chosŏn* published a list of Koreans who had contributed the most to the country; the top figure was Myung-whun Chung, a conductor of European classical music.[84] Four of the top five recognized by the journal are musicians: An Ik-t'ae (number three), Nam June Paik (four), and Yi Mi-ja (five). This fact speaks less to the South Korean love of music than to the absence of suitable national heroes in other spheres of South Korean life.

So who are South Korea's national heroes? In central Seoul there is a large monument to King Sejong, who sponsored the creation of Korean script in the early fifteenth century, and another to Admiral Yi Sun-sin, who promoted the manufacture of the "turtle boat" that figured in the defeat of the Japanese invaders in the late sixteenth century. Of the historical figures whose likenesses appear on the four major banknotes that circulate in contemporary South Korea, three—Yi Hwang, Yi I, and Sin Saimtang—are from the sixteenth century; the fourth, King Sejong, lived all but the first three years of his life in the fifteenth century.[85] In other words, no one in nearly half a millennium has qualified as a face of the national currency. (Yi I, the last survivor of the distinguished foursome just discussed, died in 1584.) Another way to put this is to say that no great hero has ever tasted *kimch'i* (at least not its modern, spicy version).[86] This dearth of national heroes accounts in part for the national hysteria over Hwang Woo-suk, the scientist who was believed to be a shoo-in for a Nobel Prize but whose career ended in ignominy when his fraudulent research was exposed.[87] In a country of hypernationalists, the unfulfilled quest for a national hero is also what accounts for the figure skater Kim Yu-na (Kim Yŏ-na) and K-pop groups as objects of exaggerated national celebration.

In short, then, South Korea is devoid of modern national heroes. And this absence of heroes—like the discontinuities of South Korean history, and the destruction of the country's traditions—is no accident.

TRADITION

"From time immemorial" is the irreproachable foundation of tradition. Shrouded as we are in the fog of time, we cannot locate the invention of a particular practice or artifact. When did we begin to shake hands, or bow, in greeting? Or bury or burn the dead? It usually matters less to know why or when we began to greet or bury people in a particular way than to recognize that our conventional rituals distinguish us, as members of an in-group, from outsiders. Our social identification in turn cannot but incorporate a temporal dimension—the acknowledgment that we come from somewhere—and tradition is the shorthand for all that has passed before us, and has therefore marked us. A shared conception of the past strengthens the solidaristic claims of the group.

Practically no aspect of contemporary South Korean nationalist discourse can bear serious scrutiny, but willing suspension of disbelief in the notion of a common national sensibility (or at least acquaintance with and acknowledgment of that notion) strikes a semisacred chord of unity among South Koreans. The ubiquitous *uri* ("our") of contemporary South Korean speech is predicated on a belief in the shared genealogy and sociology of Koreanness. The contemporary interpretation of the Tangun myth suggests that the Korean people issued from the coupling of the lord of heaven (Hwan'in) and a garlic-eating bear that transmogrified into a woman, but this interpretation misses the simple fact that before there were Koreans there were people on what we know today as the Korean peninsula. Some nationalist accounts of the Korean nation's origins place the nation not only beyond the current territorial boundaries of South Korea but also beyond those of North Korea, and these accounts also neglect movements of populations to and from the current boundaries of the two Korean nations. Only a nationalist immune to the logic and evidence of modern historiography could insist on the autochthonous and autonomous descent of the Korean people and their culture. We clothe the loose, baggy monster called "tradition" in the vestments of the modern nation-state; in so doing, we miss ancestors and influences that are almost inevitably extranational or transnational.[88]

Consider something as basic as foodways. South Koreans often stress *kimch'i* as the essence of Koreanness, but the basic contours of contemporary Korean cuisine were traced only after the seventeenth century, with the introduction of chili peppers, tobacco, and much else.[89] In Hŏ Kyun's early-seventeenth-century conspectus of Korean dishes, we find bear paws and deer tongues but nothing about the beef and pork that Hŏ's descendants devour.[90] Even now, in the early twenty-first century, *kimch'i* itself shows considerable regional diversity, from the nearly white variant in Hamgyŏng-do to the typically red-hot variety served in Kyŏngsang-do. Moreover, the persistent poverty of the agrarian majority rendered the diet of this class distinct from that of the landlord class—the class, that is, which defined our understanding of Korean cuisine. In any case, much of what South Koreans today consume with gusto—from the plethora of animal protein to the ubiquity of *ramyŏn* noodles to the almost inevitable cola, cider, and beer—tends to reflect post-Liberation tastes and trends, and to be non-Korean in origin, to boot.[91] Given the proliferation of teahouses and coffee shops in contemporary South Korea, it is bracing to learn that the first teahouse opened only in 1902 in a country that lacked a tea culture comparable to that of neighboring China or Japan.[92]

The revolutions of modernity have systematically assaulted ways of life that may have been relatively robust for centuries, such as the local agrarian way of life. The lineament of the destruction is coterminous with the history of twentieth-century Korea. Think of it as creative destruction, or as the cultural contradiction of capitalism: ostensibly robust Korean rituals and values, not to mention folktales and folk songs, are everywhere in retreat. Ethnic costumes are trotted out on special occasions; we may even sing and dance to folk tunes now and then. But the indubitable reality of massive transformation—as evidenced by a comparison between the earliest extant photographs of Hansŏng and current images of its successor city, Seoul, or between grainy daguerreotypes showing officials of the late Chosŏn era and photographs of their counterparts today—somehow coexists with the ideology of an unchanging (or at least a slowly changing) Korea, of unchanging or slowly changing Koreans. It is no exaggeration of the homogenizing effect of what is often called "globalization" to point out the striking and undeniable convergence in lifestyles—where we live, what we wear, what we eat, and what we listen to—that has occurred in the past century, leaving contemporary South Koreans and (for example) their American counterparts of today much closer to each other than to their ancestors of a century ago.

South Korea is far from unique. It would be deviant only if its industrial, post-traditional society had actually managed to retain the country's traditional forms of housing, its ethnic costumes, and its traditional people's music. Nevertheless, there is something remarkable about the speed and the extent of the transformation in South Korea, as well as about South Koreans' bedrock belief in the essential isomorphism of Korea and Koreans past and present. Tradition, annihilated, is reconstructed as an imagined past imperfect; the rhetoric of tradition and continuity casts a powerful spell on contemporary South Korea even as substantive and organic links to the past are largely expunged. Indeed, it is tradition's very emptiness that facilitates its ready invocation, for whatever purpose and at every turn.

South Korean nationalist discourse is empty because in the past century Korean tradition—any semblance of organic continuity—has been annihilated.

During the reign of the military dictators, stentorian denunciations of communism stood in for nationalism even as explicitly nationalist policies (such as the ban on Japanese culture, or the emphasis on teaching Korean script) actually alienated South Koreans from their past. The continuing dynamics of capitalist industrialization have merely accentuated this rift. The predicates of the South Korean nation in the early twenty-first century are constituted in part by formal pronouncements about Korean history and culture but also, and in a more important sense, by the culture industry that has become the face of South Korea, not just to South Koreans but to the rest of the world as well.

There are some ready tests for determining whether particular aspects of Korean tradition have survived. If one wished, for example, to gauge the survival of elements of Chosŏn Korea, one could examine South Koreans' familiarity with classical Confucian texts or their teachings. In this case, one would soon discover that it is common to meet South Koreans who have considerable knowledge of the Bible, and of the dogmas proper to specific Christian denominations, but much less common to find anyone who has read even a page of the *Analects,* or who can recite the basic principles and precepts of Confucianism.[93] Indeed, ignorance of Confucian texts and theories is surely one reason for so many random invocations of Confucianism to explain one or another South Korean particularity, when in fact it would be much more appropriate to invoke Confucianism as the explanation for many of the particularities of North Korea.[94] Likewise, as mentioned earlier, *kugak,* as an everyday pursuit, has become relatively unpopular: it is extremely rare for a young South Korean to learn to play even one *kugak* instrument, but piano or violin lessons are de rigueur. Or one might look to the built environment. Here, one would search in vain for much in the way of Chosŏn Korean structures; in fact, only one small neighborhood of Seoul still features traditional roof tiles (*hanok*). If some traditional rituals have survived—for example, *chesa* (ancestor worship)—such rituals are clearly on the wane. As for the survival of traditional foodways, today's abundance of beef and pork, and even of rice itself, makes contemporary foods radically different from those of even a generation ago, to say nothing of a few centuries ago, given the pervasive poverty of peasant life. And even though kinship ties remain powerful in South Korea (as they do around the world), I have already shown how their organization and operation demonstrate the profound transformation that has taken place in South Korea.

Lest I be misunderstood, let me emphasize that I am not a traditionalist; much of the past, as far as I am concerned, can rest in peace. It is often good to forget. Consider, for example, the almost complete lack of interest in the outcasts (*chŏnmin, paekchŏng*) and their descendants in contemporary South Korea. After the formal end of status hierarchy, with the Kabo Reform of 1894, status-conscious Koreans retained their inherited prejudices, and the outcasts engaged in an organized social movement.[95] Yet precisely because of all the turbulence and transformations of South Korean history, almost no one seems to remember the vast status inequality of the past. Given the contemporary salience of the caste hierarchy in India, and the continuing problem of the Burakumin in Japan, it is hard to lament cultural amnesia in South Korea. After all, South Korea's twentieth-century history of creative destruction and the cultural amnesia that surrounds it account at least in part for the country's ability to succeed in the ruthless competition of global capitalism, including the culture industry and K-pop. What is problematic is that the reality of change is overlaid with the rhetoric of continuity, which, precisely because it has so little basis in history or documents, often leads to random and reactionary interventions.

In South Korea, what has replaced tradition, with its function of providing a sense of continuity and coherence, is popular culture. The bonds of the proverbial imagined community of South Koreans are to be found in television waves and cyberspace, where common cultural contents are disseminated and national discussion takes place. As noted in chapter 1, listening to and singing popular songs has become an ordinary way for South Koreans to entertain themselves. The culture industry in general and popular music in particular have little concern for continuity or history for its own sake. The ultimate principles remain market demand and popular consumption; the pursuit of profit valorizes planned obsolescence and the fabrication of the next blockbuster. In this sense, even though the substance and the content of the culture industry are very different from those of the automobile industry or the mobile phone industry, all three industries operate in the same way, and each contributes in its turn to the relentless destruction of tradition.

To put this idea even more simply, the business of South Korea is South Korean business, and the making of K-pop or any other genre of popular music is not radically distinct from the manufacture of a Hyundai automobile or a Samsung cell phone. It is largely irrelevant that few of the raw materials and little of the technological prowess used in today's South Korean manufacturing were to be found in traditional Korea.[96] As noted a moment ago, cultural amnesia and the destruction of tradition may well be advantageous for capitalist enterprises bent on maximizing sales and profit. But the decline of tradition and the phenomenon of cultural amnesia do not mean that Korean traditions and ideas about the Korean nation are incapable of generating great emotion. South Koreans who have never read Confucius and who know few if any details about the colonial period may still profess great love for their country (and, in all likelihood, what little they know of either Confucianism or the colonial period reflects a distorted understanding). *My country, right or left; I love Korea and all things Korean*—but few would include North Korea in the ambit of their national romance, and fewer still would be able to articulate exactly what South Koreanness is about. It is just as well, then, that K-pop has come to exemplify South Korea, and Korean culture as a whole.

TWO

———

Seoul Calling

WHAT IS K-POP? FOR MANY PEOPLE, it is simply South Korean popular music.[1] As a result, *yuhaengga* from the colonial period and trot songs from the era of military dictatorship have been retroactively ensconced in a category that emerged only in the early 2000s.[2] Most South Koreans will readily agree that it may be unreasonable to extend the boundaries of K-pop to include, among other twentieth-century Korean musical genres, *ch'anggŭk* and *ch'angga,* or to include the *yuhaengga* maestro Nam In-su and the trot diva Yi Mi-ja. But what about the trot singer Chang Yun-jŏng, who performs like a K-pop star? If she does not belong to K-pop, then why include the soulful ballads of the indie group Busker Busker? Some Japanese K-pop fans are adamant that K-pop does not include Psy, because they consider him neither cool nor handsome. The Japanese disc jockey who was one of the first to employ the term "K-pop" used it to refer to R & B musicians, but Kim Kŏn-mo and SOLID are not stars in the firmament of K-pop. Given that neither supernatural nor secular authority is likely to issue a decree on the correct demarcations of the category—indeed, the absence of authority in popular music is one of its signature features—the ambit of K-pop is perforce contestable and essentially contested.

Philology is out of fashion, but it is not a bad place to begin any investigation. Almost everyone agrees that K-pop is a conceptual invention that substituted a "K" for the "J" in the term "J-pop," which in turn was coined in 1998 to identify a new style of music. It is safe to say, then, that K-pop is not only chronologically but also musically a post–Sŏ T'ae-ji wa Aidŭl phenomenon. It is a musical brand and style that crystallized in the course of the first decade of the twenty-first century, severing itself from earlier genres and styles in South Korean popular music as well as from J-pop. K-pop in turn is

96

intimately intertwined with the export imperative that has gripped the South Korean popular-music industry since the late 1990s. Styled as an export, K-pop underwent several permutations, its most important being as a variant of J-pop before a formula was settled on roughly the middle of the first decade of the twenty-first century, and the K-pop brand then found success across Asia and beyond. K-pop synthesized various post–Sŏ T'ae-ji wa Aidŭl trends, especially idol pop and dance pop, and polished them to a perfectionist shimmer and sheen.

In this chapter, I offer a conspectus of K-pop and elucidate its production process. I then explore the extramusical realm of political economy and global culture in order to explain how K-pop came to be produced for export and why non-Koreans began to consume it. I close with a discussion of K-pop as an aesthetic entity.

THE AGE OF K-POP

The year 2000 marked the first time that reliable statistics on South Korean record sales became available.[3] Four CDs racked up sales of more than a million copies each that year: the ballad singer Cho Sŏng-mo had the top two, and those were followed by efforts from g.o.d. (Groove Over Dose) and Sŏ T'ae-ji. The KBS Music Awards Grand Prize that year, like the one the year before, went to Cho. His "Asinayo" (Do you know) is squarely in the genre of the softly sung, slow, sentimental ballad; it would be easy to trace a straight line from Cho back to Yi Mun-se and even earlier ballad singers. In sharp contrast, Sŏ's album is a fascinating mélange of progressive rock genres; the album's top hit, "Ultramania," is at once rock, metal, and punk.[4] Cho is a clean-cut, conventionally dressed, smiling, seemingly kind young man (though it would be generous to call him gorgeous); Sŏ sports long red hair in dreadlocks and exhibits the moves and artifacts (for example, the skateboard) of the year 2000—not the sort who would have been welcome in a bourgeois Seoul apartment of that era. In the wide world of popular music at that time, Cho and Sŏ stood about as far apart as they possibly could. "Saranghae kŭrigo kiŏkhae" (Fall in love, then remember), by g.o.d., comes the closest of these best-selling songs to contemporary K-pop, but—interesting though the song is, with its mashup of rap, R & B, gospel, and other genres—it is basically a love ballad.[5]

A decade later, a new reality reigned. The age of digital downloads had ended the era of the million-seller CD. More remarkable, however, was the transformation in the kinds of songs that now became top sellers, a change readily gleaned from a reading of the names of the top ten acts: Sonyŏ Sidae, Super Junior, SHINee, JYJ, BEAST, 2PM, 2AM, 2NE1, BoA, and KARA. Except for BoA, all these acts are groups, and all but one of the acts have names that are not identifiably Korean and are written in the modern Roman alphabet; the exception here, proving the rule, is Sonyŏ Sidae (Girls' Generation), whose name in South Korea is often abbreviated as the acronym SNSD. The names of these acts are clearly indebted not only to J-pop naming conventions but also to the African American practice of employing innovative orthographies. In this they are similar to other contemporary K-pop acts, such as CL, Minzy, Dara, and Bom, which they also resemble by their inclusion of diasporic Korean and foreign members. At the risk of overgeneralization (a single album may include different styles of music, and many songs are hybrids or fusions), most tracks by these performers—inflected though they are by an extremely diverse array of musical influences, from rap and hip-hop to jazz and R & B—can be described as postdisco, post–Michael Jackson dance pop: as K-pop exports, or simply as K-pop itself. Almost invariably, a memorable refrain serves as the leitmotif in an upbeat, high-pitched, bright-timbred melody with rhythmic bass and hip-hop or techno beats. Moreover, subjective though such assessments can be, all the members of the group have been airbrushed into the K-pop aesthetic: tall and slim, with ripped abs for boys and long legs for girls and sharp facial features for everyone. Gender dimorphism prevails: cute or sexy girls, masculine and muscled boys. Each group puts on a dynamic display of coordinated movement and enacts a precise choreography. As vocalists, dancers, and physical specimens, the groups' members display polish and professionalism. Their costumes are diverse but almost always reflect the most up-to-date fashions. Their music videos incorporate all the latest techniques and trends in cinematography. In short, these performers exude style and confidence, and, like so many expensive automobiles or fancy cell phones, they communicate the sense of a complete and coordinated package. Above all, the package is readily identifiable: while I was watching K-pop videos recently, a three-year-old German girl pointed at my computer screen and declared, "Das ist K-pop."

The debut of Sŏ T'ae-ji wa Aidŭl announced the arrival of the new hegemonic tastemakers: teenagers and youths. As discussed earlier, Sŏ's trio shattered many of the conventions that had governed South Korean popular music, decisively separating young people's sonic world from that of their elders. The group's emergence also marked the moment when South Korean popular music became basically contemporaneous with trends in the United States (but this does not mean that US trends overtook those in South Korea, or that they merged). One consequence of this change was the entrance into South Korea of a diverse set of musical styles, which prospered in the South Korean popular-music scene, whether we define that kind of success anecdotally or by record sales: Kim Kŏn-mo, influenced by R & B, reggae, and rave; the jazz-fusion singer Yi So-ra; the heavy-metal, punked-out Sŏ T'ae-ji; the smooth balladeer Sin Sŭng-hun; the J-pop–influenced BoA; the bubblegum boy band H.O.T.—these were only a few of the more notable stars at the turn of the millennium. As I have repeatedly stressed, songs, stars, and genres do not disappear overnight, and all the trends just mentioned have maintained their adherents in the 2010s. Even trot isn't fading gently into the night: Chang Yun-jŏng, mentioned earlier, brings her glamorous appearance and vocal prowess to a revitalized K-poppified trot.[6] Furthermore, innovative and interesting performers continued to emerge in the first decade of the twenty-first century. Clazziquai Project, for example, fuses bossa nova, samba, and other Latin rhythms with a newly vibrant electronica, but the music of Clazziquai Project is neither a top seller in South Korea nor an integral element of K-pop abroad.[7] The term "K-pop" signifies a particular style or genre of popular music, one that even a German toddler can readily identify, and the crystallization of its style occurred in the years just after the turn of the new century.

Given what I have said about the ambiguous ambit of K-pop, it is perfectly fine to suggest that Sŏ T'ae-ji wa Aidŭl invented K-pop. Perhaps it is also possible to see proleptic moments in Kim Wan-sŏn or Sobangch'a. Nevertheless, something of a paradigm shift occurred between the advent of Sŏ T'ae-ji wa Aidŭl and the appearance of the export-oriented K-pop of the latter half of the first decade of the twenty-first century. The top K-pop acts listed on the 2010 Mnet chart reveal family resemblances as well as dissimilarities, not only between these acts and Sŏ's trio but also between the newer acts and the idol groups of the late 1990s. The original idol groups, such as H.O.T. and its female analogue, S.E.S., were speedily assembled, and their music, dance, and videos are, to put it charitably, amateurish and asinine. They modeled themselves on such boy bands as Shōnentai (1981) in Japan and New Kids on the Block (1984) in the United States, which recruited good-looking young men and endowed them with sunny songs and dance steps. H.O.T. and its successor groups, devised for domestic consumption, followed the same simple formula and applied it diligently. What H.O.T.'s producer,

SM Entertainment, did not fully anticipate was the group's success outside South Korea.

The initial stylistic shift occurred in the wake of SM Entertainment's unexpected success abroad, and of the export imperative that loomed in 1997 (discussed later in this chapter). Sŏ T'ae-ji wa Aidŭl disbanded in 1996, a mere four years after the group's explosive debut, leaving behind a vast vacuum in the youth-music scene. This era also witnessed the introduction of the mp3 player and the slow decimation of the recorded-music industry. SM Entertainment and other producers, anticipating a shift in East Asian musical tastes—a shift to which they had contributed—sought to promote their groups beyond South Korea. Therefore, in the very late 1990s, we see a move away from bubblegum pop and toward a fusion of genres, with more sophisticated choreography and cinematography. By 2000, even H.O.T. and S.E.S. had shed their innocent, infantile presentation. H.O.T.'s fifth release, the album *Outside Castle,* was ranked fifth on Mnet's 2000 top-ten chart, and the album's standout eponymous single opens with an extended orchestral prelude, whereas the highly staged, meticulous video, marked by a *Twilight*-like aesthetic—eight years before the release of the first film in that cinematic saga—seeks to attain the status of art.[8] Similarly, S.E.S.'s 1999 single "Love," from the album of the same title, which ranked sixth on the 2000 chart, begins with a scat sequence and shows a sophistication absent from the group's earlier efforts. Thus idol groups effected a convergence with the new mainstream popular music, which had entered an interesting period of incorporating disparate musical influences and creating innovative hybrids and fusions.

But where to export? H.O.T., whose surprising success abroad has already been noted, had generated an enthusiastic following in the large littoral Chinese cities. Given the relative weakness of China's domestic popular-music industry, not to mention the country's indisputably large and increasingly affluent population, the prospect of expansion both in China and in the Chinese-language sphere as a whole was more than attractive. Yet SM Entertainment's initial overture was a disaster.[9] In retrospect, it is clear not only that China was a small market in terms of profitability but also that rampant piracy made it virtually impossible to make money in that country at the turn of the millennium.

And then there was the Everest: the United States, an especially challenging market because of the country's leading role in popular music, the sophistication of its listening public, and the sheer rarity of Asian presences in the its popular-music industry. Here, the DR Music label was the pioneer. One of the label's acts, Baby V.O.X., had begun as an idol group in 1997 but quickly absorbed hip-hop and other American musical trends and now incorporated edgy dancing and sexy presentations. Baby V.O.X. garnered fans across East Asia (though not in Japan), and in 2004 the group released an album, *Ride West,* that included songs in English, Chinese, Japanese, and Korean, with cameo appearances by Jennifer Lopez and the late Tupac Shakur. "Xcstasy," a single from the album, became a video with an extended narrative, sharp images, and an urban feel.[10] It is fair to say, however, that there was nothing particularly extraordinary about Baby V.O.X.—little, in other words, to differentiate the group from any leading American act of the time. Expensive sports cars, decaying urban infrastructure, and sexy, muscled bodies may have been a combustible combination in Seoul in 2004 but probably provoked yawns on the part of the jaded American audience. DR Music's ambition—global, to be sure, and likely premature as well—came to naught.

Japan, then the second largest market in the world, shared a great deal of the South Korean musical and cultural sensibility. However, South Korea, instead of exporting music to Japan (save for occasional successes with trot music), largely imported popular music from that country. In fact, the late 1990s were a period of profound J-pop presence and influence in South Korea, and it was widely believed that non-trot South Korean popular music would not be viable in Japan. The prevailing prejudice, as mentioned in chapter 1, was not just that Japan was "ahead of" South Korea but also that there was residual discrimination against ethnic Koreans. In any event, South Korea's success in exporting music to Japan was due not to K-pop but to J-pop; that is, SM Entertainment promoted BoA as a J-pop star—one who just happened to be South Korean. The company hired leading Japanese voice and dancing instructors for the singer, investing $3 million in her debut, and in 2002 her single "Listen to My Heart" reached number 1 in Japan.[11] J-pop was characterized by its almost exclusive reliance on Western names and titles, pronounced in a way that also sounded Western (that is, they were usually pronounced as if they were being uttered in English). Thus BoA's Western-sounding name and English-language song titles were very much in the mainstream of J-pop, which had dominated the Japanese popular-music market since the late 1980s.[12] In addition, BoA had entered a particularly promising Japanese niche for adolescent *aidoru* (idol) singers. That is, she was a hybrid phenomenon—a cute girl who could sing J-pop, not just teenybopper tunes—and her positive reception spawned a series of successors. Even more remarkable is the fact that, despite not having grown up in Japan, BoA actually did learn to speak and sing like a Japanese native.[13] Her secret was intensive language training, which included an extended home stay with a Japanese family, a level of preparation that enabled SM Entertainment to present her as a J-pop act.

The apogee of this localization strategy came with Tongbang Sin'gi (also known as Dong Bang Shin Gi, DBSK, and TVXQ, among other names), which transmogrified into a J-pop group called Tōhō Shinki (the Japanese name uses the same Chinese characters as those used for the group's name in Korean). SM Entertainment found a model for its prized boy band in Backstreet Boys, the phenomenally successful American group that debuted in 1993. (Backstreet Boys, the new and improved version of New Kids on the Block, brought the power of harmony to mellifluous melodies and slow dance steps.) Tongbang Sin'gi debuted in South Korea in 2003, but after 2005 the group's activities were focused on Japan. Like BoA, the group did not occlude its national origins but sought to pass as a J-pop act. As Tōhō Shinki, the group was an a cappella ensemble, its slow, sweet harmonies usually wrapped around a love song. Polite, fan-friendly, and singing in Japanese, the group behaved like a J-pop act and compiled a series of hits. In other words, BoA and Tōhō Shinki/Tongbang Sin'gi were like Zainichi singers, who sought to pass as Japanese, rather than like those trot singers, such as Cho Yong-p'il, who were openly from South Korea. Furthermore, in their emulation of J-pop formulas, neither BoA nor Tōhō Shinki/Tongbang Sin'gi was particularly innovative, and neither projected a distinctive musical style or identity. Both acts sang slow-tempo, high-pitched ballads that fit snugly into mainstream J-pop. Roughly between 2000 and 2005, other SM Entertainment groups, such as SHINHWA, also followed this formula, both in South Korea and in Japan. Success in Japan often spilled over, though sometimes independently, to Chinese cultural domains (especially Taiwan, Hong Kong, and major Chinese cities) as well as to Southeast Asia. Indeed, followers of Tōhō Shinki/Tongbang Sin'gi regularly claim that the group has the largest fan club in the world.[14]

If Baby V.O.X. exemplified a globalization strategy that left the group all but indistinguishable from an American popular-music act, and if Tōhō Shinki represented a localization strategy that rendered the group irreducibly local (as J-pop, in this instance), then it is unclear what, exactly, is (South) Korean about South Korean popular music. As far as I can tell, no one ever consciously devised the currently dominant style, but it emerged as a fusion of the two most powerful streams in South Korea—idol pop and dance pop. By the turn of the millennium, as noted, idol pop had shed its amateurism and innocence. And by then, many elements of the current K-pop style already existed: attractive stars, youth-oriented lyrics, hybrid musical genres, ensemble dancing, and captivating videos. What pushed the musical envelope was an interesting articulation of dance pop, with its roots ranging from Motown and disco to hip-hop, Latin beats, and electronica. Koyote, for example, synthesized postdisco dance pop with techno pop and presented something of a prototype for K-pop, one that was perfected around the time of the group's 2000 hit "Passion."[15] JYP Entertainment, founded by Pak Chin-yŏng (Jin Young Park), also trod this path, which would be the proximate basis of K-pop style. Pak, sometimes called the Michael Jackson of South Korea, consistently emulated styles popular in the United States and looked to that country for inspiration.

In the small world of South Korean popular music, the major producers are alert to the trends and innovations of their competitors as well as to those of the United States, Japan, and other countries. It is bracing to realize how rapidly styles have merged and conventions have shifted. Consider the evolution of SHINHWA, easily the longest-surviving boy band. When the group debuted, in 1998, it was like any other boy band of the era. Beyond occasional notes of hip-hop, SHINHWA stayed true to bubblegum lyrics and compositions in its breakout 1998 single "Ŭssya! Ŭssya!"[16] A remake of Manfred Mann's 1964 hit "Do Wah Diddy," SHINHWA's rendition recalls the Monkees in all their simian silliness. Like H.O.T.'s 1996 hit "Candy," the song oozes a cloying sweetness. But, moving from "Only One" (2000) to "Perfect Man" (2002) to "Brand New" (2004), the members of SHINHWA not only shed the baby fat from their faces and bodies but also enhanced the coordination and sophistication of their dance routines. In the 2006 video "How Do I Say," with its self-consciously artistic black-and-white opening shot and the strumming of a guitar in the background, the group displays a level of polish utterly absent from its 1998 hit.[17] The performers' gestures follow urban American currents, and the dance steps, though far from vigorous, acrobatic, or perfectionist, evince extensive training. Yet the song remains more of a ballad, appealing to the J-pop audience. In this regard, SHINHWA resembles Tōhō Shinki, which had already become a superstar act in Japan. Although SHINHWA attempted several distinct styles, the group lacked propulsive techno dance music and vigorous, precise dance routines, despite its reputation as the premier dance group of the period.

After a three-year hiatus (2008–2011), when the group's members were serving in the South Korean military, they resumed performing, and it was only then that the group articulated the contemporary K-pop formula: SHINHWA's 2012 music video "Venus" sets an impeccably choreographed routine to the standard techno beat.[18] The group's evolution recapitulates the larger movement of K-pop performers, from their presentation as idol groups to their marketing as permutations of J-pop to their distinct branding as K-pop.

A significant shift in musical emphasis, as the case of SHINHWA suggests, occurred in the middle years of the twenty-first century's first decade. Two crucial elements were the elevation of dance as an integral part of the musical performance and the intensification of the beat, whether hip-hop or techno. Consider, in this regard, Tongbang Sin'gi. The group's 2003 debut "Hug" is very much a ballad with some dancing, in the mode of Backstreet Boys, and their J-pop debut as Tōhō Shinki stressed the group's vocal prowess. Yet by the time of the 2006 triumph "'O'-chŏng-pan-hap" ("O"-right-opposite-together—perhaps the Fichtean "thesis, antithesis, synthesis"), the group's dance routines had acquired polish and sophistication, as confirmed by the 2008 hit "Mirotic." Earlier South Korean music videos from the 1990s had featured more acrobatic moves, including break dancing. Koyote and other mixed-genre dance groups popular at the turn of the century occasionally incorporated b-boying and b-girling, but the singers mainly performed allegro steps and coordinated gesticulations, limited as they were by the need to vocalize simultaneously. Similarly, the standard K-pop routine came to rely on ensemble effects, such as contagion and grapevine, along with limb movements, but almost never used anything dramatic or even balletic, such as the fouetté or grand jeté.

But the centrality of sophisticated ensemble dancing is not the only thing that distinguished K-pop acts from J-pop acts and from the earlier South Korean idol groups. A decade after Sŏ T'ae-ji wa Aidŭl embedded hip-hop in South Korean music, the popularity of balladeers, along with the J-pop influence, continued to restrict the ambit of hip-hop; for almost all K-pop acts, hip-hop was more incidental than central. J-pop and earlier South Korean dance pop usually feature a pronounced downbeat, and in this regard these genres are no different from trot music (though trot tends to use two or four beats, whereas most J-pop and early South Korean dance pop tends to use eight beats). But hip-hop is different: the accent is on the backbeat (usually the second and the fourth), which gives hip-hop the famous kick that is conducive to dancing. In particular, with respect to K-pop, the distinct rhythm of sixteen-beat hip-hop—not so much the rapping, scratching, or beatboxing as the backbeat—accentuated the newfound stress on ensemble dancing.[19] Alternatively, some K-pop songs featured the synthesizer-driven techno or trance rhythm of a steady four beats. Here, the influence of French electronic dance music, as exemplified by Daft Punk, arrived in South Korea by way of the United States and Japan and became noticeable in K-pop tunes by the middle of the first decade of the twenty-first century.[20] At any rate, K-pop achieved an utterly different feel from that of the typical J-pop tune. Compare Tōhō Shinki's 2005 Japanese debut single, "Stay with Me Tonight," with the group's 2008 single "Purple Line" to register the group's shift away from softer J-pop harmonies and orchestral music and toward the contemporary K-pop style: faster, with a hip-hop–driven propulsive beat and more reliance on synthesizers than on strings. But even Tōhō Shinki incorporated the sixteen-beat hip-hop rhythm much less comfortably than did Girls' Generation and other later K-pop performers.

There was one more crucial turn. Wonder Girls' 2007 "Tell Me" video, with its infectious techno beat, its catchy refrain ("tell me"), and its style of dancing, serves as the archetype of contemporary K-pop style. But the real advance is that the song's hook is not just an unforgettable unit of sound but also the accompaniment to a signature dance move. That is, the listener, caught up in the compelling (though largely meaningless) lyrical and musical phrase, is also captivated as the viewer of a well-coordinated, precisely timed, interesting sequence of gesticulations and movements. Thus Wonder Girls went beyond percussive and vibratory dancing to introduce the integrated lyrical/musical hook and signature dance move, thereby creating the template for the contemporary K-pop formula.[21]

The "Tell Me" syndrome convulsed South Korea, generating copycat videos by students, police officers, and even soldiers. The video is interesting not only for its self-consciously retro flair but also for its projection of "girl power" in the form of Wonder Woman (ready allusions to American popular culture would also become an element of K-pop style). And "Tell Me" became the template for later girl-group hits, such as KARA's "Mr." (2009) and Sonyŏ Sidae's "Gee" (2009), although without the "girl power" bit: symptomatically, not only does "Gee" simplify the hook, the singers also move like mannequins (or, perhaps better, like mindless dancing dolls). The same sort of compelling refrain and signature move as in "Tell Me" can also be seen in the boy band Super Junior's smash hit "Sorry, Sorry." It was rave, but with backlighting and without the drugs. Simple lyrical refrains ("Mr." or "Gee"), combined with particular dance steps (hip dance for KARA, crab dance for Sonyŏ Sidae), entrenched Wonder Girls' successful formula, superseded it, and thus defined K-pop.

Finally, a significant shift occurred in the visual presentation of South Korean popular music. Even before television, beauty was never irrelevant; after all, the first Korean popular singers were stage actresses, and beauty was certainly an element of their appeal. But the visual became ever more important in the age of the music video. Every group—I cannot think of a single exception—shed rotundity to achieve the sculpted look. Faces became chiseled; bodies were increasingly fat-free. This was a striking contrast to pre-1980s facial and bodily norms, that is, to the culturally privileged round face and stockier body; brainwashing alone would not have been enough to make most North Koreans find the stocky, moon-faced Kim Chŏng-ŭn (Kim Jong-un) handsome. Call it maturation or masculinization, but the iconic member of the typical 1990s boy band was cute and round-faced, whereas his counterpart today seems to require a six-pack and a sharp jaw. The chiseled faces and sculpted bodies of contemporary male K-pop stars make them look almost as if they and the earlier generation of boy-band stars (such as the cuddly members of H.O.T.) belong to different races. The new look is urban and cosmopolitan: a slim face with large eyes, high cheekbones, and a straight nose, with a tall, trim body and long legs. And viewers actually get to see the abs and the legs.

Gender dimorphism, as mentioned earlier, is a distinguishing characteristic of K-pop's presentation. Although mixed-gender groups do exist in South Korea—Cool and Roo'ra, among others, achieved significant followings in the late 1990s—the accentuation of gender archetypes has solidified the practice of creating single-sex groups.[22] Girl groups can be cute or sexy, but they are all indisputably effeminate. Boys, or rather men, become ever more masculine and muscled, a trend exemplified by 2PM and BEAST. Indeed, as suggested by the latter group's name, this has been the triumph of *chimsŭng* (beast) aesthetics, an American-style muscled male sex appeal.[23] This muscular, masculine aesthetic was new to South Korea when it was pioneered just after the turn of the twenty-first century by Rain (Pi, or Bi), who was over six feet tall and well built. And the presentation of self also has an edge: the performers' dyed hair, tattoos, and suggestions of sexuality are in clear violation of the earlier sacrosanct PG-13 standard. An instructive case is Yi Hyo-ri. Her attire was invariably modest from 1998 to 2002, when she was a member of the early idol group Fin.K.L (P'ingk'ŭl). By the time she launched her solo career, in 2003, with the smash hit "10 Minutes," her hair was dyed blonde, her shoulders, midriff, and thighs were exposed, and she was gyrating in sexually suggestive ways.[24] The impact was immediate. The media gave the name "Yi Hyo-ri Syndrome" to the phenomenon of young (and old) men's inability to focus after watching one of Yi's steamy performances. The year 2003 was marked not only by the ascent of Rain but also by that turning point when the body beautiful became normative for South Korean music stars.

Beauty and cool may seem to lie beyond the pale of sober analysis, but the attractiveness of K-pop cannot be understood without them. As one member of Super Junior said in response to a query about the group's explosive appeal, "Maybe it is because of our great good looks?"[25] And then there is the story about a middle-aged Japanese woman who was baffled by her friend's raving about Tōhō Shinki: "Are they really gods? . . . If they're around, won't peace come to Asia?"[26] The woman, completely unacquainted with the group, acquiesced to her friend's plea to view Tōhō Shinki's music video: "I cannot forget how moved I was that night. Tōhō Shinki. The intense dancing by five men over six feet tall. . . . The waist movement that suggests—can only suggest—sex. . . . I was overwhelmed by the marvelous bodies of Tōhō Shinki."[27] She is not alone in her response to the K-pop brand of sex appeal, and we shouldn't miss the undercurrents of erotic projection and introjection in the rise of Tōhō Shinki and other K-pop groups.

But the K-pop formula, more or less complete by 2007, found limited success in the United States. JYP Entertainment, buoyed by its domestic success, attempted to break into the US market with Wonder Girls and Rain in the latter half of the twenty-first century's first decade. In 2004, the year after his debut, Rain had starred in the heavily viewed South Korean television drama *Full House,* and he became a pan-Asian sensation in the same year, with the release of his album *It's Raining,* which sold 500,000 copies in China and about 150,000 copies in Thailand and South Korea. But Rain would hardly make a splash in the United States.[28] Although Wonder Girls reached number seventy-six on *Billboard*'s "Top 100" chart in 2009, Rain's and Wonder Girls' initial foray into the United States fell short of resounding success.

By contrast, the "Tell Me" formula achieved a major breakthrough in Japan in 2010 with KARA and Shōjo Jidai (Girls' Generation). Although both groups sang in Japanese on their Japanese releases, they defined themselves as South Korean—that is, as belonging to the new phenomenon of

K-pop. The principal distinction was not so much that "K" had replaced "J" but that the label "K-pop" projected a brand identity. After the success of the Korean Wave, the Japanese audience had come to hold South Korean popular culture, especially South Korean television dramas, in higher esteem. But K-pop was something new: good singing and great dancing (a J-pop concert can be like a concert of European classical music) by cool, physically attractive, sexy stars. These South Korean performers radiated the excitement and edginess of American and other Western performers. With fewer tattoos and piercings, however, and with less explicit references to sex and drugs, they were easier on the eye and the ear, but with no sacrifice of sex appeal.

The news of success abroad clinched export-oriented K-pop's conquest of the South Korean market. Several ineluctable factors were at work. The rise of teenagers as the dominant segment of popular-music consumers led the industry to follow, as well as to adapt and shape, that audience's taste for idol groups. Given young people's increasing access to disposable income, not to mention the dissemination of relatively inexpensive technology for music's reproduction, the growth of the adolescent audience had been notable. At the same time, with the debut of YouTube and similar video-sharing websites in 2005, and with the explosive and roughly coeval growth of social media as well as the nearly universal ownership of video-capable phones and other portable devices for the consumption of music videos, the visual aspect of popular music came to be prized as much as the aural. When a performer was expected to please the eye as well as the ear, an attractive appearance became even more important, as did dancing and other visual elements. This valorization of the visual has been a factor in the experience of non-Koreans and older South Koreans, too. Members of the post-Sŏ generation in particular, who grew up on hip-hop, R & B, and other genres then new to South Korea, have discovered that they find K-pop performers not just palatable but actually likable: in response to a 2012 Gallup poll, South Koreans in their thirties and forties said that Psy and Girls' Generation were their two favorite acts.[29] Success abroad also spruced up the image and puffed up the reputation of more than one K-pop group or solo artist. Psy, for example, who had been only a middling performer, was transformed almost overnight into the iconic South Korean singer after his 2012 international smash hit "Gangnam Style." In the years just after 2009, the South Korean media were certainly awash in headlines about the latest heroics of this or that K-pop group.

In the course of the first decade of the 2000s, then, K-pop forged and perfected its style. By 2010 and the years just after, K-pop's sheer dominance inside South Korea, and its ubiquity outside the country, was making K-pop look like something of a monopoly, as if there were nothing else going on in the South Korean music scene. And there's no denying K-pop's large and devoted local base. But earlier genres and older stars also have continued to churn out hits and have retained their legions of fans. A diversity of music genres has never ceased to thrive in South Korea—European classical music, most obviously, but also, in the realm of popular music, everything from techno pop and punk to rap and hip-hop. For example, Skull, a South Korean reggae singer, found success in the United States and elsewhere in the latter part of the twenty-first century's first decade.[30] Indeed, K-pop owes its vitality to the existence of South Korean singers, composers, and choreographers who draw on a variety of different influences, and this is also why the current K-pop formula is likely to shift again in the near future. 2NE1's 2009 "Fire," for instance, and the group's 2011 song "I Am the Best" subtly subvert the K-pop aesthetic and ethos by incorporating such influences and elements as Bollywood music and choreography. Be that as it may, any strictly internal or endogenous history of K-pop's emergence would be incomplete. Without denying or downplaying K-pop's aesthetic choices and musical developments, it is accurate to state that the current K-pop style cannot be separated from the South Korean export imperative—and this statement takes us into the realm of political economy.

THE EXPORT IMPERATIVE

Already by the colonial period, European musical education and the spread of Western- and Japanese-inflected popular music had implanted a new soundscape and instilled a new musical competence among urban Koreans. By the immediate post-Liberation decade, South Korean musicians had acclimated themselves to American popular music and its culture. The diatonic scale had begun to supersede the pentatonic, syllabic singing had overtaken melismatic voicing, and dancing had replaced standing still. The naturalness of the Western soundscape and of American popular culture was supplanting Japanese-inflected popular music and the military-authoritarian culture of seriousness and sincerity. Almost all the thematic conventions of US (and now global) popular music, such as those related to romantic love and its rapture and rupture, were now readily legible by South Korean youth. In brief, youth of the (affluent) world were united in the structure of their feelings as well as in the infrastructure of quotidian life. By the late 1980s, almost any piece of American popular music could be understood and even enjoyed by young South Koreans.

This musical transformation was inextricably intertwined with the emergence of a leisure society in general, and with the affluent youth market in particular. The Sŏ T'ae-ji revolution brought all these changes to the fore; shocking though it was at the time, it narrowed, even obliterated, the temporal gap that had existed between South Korean and US popular music and showed that the distance between the youth culture of the United States and that of South Korea was not insurmountable. That is, by the 1990s, not only were young South Koreans ready to receive the latest US popular music, some were also capable of emulating, if not extending, US musical trends. Here, the sizable presence of the Korean diaspora, in the United States and elsewhere, provided a ready-made bridge to trends abroad as well as to pools of talent. It was only a matter of time before affluent, postauthoritarian South Korea would generate high-quality, state-of-the-art popular music, which would therefore be potentially interesting to non–South Korean listeners.

Yet the question remains: why export this music? Fame and fortune are two compelling reasons hardly unique to South Korean musicians and promoters. Although not everyone wishes to bask in glitz and glory, many South Koreans may have been just that much more eager for renown and riches. Given that the country had spent the twentieth century in the shadow first of Japan and then of the United States, it would be foolish to deny all desire to cast off the proverbial chip from South Korea's collective shoulder. Even a South Korean youth ignorant of the country's history would have had to be willfully obstinate to question the United States as the gold standard of power and prestige. In more general terms, South Korea had become a culture of ambition, celebrity, and fame. In the 1980s, an eminent South Korean journalist was shocked to discover that in France the child of a *boulanger* merely wanted to be a baker like his father; the journalist mused that this child's counterpart in South Korea would surely aspire to the presidency of a major conglomerate, if not of the country.[31] A motive perhaps even more compelling and ubiquitous than fame is profit. Although South Korea has long been an OECD country, the collective South Korean memory cannot quite shake off either the pervasive poverty and rapid industrialization that have marked the country's short history or the attendant desire to seek material comfort and enjoy accumulated wealth. All over the world, the principal message of popular culture celebrates and promotes conspicuous consumption.[32] To get rich is glorious; the pursuits of wealth and fame in fact constitute a single quest.

Nevertheless, what is striking about the worldwide music industry is the extent of its subordination to national boundaries. That is, performers' pursuit of stardom and wealth has largely been staged on domestic terrain. Some reasons for this phenomenon spring readily to mind: listeners may prefer singers who are co-nationals and songs that are sung in the shared national language; performers' legibility and likability may be enhanced by their respect for the received national conventions as expressed in appearance, behavior, and conduct.[33] More recalcitrant than listening preferences, however, are extramusical barriers to a performer's entry into a foreign market. For political or economic reasons, governments may impose restrictions on foreign singers and songs. Domestic operators, too, are understandably wary of additional competition. At any rate, whatever the concatenation of factors, popular music in the twentieth century has developed by and large along national lines. In 2012, I was embarrassed to realize that I knew only two of the ten top-grossing popular musicians listed in a French magazine; I was only somewhat mollified to learn that an American professional promoter could identify only one more.[34] Music may not have national borders, but popular music has often been national music.

The ambit of a particular musical tradition, style, or genre is largely coextensive with the expanse of a civilization, empire, or nation.[35] Much as we would like to valorize aesthetic autonomy—music's independence not just from material interests but also from social contexts—not just any piece of music, however great its boosters believe it to be, can become popular at any time and in any place. Temporal and cultural delimitations point to inevitable prerequisites of, or conditions of possibility for, music's popularity; they point, that is, to some set of conventions and infrastructures. The notions of soundscape and musical competence suggest some rudimentary horizons with respect to shared expectations. What is music (as opposed to noise)? Which sounds are comprehensible and enjoyable? Who or what is new, cool, hot? And, conversely, who or what is ridiculous or risible?[36] In chapter 1, I outlined some conditions for the possibility of a European- and Japanese-influenced popular music in South Korea; these included more than a century of elementary musical education that disseminated the Western soundscape, and nearly as long an exposure, at least in urban areas, to Western (and Japanese) popular music. These conditions are inadequate, however, in and of themselves. Also crucial were some level of affluence and leisure (foreign records were expensive and largely unavailable in South Korea until the 1980s), a propensity for devoting time and energy to aesthetic pursuits (such pursuits themselves being a feature of an affluent society), and access to the technological means of reproducing self-selected music (such means were not widely available to South Koreans until the 1980s). Before the 1980s, it was rare to encounter a South Korean who was well versed in American or global popular-music trends. It was much more common then for South Koreans to learn about the world by way of Japan. In this sense, the Sŏ Tae-ji revolution decisively shifted the primary external reference point from Japan to the United States.

Of course, not only do exceptions prove rules, they are also the rule themselves; the appearance here and there of transnational singing sensations is coeval with the history of popular music. Furthermore, the incidence of such exceptions has clearly multiplied in the post–Cold War decades, signaling an intensified globalization, as evidenced not just by the rise of the new category of "world music" but also by the interpenetration of distinct musical traditions from around the world.[37] Global pop is far from homogeneous, in terms of either its genres or its national origins; nevertheless, in spite of such British invaders as the Beatles and the Rolling Stones, or Swedish superstars like ABBA and the Cardigans, the preponderant national power in global pop has been the United States.[38] It would be misleading to equate global pop with American pop, but few would deny the impact and influence of Billie Holiday, Frank Sinatra, Elvis Presley, Bob Dylan, Michael Jackson, and Madonna in shaping a common soundscape around the world, especially among the youth of affluent countries. In popular music as in the world at large, for some time the indisputable lingua franca has been (American) English. But globalization is not mere Americanization or homogenization; counterglobalization, indigenization, and hybridization are all part and parcel of the dynamics shaping the world in general and popular music in particular. For our purposes here, the only salient point is that, as far as most contemporary young South Koreans were concerned, the United States came to set the standard for popular music.

Another exception to the rule of the worldwide music industry's general confinement within national boundaries is the emergence of transnational regional stars. Eurovision, for example, operating as a pop-music adjunct to the European Union, creates pan-European stars.[39] In the case of these stars, the language of the lyrics and the style of the music are often global in character; that is, the songs are sung in English and are similar to the regnant genres of global/American pop music. There is, however, another transnationalizing modality, which is to domesticate or localize foreign singers and songs. In the case of South Korean popular music, the predominant method of transplantation has been to acculturate a South Korean singer to the Japanese norm, whether in terms of language or in terms of behavior. Ch'oe Kyu-yŏp/Hasegawa Ichirō and Yi Nan-yŏng/Oka Ranko are the most famous in a long line of ethnic Korean singers who made it to and in Japan; yet, as their Japanese stage names suggest, they were, save for their national origins, almost indistinguishable from their ethnic Japanese counterparts. During the postcolonial period, this pattern was repeated in the two countries' enthusiasm for the same sort of music: *enka* in Japanese, trot in Korean; different names, similar music. Musicians, trot or pop, borrowed from their counterparts across the sea, and singers and composers traveled across it.[40] And even if we exclude the Zainichi singers, there were some South Korean trot stars—Yi Sŏng-ae, Cho Yong-p'il, and Kye Ŭn-suk, among others—who were household names in Japan from the late 1970s to the early 1980s, the time of the boom in South Korean songs (though they all sang in Japanese, and in a genre that South Koreans considered Japanese).[41] Moreover, thanks to the karaoke boom of the early 1980s (the karaoke machine was invented in 1971), personal renditions of South Korean trot songs became fashionable among Japanese businesspeople.[42]

Thus, as we have seen, Korean musicians have been finding success in Japan almost since the beginning of Korean popular music. Even in the inauspicious post–World War II period, when derogatory colonial attitudes toward Korea and Koreans were rife in Japan, some South Koreans in that country achieved remarkable success. And in both countries, the initial enthusiasm for popular music focused at times on the same songs and singers. It is difficult to overemphasize the geographical and cultural propinquity of Japan and South Korea. More than thirty-five years of Japanese colonial rule in Korea, with the latter half pounding an extremely assimilationist note, ensured cultural convergence, if nothing else.[43] Japanese and South Koreans alike were instructed in the modern Japanese music curriculum, which disseminated adaptations of Western choral music and children's songs. Japanese as well as Korean people lived through the US occupation, and many Japanese and Koreans eagerly embraced American popular music (as did much of the rest of the world). In short, Japan and South Korea had similar soundscapes—and, given the considerable heterogeneity in tastes and styles that emerged in both countries by the twenty-first century, what stands out more than the distance between the two countries is the diversity within each one.

Beyond the success of trot music in Japan, some groups, such as the Kim Sisters, were a big hit in the United States, and other South Korean singers, such as Patti Kim, had modest followings in Las Vegas and elsewhere. They sought to acculturate to the American norm, singing in English and in styles that recalled other American singers. And in the mid-1980s, Kim Wan-sŏn, after failing to generate much excitement in Japan, caused a stir in Taiwan. But these successes pale in significance next to the global followings achieved by US pop-music sensations, and even the followings garnered by J-pop performers in Asia and elsewhere. J-pop's success abroad, as discussed later in this chapter, was largely demand-driven: avid, astute listeners sought interesting and intriguing tunes and created a subculture of fandom across East Asia (and beyond).[44] A South Korean music executive told me something similar about K-pop—that young people around the world had discovered South Korean popular music. Yet that account is distorted. The fact is, K-pop has not been a demand-driven, quasi-organic development; rather, it has been the object of a concerted strategy for its exportation. That is, K-pop's success as an export reflects a long history of adapting South Korean singers to particular export markets.[45]

And so let us return to our earlier question, this time with renewed emphasis: *why* export this music? A common assumption, inside as well as outside the popular-music industry in South Korea, is that the domestic market is too small to be profitably sustained. Yet an OECD country whose population was 50 million in 2013 is by no means a small market; in fact, it is one of the larger domestic markets in the world (one that is, moreover, culturally and linguistically unified). And as we have already seen, not only has the popular-music industry in South Korea been thriving in the post-Liberation decades, South Korea has also become an affluent society with a youth market ready, willing, and able to consume popular culture in general, and popular music in particular. What I have been calling South Korea's export imperative, together with the conventional belief that the domestic market is small, appears to be the reflection not of any objective condition but rather of a bedrock belief that took hold during the period of rapid industrialization that began in the 1960s.[46] The embodiment of that belief was the strategy of export-oriented industrialization cemented during the Park regime, as economic growth became the panacea for mass discontent. Soon enough, the export imperative in turn became a foundational myth of South Korean political economy, giving rise to a master cultural reflex that meets any economic problem in contemporary South Korea with one simple idea: when in doubt, export.

The flip side of the export imperative was an equally zealous commitment to economic and cultural protectionism. Export-oriented industrialization required the acquisition and retention of reserves of foreign currencies, if only to purchase raw materials from abroad for production at home. In resource-poor South Korea, which lacked the fundamental fuels of industrialization, the chief comparative economic advantage was the country's relatively skilled but poorly remunerated workforce. But another essential tactic was to maximize foreign reserves by limiting their outflow. The economic-bureaucratic apparatus, in addition to making vigilant efforts to prevent the exhaustion of its reserves of foreign currencies, sought to minimize imports of consumer goods. (One consequence of this policy, as we have seen, was the paucity of foreign records in South Korea, except for pirated copies, until the 1980s.) Besides curbing imports and preserving currency reserves, the government encouraged the consumption of domestic products, thus enhancing demand and achieving economies of scale in production. The economic logic of protectionism went hand in hand with Park's commitment to combating all manner of foreign pollution and corruption—communist, capitalist, and Confucian. As a result, South Korean cultural policy became xenophobic and protectionist in the 1960s. Foreign films, for example, were strictly regulated, a policy that not only preserved South Korea's foreign reserves but also prevented the populace from being exposed to alien ideas and practices, such as political radicalism or sexual deviance. As discussed in chapter 1, the Park regime's regulatory zeal extended to popular music as well. The motivation was not purely political but also economic.

All the same, until the twenty-first century the South Korean popular-music industry did not benefit either from the country's export orientation or from cultural protectionism. The Park regime remained indifferent, if not hostile, to popular culture (with some notable exceptions, such as wrestling), and its export-oriented economic policy was single-mindedly focused on industrial production (the heavier and the more technology-intensive, the better). That is, the popular-music industry could expect little economic support, and much less in terms of freedom from control and censorship. And if economics was about factories and machines, politics was all about power—the military, national security, and domestic repression. Culture, popular or not, was marginalized, invoked only in connection with nationalism. In the early 1980s, the Chun Doo-hwan regime's famous 3S policy offered few improvements for popular music, which at the time had little to do with screens, sex, or sports. And even when culture was discussed, both the Park regime and the Chun regime belittled the entertainment industry and reinforced the long-standing elite disdain for mere "mass culture."

Beyond governmental indifference or even antipathy toward popular culture lay a key obstacle to profitability: the government's unwillingness to protect copyrights. Otherwise scrupulous and zealous governmental regulators turned a blind eye to piracy and unauthorized duplication of books, movies, and records. After all, the South Korean economy in the 1960s and 1970s benefited greatly as the work of more advanced counterparts in other countries was (according to one's perspective) borrowed, learned from, or stolen outright by South Korean operators.[47] Thus, ironically, the myth of the small market increasingly became an actuality for the South Korean popular-music industry. In 2002, the market value of popular music in the United States was $12.6 billion, and in Japan it was $5.4 billion, but the figure for South Korea was only $296 million.[48] A disproportion of that magnitude cannot be explained by the larger populations of the United States and Japan, or even by the higher prices made possible in those countries by higher per capita income. Instead, it can be traced to the weakness of copyright protection in South Korea, and to the concomitant efflorescence of piracy, with its downward pressure on the prices of legitimately produced records. In the 1980s, even a casual visitor to Seoul could not have failed to notice the ubiquity of street peddlers hawking high-quality counterfeit CDs and DVDs (these have persisted to the present). Here, the contrast with Japan is striking: not only does the Japanese market now scrupulously heed copyright laws, the typical music CD also sells now at a fixed price that is sometimes four times the prevailing US retail average.

If the South Korean government and the popular-music industry had not already failed to affect popular sensibilities regarding copyright, any belated effort to do so would have been doomed by a major technological innovation in 1996: the introduction of digitized music and the mp3 player.[49] Almost immediately thereafter, the market in recorded music went into a tailspin, not just in South Korea but all around the world.[50] Furthermore, the South Korean government's now liberalized economic and cultural policies left the door open to greater foreign competition. In 1996, after Sŏ T'ae-ji wa Aidŭl's sudden disbandment, South Korea seemed poised to be inundated by pop-singing sensations from Japan and the United States, to the detriment of domestic performers. In 1998, Kim Dae-jung's visit to Japan coincided with an influx of J-pop that made South Korean celebrities out of Japanese stars like X Japan, Amuro Namie, and SMAP.[51] The coup de grâce was the 1997 IMF crisis. The recession that followed the Asian currency crisis of the previous year was compounded by IMF-imposed austerity measures in South Korea.[52] As noted in the interlude, the effect of the IMF's intervention was more than an economic downturn; it was a shock wave that reverberated through South Korean society and left a lasting scar, which cannot be explained exclusively in terms of unemployment and a stagnant economy. The IMF crisis shattered the widespread belief in rapid and continued economic growth. For the battered music industry, it underscored the urgency of cultivating new audiences and new markets. In short, the South Korean popular-music industry was in turmoil in the late 1990s.

But the economic conditions and constraints just described—South Korea's economic and cultural propensity for exports, a market that failed to ensure steady streams of profits, and the economic recession of the late 1990s—are not in themselves enough to explain the nature and direction of music exports from South Korea. After all, economic action, however embedded in social structure, is both voluntaristic (in that several, if not many, options and directions are possible) and often successful precisely because it is unpredictable (if consequences were obvious, many others would have taken the same action).[53] In South Korea, the willingness of new popular-music impresarios and entrepreneurs to step forward and gamble on a particular successful outcome has depended on a concatenation of background factors and, at least in retrospect, on a predilection for taking risks that is more or less coherent, if it does not quite rise to the level of a consistent strategy and vision.

And it is these new impresarios and entrepreneurs who are the source of the initiative to export South Korean popular music. Their business is similar, of course, to all other businesses—they want to sell something that people want and are able to purchase—but not all production processes are isomorphic. Making hits and stars is different from making cars and trucks. The music industry remains resistant to the Fordist, top-down mode of mass production. The mature automobile market, as unpredictable as consumer demand may seem to the minds behind the latest models, exhibits enough stability to reward top-down decision making as well as the mass production that achieves production efficiency, cost effectiveness, and economic competitiveness. The same cannot be said of the music industry, where the competition is not so much over price (a teenage fan is unlikely to download a trot song, no matter how inexpensive it is) as over quality (by the standards of the targeted audience) and some level (however minimal) of innovation and inherent interest. Thus demand is unpredictable, but production still requires not only specific appreciation of a particular genre, with all its musical and extramusical conventions and practices, but also an uncanny sense of what's next. Every new single is a customized product, one that, even as a mere cover, needs a new composition and requires the assembly of singers and musicians, different types of designers, and a host of other professionals. By comparison with the automobile industry, the barriers to entry into the popular-music industry are much lower: what is needed is not so much sheer amounts of capital and advanced levels of technology as knowledge of popular music and access to talented musicians and other music makers. Particularly since the introduction of inexpensive computers and software, production processes have become financially and technologically accessible to an ever-larger circle and no longer depend on the studios that used to control the means of production. Even though popular music is often characterized as an output of the culture industry, it is in fact much more a craft product than a mass-manufactured commodity. The advantages of size, scale, and experience are much smaller in the popular-music industry than they are in automobile manufacturing or even in the manufacture of fast-changing mobile phones. And even a larger popular-music conglomerate still depends on production units that function relatively independently under top-down decision makers, and that operate as small, craftlike enterprises. Therefore, the effective unit of production in popular music is a small studio or agency, even though it may be owned by a large conglomerate.

Apart from the relatively low barriers to entry into the popular-music industry, the economic crisis of the late 1990s actually proved to be a major boon to would-be insurgent entrepreneurs, especially small and new producers. Most important, progressive South Korean governmental policy countered excessive economic concentration with legislation that limited *chaebŏl* dominance. The quasi-monopolistic dominance of *chaebŏl*, which had extended from production to distribution, ended in 1998. Thus a new space for competition opened up in the South Korean popular-music industry. It is symptomatic of this development that the three largest K-pop agencies today were all launched just before the implementation of the anti-monopolistic policy: SM Entertainment in 1995, YG in 1996, and JYP in 1997. And it is no accident that all three had already been immersed in popular music, with exposure to global trends. Just as significant is the fact that the Kim Dae-jung regime sought to promote South Korean culture abroad, branding South Korea as a creative and innovative country (and not merely as a player in construction and heavy industry, or even in high-tech production). From tax breaks to outright subsidies, the governmental policy of soft-power promotion would serve to propel the Korean Wave around the world. By 2013, the government's budget for promoting the popular-music industry was reportedly $300 million, roughly the same amount as total turnover in the industry a decade earlier.[54] Finally, the introduction of new technologies—the digitization of music, starting in 1996, and, beginning in 2005, the ascent of YouTube and other Internet-based modes of music-video dissemination—gave a momentary advantage to newer labels and agencies. As intimated earlier, the emergence of a new format often accompanies the rise of a new musical genre; J-pop, for example, arose with the new CD format in the late 1980s.[55] The South Korean entrepreneurs—by using new Internet-based technologies to market a new musical style, and by devising a new business model that relied more on the Internet than on pressed records—made South Korea the first country where sales of digitized music exceeded sales of music in nondigital formats.[56] Here again, the new entrepreneurs were willing to work with new technologies and new outlets and thus rode a wave that combined a new format with new content (that is, new genres and styles).[57]

By the first few years of the twenty-first century, the three major K-pop agencies had become the face of youth-oriented South Korean popular music. *Chaebŏl,* after an initial exodus and hiatus from the entertainment industry, would re-enter the music market in the early years of the century, but only to promote received genres, ranging from trot to ballads, and focus on domestic sales; they were not a force for innovation or exportation. K-pop was created largely by entrepreneurial firms that had to expand abroad in order to prosper. Beyond the big three, other agencies produce and promote K-pop groups, such as DSP Entertainment (KARA), CUBE Entertainment (BEAST), and Nega Network (Brown Eyed Girls).[58] Being at once new and small, these agencies carved out a new market niche, and in so doing they ushered in the age of K-pop.

To answer, then, the question of why this music should be exported: almost every developed country has a domestic popular-music industry, but few countries have both the (presumed) need to find success abroad and the capacity for systematically generating accomplished acts that can appeal to audiences beyond national borders. Thus, after the crisis of the late 1990s, intense competition combined with the export imperative catapulted the new style, K-pop.

THE BUSINESS OF K-POP (IS BUSINESS)

The founders of the three most important K-pop agencies were or are musicians.[59] Therefore, it is tempting to seek a larger and deeper artistic vision behind K-pop. But that would be a mistake, for the logic of musical innovation followed the logic of the export imperative in particular, and of the profit motive in general. These K-pop impresarios were not farsighted visionaries; they were simply in the right place at the right time, and they seized commercial opportunities rather than projecting their artistic vision. Money may be a horrid thing to follow, but it is a charming thing to meet and keep; it is the alpha and omega of K-pop.

The career of Lee Soo-man (Yi Su-man) and the trajectory of SM Entertainment exemplify the parameters of export-oriented K-pop, which Lee calls "culture technology."[60] As a student at the elite Seoul National University in the 1970s, Lee had attained renown as a folk singer and disc jockey. Given the period's regnant culture of anti-government activism, he positioned himself squarely as a progressive: against military rule and trot music. When he ran afoul of governmental authorities, he went abroad to study, and in 1980 he landed in Southern California, at California State University, Northridge. He shifted his major from agriculture to computer science—an obvious sign of the times—and also found his musical tastes profoundly shaken by his five-year stint in Northridge. From folk, his interest turned to dance pop and other genres of popular music that were thriving in the early 1980s in the United States. Above all, he absorbed the nascent and dynamic years of MTV. When Lee returned to South Korea, in 1985, he abandoned both agriculture and computers to enter the music industry. Over the next decade, he also jettisoned folk altogether in favor of producing and promoting newer sounds. At first he sought to reproduce the type of music that was then popular in the United States; as discussed in chapter 1, he found modest success with Hyŏn Chin-yŏng. Lee then changed his tack again and replaced MTV-inflected dance pop with Japanese idol pop, and here he found models in two groups that were extremely popular in Japan in the 1980s: Shōnentai (Boy Platoon) and Shōjotai (Girl Platoon). He may also have found some reassurance in the formula that had spawned New Kids on the Block and Backstreet Boys, whose US debuts had been in 1984 and 1993, respectively. After H.O.T.'s sensational success, Lee quickly trained and produced S.E.S. (1997), SHINHWA (1998), and Fly to the Sky (1998), all three of which found fans in South Korea as well as some spillover success in Chinese-language areas. These groups were largely for local consumption, however. It is possible to see them as proto–K-pop groups, but their brand of bubblegum pop and their adorable but amateurish dance moves owe more to their 1980s-era Japanese counterparts and to that era's Sobangch'a than to contemporary K-pop acts (and, as I have argued, early and late SHINHWA are quite distinct music-cum-movement experiences).

It was in China that Lee first sought to capitalize on H.O.T.'s popularity, but his effort to cultivate the Chinese market in the late 1990s was a dismal failure, as noted earlier. And, again, the most significant impediment to success in China was the impossibility of establishing a viable business model in a market rife with piracy.[61] It was only after Lee's ill-fated venture in China that he created a South Korean version of J-pop, which would also prove popular in the sinophone market.

Toward the latter half of the decade between the years 2000 and 2010, two trends brought about a shift in SM Entertainment's strategy. As discussed earlier, JYP Entertainment, depending heavily on American innovations, provided the contemporary K-pop template in the form of Wonder Girls' "Tell Me." That song's explosive popularity in South Korea led others, including SM Entertainment, to take a leaf from the Wonder Girls' songbook. At the same time, the Korean Wave—the widespread popularity of South Korean television dramas across much of Northeast and Southeast Asia—had ensconced South Korea as a popular-culture powerhouse, legitimating it as a potent brand. SM Entertainment, buoyed by confidence and the resources from its Japanese successes, revised its strategy once again to export K-pop. Therefore, even Tongbang Sin'gi, as noted above, took an American turn around 2008, away from J-pop. SM Entertainment and other agencies, pushed by the export imperative and pulled by the large and lucrative export markets, began a more global drive with the contemporary K-pop formula.

Again, the K-pop formula is driven by market considerations, not artistic concerns; the logic of K-pop is the logic of capital. Perhaps an artistic principle underlay Lee's various shifts and turns, but it seems more reasonable to conclude that he was looking for commercial success. Indeed, almost every aspect of K-pop originates in business interests. Consider, for example, the ensemble character of K-pop. In the beginning, it was an emulation of

American and Japanese groups, but it became one of the defining features of South Korean popular music. There are solo performers, to be sure, but cold commercial logic sustains the group structure. Even a casual listener notices that K-pop's ensemble singing can sound surprisingly accomplished, whereas a similar level of accomplishment is much less common in a solo K-pop singer. That is, good singers who can work together are common enough; superb soloists are few and far between. What is true for singing is true for dancing as well. Precision choreography relies less on individual virtuosity than on trainable ensemble movements. To put this idea polemically, K-pop relies less on individual genius than on collective effort. Just as significant, not only is a solo performer at the mercy of individual ups and downs, she can also be in only one place at a time. But the group structure allows a K-pop act to thrive even in the absence of one or two of its members, who may be on leave for a television interview or for an appearance on a television drama. Given the desire to appeal to a large audience—not just in terms of particular tastes for facial features, qualities of voice, or types of physiognomy but also in terms of language skills—it behooves a producer to compose a relatively heterogeneous group (the point is not to have clones, or to have everyone speaking the same language). And the group structure, which obviates a reserve army of backup singers and dancers, is not only economically advantageous but also logistically expedient. A member who drops out can be replaced. In turn, if a group should fail to thrive, then its more promising members can join another group. Individuals, therefore, are pieces in the grand strategy of a K-pop impresario. Furthermore, the group members' collective existence of living and working together sustains morale and limits divalike perturbations. In addition, a solo performer lives or dies on her own, but a group can cultivate distinct subsets of fans. The intertwined lives of the group's members give rise to ongoing narratives about them, which fans can follow, speculate about, and discuss endlessly among themselves. Thus the group structure provides a flexibility, efficiency, and reach that a solo act cannot easily offer.

Girls' Generation is exemplary in this regard. The K-pop formula is explicit, including catchy refrains, propulsive beats, and signature moves packaged and performed to perfection. The nine young women in the group—their precise selection was a protracted process—are all deemed physically attractive, but they also express a diversity of facial features and corporeal characteristics.[62] (They are nevertheless united by the group's signature feature of long, slim legs.) The group often releases the same song in four different languages. Although the musical arrangement and choreography are the same for each version, the group not only translates the lyrics into a local language (two of its members are fluent in Japanese, two more in Chinese, and another pair in English) but also makes a series of local adaptations, and discrete language sites are made available to individual fans as well as to various national fan clubs.

Commercial concerns also underlie the proliferation of subgroups. Super Junior, for example, has performed as Super Junior-M, Super Junior R.K.Y., Super Junior-Happy, and Super Junior T.[63] The idea, as with the China-oriented Super Junior-M, is to have the group come and go, to maximize its exposure (and producers' profits). Along this line of thinking, the latest trend has been to create multinational and multiethnic groups, not for the sake of political correctness but principally to extend their appeal to neighboring Asian countries. SM Entertainment promotes EXO, which debuted in 2012, as two subgroups, EXO-K and EXO-M, and these operate primarily in South Korea and in sinophone areas, respectively. The group 2PM includes Nickkhun, who is from Thailand, where K-pop is extremely popular.[64] There is a trend toward including ethnic Chinese performers in K-pop groups, such as f(x) and Miss A. The blatant appeal to co-ethnic affinity is a permutation of the foundational logic of K-pop.

Other features of the group structure also reflect the cold calculus of business. Given the profound popularity of Wonder Girls and Girls' Generation, it would seem obvious to produce all-girl groups. Yet the initial motivation for forming them, at least according to a senior SM Entertainment executive, was because the South Korean military conscripts almost every male South Korean citizen for a minimum period of twenty-one months.[65] The draft, needless to say, strikes many idol singers in their prime, since they must enlist before they are thirty years old. The effects of universal male military service on the world of K-pop range from the short life of a boy band (and of a garage rock band, for that matter) to the emergence from military training of a masculinized rock star.[66] Thus SM Entertainment assembled girl groups, which are not subject to the problem of dissolution caused by compulsory military service.

In response to the nascent global demand for K-pop, the genre's stars differentiate themselves from the vast majority of American acts (beyond the obvious ethnonational distinctions) by projecting a polite suburban gentility beneath an edgy urban veneer. K-pop offers kinder, gentler versions of some of the more outré performers from the United States and elsewhere, but it also presents itself with a professional sheen. Once again, both elements—politeness and professionalism—are intended to appeal to a particular segment of the world music market. Certainly a significant slice of what is currently the largest market (Japan) and of what is likely to be the largest market in the future (China) seems smitten with the package. But the politeness and gentility (smiles rather than sneers), instead of reflecting a Confucian cultural trait, are the systematically cultivated expression of a calculated decision to appeal to the targeted audiences. It is possible to interpret this gentility as a matter of regional sensibility—as something along the lines of East Asian cultural conservatism. However, it is probably more reasonable to regard this presentation as an edginess that is not *too* edgy, a sexiness that is not *too* sexy, an urban quality that is not too "ghetto." Just as rock 'n' roll achieved mainstream acceptability in 1950s white America by shedding its mantle of "Negro" music, K-pop appropriates all the elements of urban American (often African American) sound, movement, and energy and tames—bleaches—them for popular consumption around the world.[67] And, as diligently seductive and charismatic as K-pop stars are in performance, they present themselves as humble and modest. In addition, it does not take much exposure to K-pop performances to note the frequent nods and winks directed at viewers (supporters or customers, according to one's perspective). Made up and dressed up, K-pop stars nurture their fans and fan clubs, not only in concert and on websites but also in direct encounters.[68] In other words, they work as employees, not as self-regarding artists. Like solid professionals, they have been trained in the business of K-pop, which includes good customer service.

The most distinctive aspects of K-pop, in terms of the popular-music business, are its almost complete eschewal of the independent musician-artist, its embrace of the studio system to develop talent, and an extreme division of labor in the creation of songs and videos. The K-pop formula relies on a particular mode of production. The incubation system dedicated to spawning K-pop stars is a contemporary South Korean analogue of the famed Hollywood studio system.[69] Needless to say, all music agencies recruit talent and train their stars to some extent, but the K-pop system is extremely comprehensive. Agencies differ in their levels of organization and in their curricula, but there is a broad family resemblance across the agencies. The recruitment process is highly selective. SM Entertainment, for example, chooses about 1 trainee for every 1,000 applicants (other agencies claim roughly 1 acceptance for every 250 applicants). There are three classes of trainees: *chunbisaeng* (preparatory students), *yŏnsusaeng* (practicing students), and "project group" members. Those at the preparatory stage may still be young enough to attend primary school, and their participation may be a casual extracurricular activity. The second stage, that of practicing student, is much more serious; here, the aspirant may spend five or more years training to be a K-pop star. At least four of the nine members of Girls' Generation spent more than six years as *yŏnsusaeng*.[70] Because many of the *yŏnsusaeng* attend school, they can take part in training only in the afternoons, and they often end up returning home on the last train, around midnight. They may spend up to twelve or more hours every day in group and individual lessons, in every sphere deemed necessary for K-pop stardom—singing, dancing, foreign languages, etiquette, and so on. A JYP executive claimed that the agency's training center offers sixty-seven different subjects. The regime is akin to that of a well-disciplined military camp or a training institute for Olympic athletes. According to several *yŏnsusaeng*, the most nerve-racking routine is the monthly examination in which each trainee's progress is judged. After three to five years (the full range seems to be from two to eight years), the most promising *yŏnsusaeng* are organized into project groups preparing to launch their professional careers. An SM executive claims that perhaps 5 percent of the trainees turn professional. Even at the project-group stage, individuals drop out for a number of reasons; for example, one potential member of Girls' Generation joined another group, T-ara, whereas another decided to pursue academics and was admitted to the prestigious Korea Advanced Institute of Science and Technology (the MIT of South Korea).[71] The agency invests heavily in its trainees, spending an average of about $300,000 per person—roughly twice the average annual income of a college graduate— over a five-year period. The money goes not only to musical instruction and dancing lessons but also to plastic surgery and other efforts to enhance the attractiveness of the final product.

After his or her debut, the K-pop professional inhabits a total institution. In spite of their fame and their fan clubs, K-pop stars live together, often sharing bedrooms, and they work without much free time. One K-pop star claimed that the lack of personal freedom and free time meant that the only readily available source of entertainment was to "hang out with other K-pop stars." Thus the widely publicized life of a K-pop star seems more like the life of a low-wage foreign migrant worker than like the life of the proverbial rock star. According to a governmental report, the average salary of a K-pop performer was about $10,000 per annum, but music executives point out that they have invested a great deal in making their trainees into stars and continue to cover all their considerable expenses.[72] Poor remuneration and adverse conditions have led to lawsuits that have entangled agencies and stars.

The heart of the popular-music industry is planned obsolescence, and the same principle is central to K-pop's star-maker machinery. Just as no music producer can expect a hit to keep selling after months on the charts, SM Entertainment and other agencies are not betting that any of their acts will survive beyond five years or so. In spite of the agencies' relatively heavy investments of money and time, they assume that rapidly changing tastes will render even the most successful group passé after a while. In South Korea, given the stiff competition and the constant streaming of songs, it has become rare for any song to hold the top spot on the charts for more than a week. As each act struts its short half-life upon the stage—and lucky are those who debut and then stay in business for even a year—the factory keeps on churning out new acts. Music fashions change, markets may change, and all these permutations are part and parcel of the strategic vision of SM Entertainment and its peers.

To be sure, there are other avenues of popular-music stardom in South Korea. Several well-publicized audition programs exist. Arts high schools and special majors at several universities prepare students for careers in musical entertainment; Rain and SE7EN are graduates of the renowned Anyang Arts High School. Other stars are simply found by talent scouts and record executives. However, because K-pop is essentially an oligopoly (though this situation may change in the future), there is currently only one royal road to K-pop stardom: the training institute of one of the major K-pop agencies. The agencies also seem to be expanding their influence; in 2009, for example, SM Entertainment was instrumental in establishing Hallim Entertainment Arts High School.

Given the realities—an oligopolistic industry, with few competitive entertainment agencies; the weakness of the independent music scene; the industry's intimately intertwined elements—and the lack of viable alternatives, most K-pop stars are doomed to live out their short careers in thrall to their managers. And, apart from military conscription and other reasons for ending a career, there are the challenging and demanding working conditions. The stars work long hours without any sustained rest or relaxation, in a state of semipermanent sleep deprivation. The physical demands—constant training, vigorous dancing, incessant traveling—also lead to physical injury and illness, not to mention mental stress.

In this regard, the ethos behind the stars' impeccable public behavior is less Confucian than authoritarian. K-pop stardom is hardly a charmed life.

Its fragility can be gauged by the plethora of suicides among successful performers.

The success of K-pop as an export is not merely about the thorough training of singer-dancers but also about the assembly of high-caliber professionals. Whether we look at Hyundai Sonata or Samsung Galaxy, South Korean corporations have brought together technically proficient individuals—at times foreign experts, but more often nationals trained at top universities abroad, usually in the United States—who seek to emulate and, over time, to supersede the leading brands and models. Although there is a strong desire for insourcing, or doing everything in house, the reality in K-pop is that outsourcing is constant. K-pop producers seek to hire world-class artists and professionals to do everything from writing lyrics and composing music to choreographing and costuming; Swedish popular-music composers in particular are highly desired by K-pop agencies that seek global acceptance. In addition, given South Korea's drive to be a world center of fashion and design, the South Korean popular-music industry draws on domestic (and, at times, foreign) talent in fashion and even CD sleeve design. K-pop agencies are blessed with an oversupply of highly trained musicians and entertainment-industry professionals, many of whom have studied and worked abroad as performers, composers, choreographers, stage managers, and so on. The agencies also draw on the far-flung populations of the South Korean diaspora.

Production in and of itself is incomplete, of course, without distribution and marketing. A corporation like Hyundai or Samsung, before it establishes brand recognition (that is, a mark of sheer visibility but also of reliable reputation), spends enormous energy and money on establishing links to local distributors, marketers, advertisers, and allied professionals. Quite often, such a corporation extends extremely advantageous deals, and not just pecuniary rewards, in order to crack a particular national market. Much the same can be said of SM Entertainment and other agencies, which perforce rely on foreign partners who have access to distribution and promotion mechanisms that are often idiosyncratic to the countries in question. K-pop agencies seek close collaboration with local promoters, and with the prevailing modes of operation in local markets. For example, contemporary East Asian business practices are characterized by the rhetoric of human relations, and K-pop agencies devote considerable time and energy to cultivating their business partners and counterparts. Many resources are expended on encounters with these partners, who are offered not only elaborate and expensive meals and drinks but also sexual entertainment.[73] By offering financial incentives for local promoters to sell K-pop, K-pop agencies frequently sacrifice short-term profits in favor of longer-term gains. One high-level executive said that though the usual split is fifty-fifty, his agency was willing to strike a "crazy" deal that gave 90 percent of first-year profits to a Japanese partner.[74] These and other aspects of South Korean business practices are in fact deeply influenced by Japanese business customs and conventions.[75] This aggressive courting of local partners has inevitably generated criticism of K-pop agencies' business practices.[76]

Localization strategy remains a cardinal feature of K-pop marketing. Most agencies are acutely conscious of the distinct demands of different national markets. In this regard, K-pop's success in Japan is indistinguishable from the K-pop agencies' concerted efforts to adapt to the particularities of the large but challenging Japanese market. For example, the CEO of SM Entertainment, who grew up in Japan and is fluent in Japanese, is, not surprisingly, keenly aware of the necessity of heeding Japanese conventions. And not only are there Japanese-language websites for fans, and lessons in Japanese language and culture for K-pop performers, these websites and lessons also hew closely to the prevailing conventions of the Japanese popular-music industry, ranging from elaborate packaging (including gifts added to packaged CDs and DVDs) to active cultivation of devoted fans and fan clubs. Whereas South Korean fans employ the language of kinship to address the stars, their Japanese counterparts purchase large amounts of fan-club paraphernalia and generate a distinct subculture.[77] In short, market research and local knowledge contribute, in however small a measure, to the dissemination of K-pop in Japan.

Yet another critical component of K-pop marketing is its embrace of the Internet and social media. In the post–World War II decades, the classic route to pop-music success in the United States or Japan was performing at local venues and seeking airplay on local radio stations, thus generating record sales. K-pop acts take part in these received activities, but the emphasis has been less on promoting the sale of physical CDs than on eliciting downloads of digitized music. More recently, much of K-pop marketing has been taking place on YouTube and has relied on social media to disseminate K-pop content, a process that leads both to royalties, however limited, and to loyalty among the fans who purchase paraphernalia, attend concerts, and contribute to other sources of income. The explosive growth of YouTube, social media, and smart-phone use between 2005 and 2010 was especially important in making K-pop a pan-Asian and, indeed, global phenomenon.

Here again, K-pop was in a favorable position. In the years that followed the 1997 IMF crisis, one of the major governmental initiatives was to embrace and enhance the digital economy. After Kim Dae-jung's Cyber Korea 21 program proposed a massive expansion of Internet infrastructure, by 2002 South Korea had become the country with the world's most extensive broadband penetration.[78] Beginning in 2000, the website Soribada experienced explosive growth as a file-sharing site, one that, after a government crackdown, transmogrified into an extremely successful music-download and subscription service. By 2003, all the major South Korean producers of cell phones had incorporated mp3 players into their devices, thus anticipating iTunes and Spotify. By 2011, more than 20 million South Koreans (in a country of 50 million) owned smart phones. Thus South Korea's early adoption of digital technology not only brought a crisis to the South Korean popular-music industry but also paved the way for a new mode of music dissemination. In short, South Korea was something of a pioneer in the brave new world of the digitized information economy, and the country was therefore in a position to benefit from the new way of conducting the music business.[79]

It would be a mistake, however, to characterize K-pop agencies as either purely entrepreneurial or strictly formal-rational organizations. K-pop agencies, like the film studios of Hollywood's golden age, are extremely organized in disciplining their stars-in-the-making—but, again like the old Hollywood studios, they are also rather capricious and idiosyncratic in their decision making, as a consequence of the charismatic authority accorded to founder-entrepreneurs and of the general cultural propensity for hierarchical management in South Korea.[80] Many elements of the South Korean entertainment-business model also exist in the United States (recruitment and training of stars, and so on). Despite certain similarities, however, the business model in the world of K-pop entertainment is in many ways antipodal to that in the world of US entertainment (for example, a US agency typically "represents" its "talent"). Moreover, in the ideal type of US arrangement, the aesthetic autonomy of the performers is valorized.[81] In addition, aspiring performers under the US model manage and assume the course and costs of preparing for their own careers, whereas a K-pop agency insources the career-preparation process. This is not to say that K-pop stars are powerless and mindless puppets of producers' vision and incubation but rather that the K-pop industry's structure privileges producers over performers. In short, then, K-pop emerged from a South Korean version of the old Hollywood studio system. It is predicated not on faith in the artist's autonomy but on extreme division of labor and massive dispersion of expertise. The production agency creates acts and songs from diverse sources, and the agency's performers, after years of in-house training, ultimately execute what has been conceived for them. The "K" in K-pop has more to do with *Das Kapital* than with Korean culture or tradition.

INTERNAL AND EXTERNAL TRANSFORMATIONS

A studio system does not exist in a vacuum. It must have the means to populate and sustain itself, and it must be able to sell its products beyond its national market. By the turn of the millennium, both of these preconditions were in place for the K-pop system.

A studio system, no matter how perfectly conceived and executed, cannot recruit potential stars in a country devoid of talent, or in a culture that devalues talent—and, as it happens, contemporary South Korea has a large reserve army of potential K-pop stars. In the affluent South Korea of recent decades, popular entertainment has entailed not just listening passively to professional singers but also actively performing in quotidian settings. Although *noraebang*—specialized establishments for karaoke singing—did not open in South Korea until 1991, the karaoke machine, invented in Japan in 1971, had already become a household fixture as well as a ubiquitous feature of bars, churches, restaurants, and virtually every other kind of establishment where South Koreans congregate. Communal singing at family gatherings and religious rituals or in public places is hardly unique to South Korea. As noted in chapter 1, Koreans learned to sing choral songs from Western-inspired musical educators and Christian missionaries. Furthermore, people often entertain themselves by performing music, and in East Asia singing certainly occupies a major role in that regard. Yet South Korea is remarkable for the way in which the primary postprandial entertainment seems to require heading to the nearest *noraebang*. Of the scores of suppers I have had in South Korea over the past two decades, I can hardly recall a single instance in which this second stage (*ich'a*) was not suggested, and almost always at an establishment where singing was compulsory. To be sure, television viewing remains a default mode of evening entertainment for adults at home (precollege students are busily studying, by and large, at *hagwŏn,* the so-called cram schools), and almost every South Korean seems to be staring incessantly at one screen or another, but it remains the norm for urban work colleagues to eat dinner together and possibly engage in a spot of drinking. The night out (more common during the week than on the weekend) tends not to be just about drinking and conversing (even imbibing without simultaneously eating is uncommon) or dancing or other escapades, and the typical destination, across all age groups, is the *noraebang*. Indeed, *noraebang* culture is hegemonic, forcing nearly everyone to participate in a collective songfest (even as many South Koreans insist that they hate doing so). Yi Ch'ang-dong's 2007 film *Miryang* (Secret sunshine) captures the inextricable intertwinement of everyday life and singing in contemporary South Korea, whether one is crooning alone at home (accompanied by a karaoke machine) or with friends at a local *noraebang*. Thus did South Korea become a nation of singers, and the singers perform mainly pop songs. It is also not uncommon for young people (and even some old ones) to reproduce K-pop dance steps in public. Furthermore, there are innumerable televised auditions for identifying potential stars, and they are some of the most-watched shows.[82] At any rate, as far as the supply of potential South Korean singing stars is concerned, there appears to be, in a word, a surplus.

The sheer scale of this supply is inadequate in and of itself, of course; after all, if South Koreans were still singing trot songs, these potential stars' international appeal would be largely restricted to Japan. But the South Korean soundscape, at least for people born after the struggles of the Park years, has become firmly and naturally Western. Whether we look at standard sartorial habits or the dominant discourse about life and love, young South Koreans' adherence to Western and specifically American norms would be difficult to deny (much as that adherence *is* constantly denied). The Confucian ideology that devalued singers—recall the abysmally low status of *p'ansori* singers, or the attempted and successful suicides among the first Korean stars in the colonial period (see chapter 1)—has waned significantly, to the point where, by the early 2010s, the most desirable occupation for a young South Korean girl had become that of singer or K-pop star. Although a survey of preteens and teenagers about what they would like to be when they grow up is hardly predictive of their future occupations, responses to a survey can strongly suggest what is popular and admired at the moment. What is more relevant for would-be K-pop stars is that some parents now encourage their children to pursue careers in K-pop, just as eager mothers (and the occasional father) have sought to enhance their children's performance at school, or perhaps in classical music.[83]

We should also take note of the particular nexus of schooling and employment in South Korea. Given the salience of entrance examinations for matriculation at an elite university—and admission to an elite university is widely believed to guarantee an elite job in a corporation or in government—"diploma disease" has spread as an incapacitating condition of life for many young South Koreans. Although school classrooms are now less martial and intimidating than in the past, many children find themselves going to school after school: *hagwŏn*. Facile commentators have been eager to trace this phenomenon to the Chinese meritocratic examination system (*kagyo* in Korean), but the system of cram schools is in fact more of a modern Japanese invention, which South Koreans have emulated. Meanwhile, young people, devoid of free time and entertainment, find that popular music serves as one of the few respites they can enjoy privately or with peers. Even more striking is the fact that, because few viable employment opportunities exist for those who are left out of the paper chase, K-pop stardom has become the South Korean dream, a beckoning and lucrative opportunity for young, non–university-bound South Koreans, particularly since there have been few visible outlets for independent musicians in South Korea, unlike in the United States or Japan, with their respective garage-band and live-music (*raibu*) scenes.

Moreover, South Koreans have undergone a physical metamorphosis as they have become taller and, at least by the standards of Western pop culture, more attractive.[84] This is to say nothing about the ubiquity of plastic surgery.[85] The traditional Confucian mores sharply condemned alterations to the face and body bestowed by one's parents, but conventions shifted so rapidly that by the 1990s it was becoming more and more acceptable to undergo facial cosmetic surgery, whether to make one's eyes appear larger and more vivid by the construction of so-called double eyelids (accomplished with an incision of the encephalic fold) or to make one's nose more shapely and distinct.[86] The widespread yearning to be beautiful (or at least not ugly) became enshrined as something of a basic human right. The 2006 film *Sigan* (Time), by Kim Ki-duk (Kim Ki-dŏk), emblematically captures this pervasive South Korean turn toward cosmetic enhancement. As one measure of this rapid change, in 2000 there was still a public outcry when the actress Pak Nam-ju (Park Nam Joo) acknowledged having gone under the knife, but in the early 2010s such a revelation is no longer major news.[87] The past few years have seen a series of K-pop stars reveal their past cosmetic improvements.[88] According to one survey of Seoul women between the ages of twenty-five and twenty-nine, more than 61 percent had undergone some form of plastic surgery, and more than 77 percent said that they needed some form of artificial enhancement.[89] Indeed, South Korea is a world leader in plastic surgery, in terms of both medical practice and popular consumption.[90] The proliferation of makeovers in physical appearance, fashion, and everyday demeanor has made the wealthy Gangnam area a place that strikes outsiders as a hotbed of fashion models and movie stars. (On a South Korean television show, a young Thai woman gushed, "I have never seen an ugly woman in Gangnam.")

In fact, changing aesthetics have permeated every dimension of South Koreans' appearance. In the matter of hairstyles, for example, the 1980s were a time when the rules were simple and finite. Boys had crew (or near crew) cuts; lengths varied, but almost all men had well-trimmed hair. Girls had straight hair; women permed their hair and kept it short. Long, straight hair was extremely rare (and an identifying mark of Japanese girls and women who were in South Korea). Some women had more hair than others, but the color scheme was black and blacker—a point of traditional pride for Korean women.[91] Then, in the mid-1990s, the rules became confusing and complex; lengths, styles, cuts, and colors began to vary. The changes are evident in music videos: if it was hard to find dyed hair before the year 2000, it was very hard to find undyed hair just a few years later. In the late 1980s, young Japanese tourists with dyed blond hair prompted exclamations that such a thing would never be seen in South Korea; today in Seoul, it has become reasonable to assume that young women who haven't dyed their hair are most likely not South Korean.

Until the 1980s, in the name of Confucian tradition, sartorial and sexual modesty were the unquestioned norm in South Korea. In roughly the same way that American television audiences of the 1950s saw Elvis Presley as indecent, the performer Kim Wan-sŏn, who was almost always fully clad, was often considered obscene in the mid-1980s, but two decades later she would have seemed quite modest, if not altogether quaint. South Korea became much more open in the post-Liberation era, as described in chapter 1; it was the dark decades of military rule that made Kim's clothing and dancing seem so risqué, so un-Korean. In contrast, the conservative Lee Myung-bak regime went so far as to promote K-pop as one aspect of South Korean soft power, at a time when K-pop was even more un-Confucian in appearance. The onslaught of US popular culture—in the generalized context of sexualized bodies and sexual imagery—shaped South Korean tastes, from movies to music videos. Before the 1980s, even a chaste kiss was seldom seen on screen, but quasi-pornographic scenes proliferated thereafter. Greater bodily exposure and sexual suggestiveness were slower to appear in popular-music shows and videos because, unlike movies, they were open to South Koreans of all ages. Singers, especially women, remained reluctant even to show bare arms and legs until the 1990s, but after the advent of Yi Hyo-ri Syndrome, in 2003, exposing the body became the norm, however delayed its emergence.

Apart from domestic transformations, K-pop's trans-Korean success was predicated on changes beyond the Korean peninsula. To paint with a broad brush here, the making of modern national identity in East Asia in the twentieth century was coeval with the creation of national popular culture. Notwithstanding the hybrid and transcultural origins of Chinese, Japanese, and Korean popular music, much of each nation's popular music was sung in that nation's language, by actual or presumed ethnic natives of that country.[92] Certainly South Korean popular music had an ethnic Korean veneer.[93] Soft xenophobia was one facet of the phenomenon of national popular music, but a more important factor was the interest of a nascent national audience (sustained by family and friendship circles and by a nationalized mass media) in listening mainly to popular music sung in the nation's language; thus national audiences made stars of their co-ethnics.[94] Musicians and producers found inspiration and examples from everywhere in composing and performing popular music. Yet much of Northeast and Southeast Asia was not only impoverished but also protectionist. Foreign popular music, when not censored or heavily taxed, long remained a luxury good. In the post–Cold War period, many of the conditions that had sustained national popular music became weakened. The collapse of state socialist societies went hand in hand with the financial and economic globalization that sought to eliminate nationalist barriers, including economic and cultural protectionism. There were also related efforts to protect copyrights, to market music across national borders, and to denationalize and globalize popular music. Rapid advances in the technological means of reproducing music—above all, the creation of the World Wide Web and the development of web browsers, which led in turn to the diffusion of digitized music—accentuated this political-economic-cultural globalization and convergence, at least among the affluent nations of the world.

Furthermore, the socioeconomic conditions that made it possible to consume popular culture spread across Northeast and Southeast Asia. Here we see many of the same trends that established popular music in colonial Korea, such as urbanization, industrialization, and the rise of the middle classes and youth culture. And not only did the economic and political preconditions exist, increasingly affluent Asians had also been schooled in the musical competence and cultural sensibilities associated with Americanized popular music, an education that entailed familiarity with the Western soundscape and the domain of recent American popular music as well as with its cultural assumptions, ranging from its rhetoric and poetics to its valorization of romantic love. The inevitable companion of financial globalization was global consumerism, or the globalization of consumption.[95] In brief, South Korea's neighboring countries, in addition to Europe and much of Latin America, were ready for something like K-pop.

Consider the Japanese attitude toward South Korean popular culture. As we have seen, Japanese listeners had been receptive to ethnic Korean singers since the colonial period. This convergence of musical taste undoubtedly helped, as did numerous points of physical, linguistic, and cultural similarity. Yet the success of trot/*enka* singers notwithstanding, it had long been believed, as discussed earlier, that mainstream Japanese listeners would resist and reject Korean singers. From roughly the mid-1980s on, however, South Korea's dynamic economy and democratic politics, as well as the nation's cultural resurgence, steadily enhanced the general image of South Korea in Japan.[96] The 2002 World Cup, which South Korea and Japan jointly hosted, would prove to be something of a turning point. In 2003, with the spectacular success of the television soap opera *Uintā sonata* (The winter sonata; *Kyŏul yŏn'ga* in Korean) the Korean Wave (Kanryū) swept over Japan. The powerful trend of obsessive fandom, especially endemic among middle-aged women, was acute enough to generate a countertrend: the Counter-Korean Wave (Ken-Kanryū).[97] This was fueled less by older Korea-haters than by younger Japanese men seemingly troubled that "their" women (usually older sisters or mothers) were expressing unabashed enthusiasm for South Korean stars, such as Pae Yong-jun (Bae Yong-jun, widely called Yon-sama in Japan). But even Counter-Korean Wave activists were loath to engage in outright racist discourse, and their ineffectuality can easily be gauged by the continuing popularity in Japan today of South Korean TV dramas (often aired in the original Korean, with Japanese subtitles). Even a casual visitor to South Korea is bound to notice groups of Japanese women who are making pilgrimages to the filming locations for their favorite dramas; hundreds of Japanese fans attended the funeral of one of the stars of *The Winter Sonata*, but hardly any South Korean followers were present.[98] By the time that KARA and Girls' Generation found success in Japan, in the guise of K-pop, South Korean popular culture was already a well-recognized, well-respected brand in Japan.

Beyond Japan, K-pop has a significant following in the Chinese-language spheres as well as in Southeast Asia, especially Thailand, Cambodia, and

Vietnam. In Europe and Latin America, however, despite pockets of enthusiasm, K-pop is hardly a commanding presence. Yet it is remarkable that K-pop should have any fans at all in Paris or Lima beyond those cities' expatriate or diasporic Korean (and possibly East Asian) communities. To be sure, the explosive enthusiasm that "Gangnam Style" generated across the world in 2012 cannot be gainsaid, but it remains to be seen whether Psy or his coterie will experience a systematic breakthrough in the largest and most competitive market: the United States. In fact, one major OECD country where "Gangnam Style" failed to go viral is Japan, where K-pop's popularity is second only to its popularity in its native South Korea, and so it's possible that K-pop will instead remain a niche genre across Europe and the Americas.[99] This speculation is strengthened by K-pop fans in Japan who see Psy as neither hot nor cool and thus as not really belonging to K-pop. At the same time, as Psy's success has demonstrated, South Korean popular music is bigger than the contemporary K-pop formula.

THE PLACE OF JAPAN AND J-POP

We have already considered some of the reasons why K-pop became a South Korean export. The success of K-pop in Japan and elsewhere raises another question: why didn't J-pop generate a following in South Korea and beyond? To focus, for the moment, on South Korea, the continuing ban on Japanese cultural exports in that country—a ban lifted more or less completely in 2004—blocked overt public performances of J-pop, such as on television or radio shows. Even as recently as the last several years, several clerks in CD stores told me that they were wary of playing J-pop songs, for fear of anti-Japanese men stridently denouncing these clerks and the stores for their collusion with Japanese colonialists. At the same time, however, Japanese popular music has long been widely available and popular in South Korea. For example, Ishida Ayumi's "Blue Light Yokohama," a captivating 1968 hit, could be heard across South Korea in the 1970s.[100] In the 1980s, Itsuwa Ayumi's "Koibito yo" (Lover) and Anzen Chitai's string of melodious love ballads became difficult to avoid, as evinced by the large circulation of pirated CDs available in Seoul and elsewhere.[101] In the 1990s as well, despite the shift to American music, J-pop still had a large following in South Korea; indeed, South Korean performers openly emulated, performed, and at times lifted J-pop tunes. (As already mentioned, murmurs of a J-pop invasion of South

Korea were sounded in the late 1990s, when the South Korean popular-music industry was in crisis.)

One might also ask why J-pop did not conquer East Asia in general. It would be easy to invoke the memory of Japanese military aggression, which kindles nationalist passions. In spite of occasional flare-ups of jingoism, however, anti-Japanese sentiment cannot account for J-pop's limited penetration into East Asia.[102] Neither does it make much sense to insist on the musical shortcomings of J-pop, J-pop singers, or performers in other Japanese popular-music genres. Rather, we should look to the involuted character of post–Cold War Japan, which became an affluent, culturally differentiated society.[103] However diverse South Korean musical culture may be, it is still no match for Japan when it comes to the range of musical genres, the enthusiasm of the fans, and the propensity for participating in making music. That is, K-pop is the name of the game in South Korean popular music, but Japan has many different games in play. Contemporary Japan is a realm of subcultures and a culture of *otaku*, a term that surfaced in the late 1970s to signify the fanatical followers of science-fiction manga and anime but was soon applied to those with any type of avid subcultural interest.[104] It is an archipelago that exhibits Galapagos Syndrome: the existence of distinct ecological niches, which generate flora and fauna of popular culture that occur nowhere else in the world.[105] Furthermore, the Japanese popular-music industry, which experienced a decade of rapid growth after the introduction of CDs in the early 1980s, became intimately intertwined with indigenous broadcast television, and thus with corporate sponsorship.[106] In this context, there has been a powerful inward pull toward satisfying the large domestic market as opposed to seeking risky export opportunities. In other words, Japan's large domestic market creates a disincentive for music exports. Following the money has meant staying in Japan.

J-pop arose along with the new audience for popular music, which in turn arose from the spread of digital music in the form of CDs, and from the availability of relatively inexpensive CD players starting in the mid-1980s.[107] The record-buying audience became younger and more dominated by women, a circumstance that led, predictably, to the rise of singers who appealed to the new customer base.[108] Songs were often written in *katakana* (Japanese script used for foreign words) or even in Roman script, a practice that K-pop adopted. J-pop also anticipated K-pop in absorbing R & B, dance pop, and other American and world music trends in the 1990s. The music, because it appealed to younger listeners, immediately became distinct from older

Japanese popular music as well as from Western (especially American) pop music: it was more upbeat, faster, and louder than the older Japanese music but less upbeat, slower, and quieter than mainstream American pop-rock.[109] J-pop was mellower music, often sung at a high pitch but incorporating melisma and other characteristics of African American singing.[110] Despite some generic characteristics, it would be misleading to overgeneralize about J-pop. For example, PUFFY, a popular late-1990s group, instantiates post-modern pop music with its lyrics and compositions, which often recapitulate and incorporate the very history of popular music. Amuro Namie has infused mainstream J-pop with an Okinawan sound.[111] The so-called Queen of J-pop, Hamamura Ayumi, carries the mantle of Matsutoya Yumi and Nakajima Miyuki, two vocalists of feminine sensibility. There are also numerous idol singers and bands—Utada Hikaru and Arashi, for example, or EXILE and L'Arc~en~Ciel—with interesting and innovative hits, some of which have spread J-pop well beyond the Japanese archipelago.

Diverse though J-pop may be, its insistent undercurrents and idiosyncrasies render it distinct from American and global pop, and it was a sense of pride in this reality, not a sense of the new genre's being inferior to or derivative of foreign popular music, that led to its name.[112] But, as with the popularity of "Western food" (*yōshoku*) in Japan, no one can say that J-pop is in any way traditionally Japanese, and yet it is difficult to find J-pop outside Japan except where Japanese people congregate. The group AKB48—in the lineage of Onyanko Kurabu (Kitty Club), which was exceedingly popular in the late 1980s—is emblematic in this respect and is easily the most popular group in contemporary Japan.[113] Its members, all demonstrably amateurs, are chosen by fans, who become eligible to vote in an annual election by buying CDs (voting proceeds on the principle that one purchased CD affords one vote). The top vote getters are the ones who perform onstage in any one year. As for the annual election, which entails campaigns featuring handshakes with potential voters, it has become a national media circus that makes newspaper headlines. The democratic character of AKB48 is of a piece, alas, with the rather demotic nature of the performers and performances; in spite of some talent and training, they are not particularly skilled at singing, dancing, or playing musical instruments.[114] Indeed, it is said that they are not particularly beautiful, either; beauty, it is also said, would "threaten" fans who prefer "cute" girls—that is, the proverbial girls next door. Nevertheless, the group's popularity is nothing short of sensational. In fact, the title of a book about the group's leading member asks whether she has transcended Jesus.[115] What sustains the group's phenomenal popularity is that its members are the stars of their own long-running social drama, which in turn relies on extensive marketing that uses physical contact (the aforementioned campaigns and handshakes) and social media.[116] The overwhelmingly male fan base idolizes and idealizes these girls, who resonate with the dominant Japanese *kawaii* (cute) aesthetic à la Hello Kitty.[117] AKB48 fans, somewhat like television viewers who immerse themselves in long-running soap operas or reality shows, avidly follow the vicissitudes of the cast of characters; that is, extra-musical contexts and offstage narratives entangle AKB48 and the group's fan base. But the group is illegible to cultural outsiders, who are merely baffled by its popularity.[118] Moreover, although the concept of AKB48 is itself eminently exportable, the reality of moderately attractive, middling singer-dancers can hardly be expected to generate much enthusiasm outside Japan.

Elsewhere in Asia, as well as in Europe, there is a cultlike devotion to Japanese manga, anime, and video games that is not a consequence of governmental policy or corporate ambition; rather, it is largely a demand-led phenomenon known as "Cool Japan," the Japanese equivalent of the Korean Wave. But until quite recently the Japanese government was strident in its dismissal of popular culture in general and manga in particular. Almost no one—not government bureaucrats, musical promoters, or popular singers themselves—sought to promote or export Japanese popular culture.[119] The contrast here to the South Korean government of the twenty-first century could not be more pronounced. But Japan's inward orientation is not a long-standing cultural characteristic; post–World War II economic growth in Japan was, like its counterpart in South Korea, led by export-oriented industrialization. After Japan's bubble of property-led speculation burst, in 1991, the country entered a period of stasis. One of its manifestations was a general disinclination to return to an export-oriented growth strategy and society. Japanese businesspeople had long bemoaned the country's small market, but now they found it big enough, and adequate to their modest aims.

Finally, the intensely competitive global music market, which prizes what is cool or hot, demands perpetual innovation and superior quality. In the first decade of the 2000s, while K-pop was forging a distinct style, J-pop was rehashing established genres and routines. Neither a strong infusion of hip-hop, as in BIGBANG, nor the powerful combination of compelling refrains and memorable dance routines that marks K-pop groups, such as KARA, appeared in or affected J-pop, which is precisely why those K-pop acts were so popular in Japan.[120] In other words, the factor of aesthetic innovation, at least from the standpoint of fans, cannot be overlooked in any analysis of why J-pop has not spread outside Japan, especially since the same factor has played such a major role in propelling K-pop to the status of a transnational phenomenon.

THE AESTHETICS, BRANDING, AND CHARACTER OF K-POP

K-pop, as we have seen, is a commercial product, an output of the South Korean culture industry that seeks to satisfy consumers. It has no overriding cultural, aesthetic, political, or philosophical agenda—or even any ambitions along those lines. At least in intent, K-pop is not about art, beauty, sublimity, or transcendence. The business of K-pop is simply business. Even so, K-pop is not just an interesting social phenomenon; it is also an aesthetic achievement. It may seem paradoxical that a thoroughly commercialized music, geared to ephemeral enthusiasm, should prove to have aesthetic virtues, but the same mercenary impulse did not preclude the triumphs of a Mozart or a Verdi. To say that the alpha and omega of K-pop is crass commercialism is not to deny that it can also be physically attractive as well as artistically accomplished. But before we examine K-pop's interesting and innovative aspects, let us pause to thoroughly absorb its profoundly commercial character.

As I have been arguing, K-pop is a post–Sŏ T'ae-ji wa Aidŭl development in South Korean popular music, a development that at once diverged from past Korean and South Korean soundscapes and converged with regnant American and global popular-music conventions. K-pop, in its visual emphasis and its fusion of singing and dancing, represents one terminus of the MTV revolution and the age of music's digital transmission and reproducibility. K-pop, as we have seen, is a package that depends on an extreme division of labor, one that integrates various types of expertise and places high value on polishing itself to a perfectionist sheen. Or, to put this in a less than flattering way, K-pop is utterly lacking in authenticity, autonomy, and originality.

K-pop is inauthentic in that it is neither Korean nor South Korean. Not only is it different from traditional Korean music, it also diverges from the long tradition of Korean popular music. But most K-pop fans don't care about that kind of inauthenticity. Rather, the kind of inauthenticity that might concern a K-pop fan is the kind associated with phoniness, that foible identified and excoriated in J. D. Salinger's 1951 novel *The Catcher in the Rye* but more completely articulated by Lionel Trilling and Charles Taylor.[121] Modern authenticity, tied to notions of sincerity, of staying true to oneself, is understood as the outward expression of an inwardly experienced correspondence between the true self and the self in the world—a unity between the two that is uncompromising with respect to the movement of time and to external contingencies. To put this idea another way, K-pop, as a mercenary pursuit, does not stay true to its art (such as its art may be). In this sense, K-pop flatly contradicts the European Romantic ideal of the artist as a seeker after Beauty and Truth (and, for that matter, the Socialist Realist goal of an art that represents an objective reality in hopes of transforming it). Surely Lee Soo-man is worlds away from Wackenroder and Tieck's art-loving friar, at once ascetic and aesthetic, and remote even from such radical rock musicians as Radiohead and Rage Against the Machine.[122] Nearly every aspect of K-pop is functional, intended to satisfy the market rather than fulfill some deep artistic or political urge. Indeed, customers' expectations play a significant role in the constitution of K-pop. Consider something as seemingly trivial as K-pop performers' general reluctance to lip-synch, which stems from producers' awareness that audiences reject inauthenticity in general, and lip-synching in particular. K-pop performers' avoidance of lip-synching is akin to the practice of concert pianists, who tend to play from memory in part to satisfy the expectations of the audience. But whereas an aesthetic ideology in classical music underpins the practice of performing from memory, the only reason for a K-pop performer to resist lip-synching is to fulfill the audience's expectations for the performer to sound authentic, and thus to fulfill the commercial imperative of pleasing the audience.[123]

As for autonomy, K-pop stars, by and large, only sing and dance. They execute what has been conceived for them; they wear what they are told to wear, they sing what they are told to sing, and they move and behave as they are told to move and behave. For this reason, some critics deride K-pop performers as robots because they seem to lack artistic autonomy and personal will. One gauge of an act's autonomy would be its sense of group identity and continuity, its commitment to a particular aesthetic principle or musical style. But K-pop groups tend to move with contemporary currents, and thus they are anchorless. As already noted, SHINHWA began as a boy band but became masculinized when it was fashionable for the band to do so. R & B was a significant influence on KARA's early music, but the group shifted to dance pop when that became the genre of the moment. SM Entertainment's

J-pop emulations ceased as its rivals, JYP Entertainment and YG Entertainment, incorporated the latest American trends to win a larger market share. When Wonder Girls' "Tell Me" proved to be what people loved, SM Entertainment was happy to cast Girls' Generation in that mold. In short, K-pop follows trends and does not seem to value music in and of itself; it is a heteronomous entity.

And finally there is the question of originality. K-pop is indistinguishable from American pop music in virtually every way: in its ubiquitous but shallow historical references to and mashups of recent pop hits, stars, and genres; in its fusion of upbeat cheerfulness with danceability; in its modes of singing and dancing; in its sartorial styles; and in its immersion in urban youth and commercial culture. There may be exceptions, but K-pop performers in general, unlike American stars, did not start out playing music in the family garage or composing songs in their bedrooms. Instead, they auditioned and were trained to be performers. In the K-pop studio system, perspiration is worth more than inspiration. Originality is valued only to the extent that it represents something new, cool, and exciting for the paying public.

To summarize, the elements of authenticity, autonomy, and originality are the essence of the Romantic ideology of the artist, an ideology diametrically opposed to the logic of K-pop. K-pop is a particular mode of popular-music production, consciously and commercially conceived and expertly and effectively executed. It is predicated on the belief that comprehensive and prolonged training can be combined with a highly professionalized division of labor to generate popular-music success. That is, K-pop embraces its status as a culture industry. It may be faint praise to say that K-pop, as a product of Brand (South) Korea, is as good as a top-of-the-line Samsung cell phone: engineered to (near) perfection, reliable but affordable, stylish yet functional, and easy on the eye (as with K-pop, no one would say that South Korea has a long tradition of crafting cell phones, or that Samsung has thus far been noted for originality). K-pop, as an export-oriented industry, trains and cultivates promising raw talent and produces performers with attractive faces and bodies who can sing and dance well while collaborating seamlessly and harmoniously. K-pop groups are rendered compelling precisely by this professionalism and this perfectionist impulse. But aesthetic judgments are ultimately beside the point. People would not purchase Samsung cell phones if the devices were not functional and dependable, presentable and pleasurable. In the same way, popular-music fans would not download a track or attend a concert if they didn't get their money's worth, so to speak. Again, the logic of capital is the logic of K-pop.

Thus the corporate discipline of the star factory runs counter to the Romantic ideology of the artist-genius, but we might question that ideology itself. Ethnonational authenticity is a matter of cultural criticism, as discussed in the interlude, but it is also a topic that few people seem to become exercised about. No one has found the roots of cell phone production in traditional Korea, but that worries neither Samsung executives nor global consumers. The idea of authenticity as the state of being true to oneself may valorize untutored genius, but the mundane reality is that few if any stars emerge completely out of nowhere. Stories of unheralded geniuses, such as Britain's Susan Boyle and her South Korean counterpart, Ch'oe Sung-bong (Choi Sung-bong), are compelling and certainly promote TV viewership and music sales.[124] Yet even in televised talent contests like *The X Factor,* and even over the course of a short broadcasting season, the hands of voice coaches, dance instructors, and makeover professionals are visible. The romance of the *orecchiante,* the person who cannot read music but performs it beautifully, is a nostalgic ideal; but even in the United States, this putative diamond in the rough is repeatedly ground down before she is allowed to make her professional debut. The point here is not to deny the possibility of musical genius but rather to observe that the inborn talent of almost all successful musicians, past and present, has been enhanced and transformed by teachers, formal or informal, over an extended period of preparation. Whether we are talking about Herbert Simon's ten years or Malcolm Gladwell's ten thousand hours, the K-pop system is testament to the power of training over genius.[125]

The contemporary arts, especially in the United States, are still under the reign of Romantic ideology. Talent and genius are said to trump training and effort. Cineastes glorify the auteur and love to bash Hollywood and the studio system. Musical excellence, for its part, is widely believed to be unteachable, even though teaching institutions proliferate, and even though it would be almost unimaginable for a composer or a singer to emerge out of thin air.[126] Amateurs are thought to exude authenticity; conversely, excessive training smacks of inauthenticity. Moreover, the longing for the undivided whole ignores the inevitable reality of artistic divisions of labor. Billie Holiday, for example, neither wrote the lyrics nor composed the music of her incandescent interpretations, yet who would deny that she was a great singer?

Romantic ideology not only distorts the production of music and art but also suppresses the role of the audience and the market. According to the

Romantic line of thought, the true artist creates in splendid isolation, communing with his own genius (and perhaps with the predecessors who are his equals) and ignoring if not damning his potential listeners. The egoistic sublime, however, is mere solipsism; originality in and of itself is useless as a metric of musical greatness. Without heeding the regnant soundscape, one may well compose noise or nonsense; a measure of imitation is the condition of music's possibility.[127] At least implicitly, a poet or a singer has readers or listeners in mind, who in turn shape not only the performance but also the creation of the poet's or singer's art. If poets are singing in solitude, then they cannot be the unacknowledged legislators of the world. The relationship between the artist and her audience is mutually constitutive. On the one hand, the desire for a large audience virtually guarantees that the work will cater to demotic tastes, though a large listening public is not necessarily a guarantee of the work's aesthetic merit or longevity.[128] On the other hand, the artist's annihilation of the audience all but guarantees that the work will be solipsistic if not entirely unsustainable; the occasional masterpiece may be produced (Beethoven's *Grosse Fuge*, perhaps), but the work is more likely to resemble that of the painter Frenhofer in Balzac's "Le chef-d'oeuvre inconnu" (The unknown masterpiece) or, in the case of music, any number of contemporary classical pieces that usually go unperformed and are sometimes unperformable. Artistic success is a *collective* sublime, entailing the aesthetic and social concourse of the audience and the work of art.

In short, it is possible to view K-pop performers as inauthentic automatons singing unoriginal songs or performing East Asian versions of various kinds of American and global popular music. In one sense, this kind of disdain is simply prejudice.[129] K-pop performances are also dismissed for their polish and perfectionism, and K-pop itself is regarded as a flash in the pan. Here, we might recall the earliest music videos, which were criticized for privileging style over substance and thus elevating impermanence over immortality.[130] The Internet is awash in the backlash to the Korean Wave, with K-pop derided for inauthenticity, heteronomy, unoriginality, and many other failures. K-pop does strike many self-proclaimed lovers of music as artificial and superficial, simple and simplistic, even comical and vulgar. But an appreciation of K-pop, like an appreciation of virtually everything else in life, depends on the momentary suspension of disbelief and the willingness to enter into another world and sensibility.[131] 4Minute and f(x) are not Beethoven. K-pop is as different from European classical music as a Krazy Kat short is from *Andrei Rublev*. But we would be shortsighted if we could find nothing of value in either the short or the longer film, in either f(x) or Beethoven. If we can move beyond the fact of K-pop as an unabashed culture industry, and if we can liberate our senses from Romantic ideology and its associated shackles, then it may become possible for us to appreciate K-pop's interesting and innovative features.

In the regnant structure of the K-pop lyric we find the popular-music equivalent of the villanelle (or perhaps, as a very critical critic might have it, the equivalent of that parodic form known as the paradelle).[132] The strophic structure of all popular music is accentuated in K-pop. The hook—"Tell me, tell me," "Sorry, sorry," "Gee, gee, gee"—anchors the song, and the song's emotional and artistic gravity then resists erasure from the mind's recorder. Lyrical and musical refrains in turn are articulated and enhanced with signature gestures or dance steps as the performers produce kinetic equivalents of lyrical refrains in what is sometimes called "point dance."[133] Thus crab dance accompanies the refrain "Gee, gee, gee," or physically onomatopoeic movements replicate the beating of a heart in 2PM's 2009 "Heartbeat," or the "la-la-la-la-la" refrain in KARA's "Mr." is accompanied by the performers' swinging hips. The effect of this unity is memorable, especially since its performance is almost always perfect. This synthesis is, in a sense, productive of a particular structure of feeling; the K-pop formula achieves what Wallace Stevens points to in "Peter Quince at the Clavier": "Music is feeling, then, not sound." The synergistic hook, with its fusion of lyrics, music, and movement, is K-pop's signature innovation and contribution.

"Formulaic" is a dirty word among many music aficionados. On the one hand, almost any good song (or poem, or other work of art) is constituted by a form and is therefore formulaic; it is simply a matter of how the form (and the formula) are employed, developed, and articulated. On the other hand, if a song is merely repetitive (in the pejorative sense of being formulaic), then it is unlikely to be as successful as K-pop songs are. Music, especially art music or classical music, is formalist: much of its beauty resides in the precise articulation (and performance) of an established syntax. Yet what makes art music or classical music incomprehensible to many listeners, and therefore unenjoyable, is that it lacks a ready-made vocabulary. What popular music achieves— and the K-pop hook heightens this effect—is the presentation of a comprehensible vocabulary, an articulation of phonemes and words (even if they are phatic and ultimately meaningless) that listeners can begin to make sense of so as to enter the K-pop song's sonic world and hermeneutic circle.[134] Thus the language of K-pop, with its simple, almost universally understandable grammar and vocabulary, is akin to Basic English, or Globish.

Most K-pop lyrics are eminently forgettable, but the predominant theme of passionate, romantic love and its permutations—that the course of true love never did run smooth—generates some memorable anthems or poems for young people, as when 2PM sings of heartache in "Heartbeat" or when 2AM voices undying love in 2010's "Chugŏdo mot ponae" (I can't let you go even if I die). A jaundiced elder finds such lyrics difficult to take seriously, but they do convey the almost inexpressible turbulence of youthful emotion and serve as a poetry of the heart (or so I interpret what these groups' youthful fans have to say). These lyrics veer wildly between the love that dare not speak its name (and therefore cannot be named) and the love that must be expressed simply and straightforwardly; the alternation is not entirely unlike the dialectic between apophatic and cataphatic theology. What is remarkable, however, is that some K-pop songs go well beyond the seemingly evanescent emotions of the adolescent heart and articulate personal troubles that in turn are related to serious social issues. For example, H.O.T. (if, for the moment, we can consider that idol group, in all its bubblegumminess, as belonging to K-pop) sang about the educational dysfunctions of South Korea (see chapter 1) in the 1996 hit "Chŏnsa ŭi huye" (Descendants of warriors). Tongbang Sin'gi's 2006 song "'O'—Chŏng-Pan-Hap," mentioned earlier, articulates a hard-hitting social critique, decrying the absence of "absolute truths" in a reality that is empty ("O"); the video, apart from its well-choreographed dance routines and its picturesque shots of Tokyo, Bangkok, Prague, and other locales, uses rapid flashes of imagery to portray social problems that include alienation, poverty, and violence.[135] Wonder Girls' 2007 megahit "Tell Me" is plainly a girl-power anthem—and we should not underestimate the presence or the power of such elements in the performances of K-pop girl groups, especially for young female listeners and viewers who are aware of the gender-based double standard and yearn for more freedom. It is true that popular-music fans (the word "fan" is, after all, short for "fanatic") often hear messages that a song has not sent, feel emotions that the song has not conveyed, and grasp meanings that the song has not intended. Nor is resistance or empowerment central to K-pop, whose logic is, again, the logic of capital. It would still be a mistake to dismiss the emancipatory moments that eager or even casual listeners experience in connection with K-pop. K-pop songs are not political manifestos, but devoted fans are not the only ones who have discovered optative moments in these songs, which in their most captivating renditions present counterfactual possibilities, not just escapist fantasies. Nor are K-pop songs hermeneutics of suspicion, but attentive listeners endow them with meanings and dreams or just with simple phatic pleasures and thus experience them as shining some light into the darkness.

In general, popular music provides the compass and comfort of musical order, which almost any novice listener can grasp, and the very banality of the lyrics facilitates and encourages the listener's engagement with a song's sense and sensibility, its sentiments and passions. As Edmund Burke noted, "We submit to what we admire, but we love what submits to us."[136] Everyday beauty, not sublimity, is what K-pop presents. If K-pop lyrics are not quite poems of quotidian life, they manage to assert, clarify, and even deepen listeners' inchoate emotions and thus prove purgative, if not cathartic. Although K-pop lyrics are closer to ditties than to poems, a moment's immersion in a discussion group for K-pop fans reveals that the lyrics are far from simple fixed clichés.[137] As in Schubert's "Lob der Tränen" (In praise of tears), or at least as in August Wilhelm Schlegel's lyric text, K-pop music goes beyond mere words to express and explicate tears or smiles, the pain or pleasure of life. And pain and pleasure are intelligible, even enlightening, states.

As musical compositions, most K-pop songs are not only well executed but also well crafted, and some are in fact innovative, at least in the context of popular music. Girls' Generation's "Genie," for example, incorporates the Dorian mode: by not resolving its chord progression, the song gives a sense of being unsettled—appropriate when a feeling of floating is what the song is intended to project. The song's composer and lyricist, Yu Yŏng-jin (Yoo Young-jin), began as a ballad singer in the 1990s, and his work now incorporates disparate musical styles. Yu is often dismissed as a hack, but his compositions are sometimes truly fascinating, if only because of the need to be competitive, and therefore innovative. "NuABO," Yu's 2010 song as performed by f(x), has a surprising moment in which the musical theme (or formula) is suddenly reversed, and the video also goes to black and white.[138] This reversal in the music and the reversion to retro black and white in the video create a surprising synergy that even a casual listener/viewer could not help noticing. The time dilatation seems especially apt in the world of popular music, where the dictum of carpe diem, in the sense of a lifetime burning in every moment, is normative, and where the insertion of the past or a reversal of this kind is necessarily unsettling—a small surprise, but no less an artistic achievement for that.

K-pop choreography, too, is expertly conceived and at times sumptuous and sophisticated. Its execution is all the more astonishing for seeming to require no special effort from performers who are not just singing (recall the reluctance to lip-synch) but doing so with real élan. When K-pop performers dance, they may not have the grace of a Fred Astaire or the charisma of a Michael Jackson, but the number of groups capable of first-rate ensemble dancing is remarkable.

K-pop music videos are cinematic short stories that are necessarily limited, not just in duration but also in their artistic ambitions. As such, if they don't quite attain the grandeur of the greatest films by South Korean directors, they range from competent to excellent, and they employ almost all available cinematographic techniques. Given the importance of the music video in the age of YouTube, K-pop producers have sought to revitalize the genre. To be sure, K-pop videos are mostly simple narratives that showcase the body and highlight dance, but they also represent a great deal of diversity. Some are lighthearted, like AFTER SCHOOL's 2012 "LOVE LOVE LOVE," which encapsulates a miniature romantic comedy using the theme of Max Ophüls's 1950 film *La Ronde*. Others are much more serious and self-conscious about pushing the envelope, such as Brown Eyed Girls' 2010 "Abracadabra," which walks the line of what is sexually permissible by flirting with themes of erotic empowerment and recalling both Just Jaeckin's 1975 film *Histoire d'O* (*The Story of O*) and Paul Verhoeven's 1992 film *Basic Instinct*. Modest though these music videos are by comparison with great works of cinema, many also mesmerize as they rapidly engage the viewer and make the most of their three minutes' running time.

In short, then, K-pop is a commercial enterprise whose products, like cars and cell phones, are designed and intended to be sold, but it would be a mistake to deny or denigrate K-pop's triumphs. The current style, which solidified toward the end of the twenty-first century's initial decade, embodies a moment of particular but necessarily evanescent perfection. Given changing tastes and omnipresent competition, K-pop producers will relentlessly pursue innovation, especially as we move toward the next great disruption imposed by a major social change or technological transformation. For the moment, though, K-pop's current aesthetic achievements are here to behold, and it would be a pity to miss them.

THE LEGIBILITY AND LEGITIMACY OF POPULAR MUSIC

Popular music's severest critics are absolutely right: it is the product of a culture industry. What they forget, however, is that music has been a commercial enterprise for centuries.[139] The sheer variety of the professions that spiral around the enterprise is simply staggering, encompassing everyone from dancers and choreographers to stagehands and set designers, from audio and hi-fi inventors and manufacturers to disc jockeys and composers and lyricists. It is a big, oligopolistic business, too: in the early 2010s, the four largest popular-music corporations controlled roughly 85 percent of global sales.[140] What is curious, however, is how focused this big business is on churning out highly crafted songs and accomplished stars, especially since no one seems to be able to articulate an abstract definition of a star, although any number of people in the business can point to any number of concrete individuals who have achieved stardom. Nor does anyone in the business seem to have mastered the process of creating a hit or a star, at least in the sense of working from a business plan or a blueprint. But if people in the business don't know what they're doing, they do know what they want—hits and stars, fame and fortune. Few stars, admittedly, are born famous; some achieve fame, and some have fame thrust upon them, but the reality is that the moment of a future star's discovery would be meaningless without the subsequent process of cultivation: the makeover.[141] The sempiternal temptation is to perceive a seed of pure genius in the act of making music, one that commodification and capitalist industrialization have sullied by introducing not just alienation and exploitation but inauthenticity and unoriginality, defiling innocence from its original Edenic state to fall into the corrupt present. But the industrialization and commodification of popular music are coeval with popular music itself. A star is born with the help of myriad midwives, most of whom seem to have a singular fixation on their own slice of fame and fortune. Popular music, alas, was born in a state of original sin, for its widespread dissemination would be impossible without its entanglement in capitalist (and necessarily technological) industrialization and the consumer society.

And the original sin that stains the soul of popular music is further darkened by the question of popular music's legitimacy. The European Romantics, in revolt against the facile universalism of Enlightenment thought, generally located the soul or essence of a people in that people's language but sometimes also in its folk music and folklore. Speech, music, and narrative, arising organically, as it were, from a way of life, were believed to express and exemplify a people and its distinctive lifeway; hence the Grimm Brothers' famous collation of tales of the German people (however mediated and transformed those tales may have been).[142] The conservation or revival of folk songs, too, as emblems of authenticity, was never far behind any initiative to preserve or recapture the soul of a people. In the course of the nineteenth century, the

European Romantics and their cultural heirs also established the crucial divide between the authentic (real, natural, organic) and the inauthentic (artificial, industrial, commercial).[143] Today as well, the criterion of authenticity remains very much alive in every sphere of musical discussion, whether in connection with early music (the temporal test) or world music (the ethnographic test). Whereas folk songs were said to have emerged—organically, collectively, mysteriously—from the genius of the people as a whole, popular music was clearly a conscious construction, an industrial invention. From this polarizing perspective, folk music is a bottom-up phenomenon, and mass music is a top-down production. Thus folk music, according to the terms of this binary, is inextricably intertwined with tradition and embodies the entire community; it endures over time and invites participation. Popular music, by contrast, is new and fleeting; it often appeals to youths who are susceptible to fashions and fads, and it induces passive listening as well as social alienation. Moreover, whereas folk music is local or national in origin, mass music is definitely not local, may be foreign, and is certainly cosmopolitan. What is most damning, popular music is a commercial product—a commodity.[144] Folk music, in short, is of, by, and for the people; popular music gives the people what they want but is not of or by them. Art music and folk music can aspire to the status of art; mass music is relegated to the status of a commodity.[145]

In the received judgment of musicological scholars and music critics, popular music almost always fails the test of authenticity. The ethnomusicologist Bruno Nettl, for example, proposes a commonplace criterion of authenticity, one that "is rooted in the idea that each culture has a primordial musical style of its own.... An authentic song is thought to be one truly belonging to the people who sing it, one that really reflects their spirit and personality."[146] Unfortunately for Nettl, however, most of what people sing did not arise organically and endogenously but frequently came from far away; in Italy and Hungary, for instance, folk songs were often Arabic and were clearly not indigenous.[147] Moreover, as we have seen, famous folk songs in Korea were standardized and nationalized versions. In addition, they were often sung to the accompaniment of European musical instruments, and so their contemporary articulations are quite remote from any past state of regional diversity and any quality of truly authentic performance. By Nettl's criterion, we might also transpose Richard Wagner's notoriously anti-Semitic remarks to South Korea and conclude that K-pop may be inauthentic because it is not rooted in the musical traditions of the Korean people.[148] But K-pop is what most young South Koreans grew up listening to; it is what they have known all their lives—and if we had to identify the one essential root of K-pop, it would not be Korean music, traditional or popular, but rather US popular music, specifically its African American strains. That is not a bad lineage, musically speaking, but it does suggest that K-pop would fail the ethnonational test of authenticity.[149]

What is perhaps most significant, the besetting sin of popular music is simply that it *is* popular. The idea that the vast majority of people have been shaped by popular music, as well as by television and movies, is seen as a concern in and of itself. If a medium happens to offer sociological insights into how people live and what people feel and think, but if it also shapes quotidian morality and metaphysics, then it should come as no surprise that intellectuals and educators get so worked up over it.[150] Popular music satisfies hungers not only for fun and relaxation but also for meaning and even salvation, appetites for everything from the silly to the serious. Like Verdi's *tinta* (color), it seems to bleed and blend into the whole world.[151] Popular music has become not merely the noise of life but something akin to its master key.

Theodor Adorno famously wrote that popular music is inevitably doomed to standardization, to the mechanical reproduction of certain memes and the hapless quest for pseudo-individualization—doomed, that is, to be passively consumed, to be at once distracting and indistinctive, to be mere white noise.[152] In other words, popular music, for Adorno, is a sedative, an opiate to help the masses cope with the unpleasant realities of capitalist modernity.[153] To be sure, European art music has frequently been popular music; and for the European aristocracy and bourgeoisie, there certainly was and is nothing inorganic or inauthentic about European classical music.[154] And opera—today the word virtually denotes snobbery—was the functional equivalent of popular music in Italy and elsewhere in the eighteenth and nineteenth centuries.[155] Moreover, despite the enduring insistence on making distinctions between and among opera, musical theater, and musicals, such interstitial works as *Les Brigands, The Mikado, Porgy and Bess,* and *West Side Story* suggest that these distinctions are something less than hard and fast.[156] Be all that as it may, the question of whether sublimation or the musical equivalent of opium is actually such a terrible thing is a matter of perspective, but Adorno also articulates another, aesthetic critique: that whereas Beethoven's late style struggles with death and thus with eternal, universal issues, popular music remains ensconced in the here and now and is thus doomed again, this time to ephemerality and oblivion.[157] But even though popular music is a product of the culture industry and an object of conspicuous consumption, it is almost always polysemous, as any extended colloquy with its listeners would reveal, and its meanings are almost always profound.[158]

Personal choices in the realm of popular music—as instances of the articulation of the modern ethos of choice, which in turn confers both individual and group identity (What sort of person am I? To which group do I belong?)—take place in a realm of existential freedom and have decisive consequences. However derided mass music may be as a commodity churned out by the culture industry, it can capture the soul, according to people who profess to love popular music as something to live by, live with, and even live for. What other contemporary phenomenon gives rise to what Chateaubriand called "le vague des passions"?[159] As with yesteryear's wine, women, and song, so also with yesterday's sex, drugs, and rock 'n' roll: popular music was and is inextricable from life's emotions and from enjoyment of life. Popular music would pass almost any test of authenticity that revolved around the idea of a music's belonging to and being meaningful to people.[160] Indeed, the fundamental distinction between folk music and popular music may be that folk music is older and less popular, and therefore less meaningful to most people. To put this idea in polemical terms, when an aging Briton hums "Yesterday," is her experience somehow less authentic and less meaningful to her than if she were humming "Greensleeves"? Would we even remember "Scarborough Fair" if not for Simon and Garfunkel? (And who can recall one of that song's likely precursors, the Scottish ballad "The Elfin Knight"?) Or, again, for the Zainichi writer Kyō Nobuko, when an ethnic Korean woman in her eighties bursts into a rendition of "Kachūsha no uta" (Song of Kachūsha, perhaps the first hit in Japan), that song may be more meaningful to her than any other song or form of music she has encountered in her long life.[161] A common trope in modern novels and films is the popular song that recovers a deeply grooved memory. For example, in Im Ch'ŏr-u's novel *Kŭ sŏm e kagosipta* (I want to go to that island), we readily comprehend the significance when a woman farmer sings the popular song "Mokp'o ŭi nunmul" (Tears of Mokp'o), which expresses something deep and meaningful in that character's life.[162] Needless to say, we shouldn't ignore the tremendous variation across individuals; it is not unusual for European art music to be, effectively, soul music for some ethnic Koreans, the music they grew up with, the music that embodies something deep and meaningful about their personhood. For the vast majority of the population in the affluent world and increasingly in the nonaffluent world as well, however, popular music is the ambient reality that structures meaning and feeling, the sense of self and reality. It is, in other words, the world of everyday sociology and philosophy.

If the aesthetic or emotional legitimacy of popular music remains a topic of controversy among academics, among nonacademics there is no need for an apologia, since popular music *is* music. (And does anyone really need to defend or justify music of any kind?) Of late, many critics have shown themselves ready to vouch for popular music's aesthetic magnificence; for others, popular music betokens the decline of civilization.[163] But aesthetic judgments, if they are not merely to reproduce an existing social order by reflecting assumptions about socioeconomic or sociocultural superiority and inferiority, must rest on appraisals that are both formal and commensurable.[164] The philosophically grounded articulation of an aesthetic judgment valorizes particular formal criteria—for example, complexity over simplicity, refinement over rusticity, innovation over convention—in a way that more or less objectively proves some piece of music or some musical style better than another. And the modern European discussion of aesthetics, usually said to have begun with Alexander Baumgarten's ponderous *Aesthetica* (1795), symptomatically produces and reproduces similar sets of hierarchies—in the case of Baumgarten, logic over beauty (the latter associated with the aesthetic/imaginative faculty, itself characterized as "facultas cognoscitiva inferior" or "gnoseologia inferior").[165] Yet not only are such criteria historically and culturally variable, they are often endogenously constituted within a particular genre.[166] In any event, the deployment of formalistic criteria would do little to persuade folk aficionados that Schoenberg's *Moses und Aron* is superior to the Cuban folk song "Guantanamera," and even those few folkies who could be convinced of the opera's aesthetic superiority might still prefer to hum "Guantanamera" in a moment of repose. Moreover, folk aficionados probably like their folk songs simple, rustic, and conventional and would certainly rather hear "Guantanamera" performed by a banjo-strumming Pete Seeger than by a full symphony orchestra, to say nothing of how perplexing they would find a dodecaphonic or micropolyphonic version of the song.

Everything considered, the standard explanation for popular music's appeal is, to put it crudely, the underdeveloped taste of the masses (or—which is to say much the same thing—their unfortunate ignorance). According to Gunther Schuller, who would write brilliant books on jazz and Alban Berg, "The commercial, made-for-profit musics have . . . moved into the vacuum left by [the] massive failure of the whole educational environment."[167] But would systematic instruction in the theory, history, and appreciation of European classical music have been enough to prevent the appearance of Schuller's "made-for-profit musics"? To put this question differently, if European art music were to lose its value for the wealthy and powerful, would it still have any value at all? There is no way to be certain, but clearly the sedulous pleasures of popular music have triumphed everywhere. In the future, independent thinkers on the model of Kenneth Rexroth surely won't be the only ones to find the sensibility and artistry of a Catullus in a popular singer like Bob Dylan.[168]

Then there is the question of moral psychology. When I was endlessly playing and replaying études from Hanon and Czerny, it was to the leitmotif of my Japanese piano teacher barking, "Mit Gefühl!"—as if those finger exercises had ever been meant to evoke profound emotional responses. She was convinced that European art music, especially pieces associated with nineteenth-century Vienna, was a path toward the virtuous and moral life.[169] But we have not had a totalitarian society that promotes popular music; and many authoritarian societies, such as South Korea under military rule, have actively censored popular music as immoral and decadent. This is not to suggest, of course, that the culture industry or even folk music is on the side of angels; in the future, Adorno's dystopian view of popular music as an opium of the people may come to be validated. Moreover, an art form, no matter how autonomous, cannot exist in splendid isolation, and it takes considerable suspension of disbelief to hope that humming a Beethoven melody or a tune by Girls' Generation or, for that matter, engaging in any form of prayer will deliver us from evil. Even though it is unlikely that people are dying miserably every day for lack of what is found in popular music, hardly a day goes by without someone finding pleasure, joy, and even moral compass there.

The devaluation of the popular is, in a word, overdetermined. In critical discourse, ancient or modern, Eastern or Western, rare is the intrepid intellect who privileges comedy over tragedy, lightness over seriousness, the ephemeral over hoped-for immortality, *Weltfreude* over *Weltschmerz*. The occasional exception notwithstanding, to assert that popular music is squarely in the camp of comedy, lightness, the ephemeral, and *Weltfreude* is surely to offer a robust generalization. At the same time, bound up as popular music is with pleasure, fantasy, and relaxation, it is also a realm in which many people contemplate and express their innermost sentiments and ponder life's joys and travails and meanings.

And so it is the revenge of popular music to reign supreme among the arts for today's affluent youth. Intellectuals may bemoan young people's failure to read prose, much less poetry. They may complain that young people don't know much about history, and that they probably know even less about painting and architecture. But no one can deny that almost all young people listen to a great deal of popular music, and that, at least in this respect, appreciation of music is nearly universal among them.[170] The philosophers of aesthetics are right about one thing: art is a cognitive endeavor. It is not altogether impossible to enjoy an illegible, incomprehensible work of art (contemporary classical music, that virtual oxymoron, comes to mind), but enjoyment of a work generally depends on its being legible and comprehensible, and many people do understand and enjoy popular music and its conventions.[171] Popular music is omnipresent—cacophonous in public spaces, sonorous in private spheres—and it has come to define contemporary lifestyles in the affluent world. Whatever one may think of hip-hop or K-pop, both are recognizably music even for those who listen almost exclusively to European art music.

All this is to express an indisputable reality: that many people enjoy K-pop in particular, and popular music in general, for good reasons, and that no amount of social snobbery or supercilious philosophy is going to change their tastes or their minds. K-pop fans say many things; in my translation, they are saying that K-pop can soothe and massage the soul, thus assuaging or fulfilling desires and longings, or offering (or selling) hope, or comforting and satisfying the conscious self, or providing the means of a measured resistance to overbearing parents, or stimulating the craving to be creative or grown-up or sophisticated. K-pop offers fodder for conversation, enables people to pass the time pleasantly, helps them make new friends and acquaintances, invites them into a new world of sound and movement, satisfies the urge to belt out a song or dance to the beat, and even gives people reasons to forge ahead. Some fall in love with K-pop stars and songs; others find friends who live in the same subculture. K-pop, like popular music in general, marks the beautiful in ordinary life: a promise of happiness, the anticipation of bliss. To say that K-pop is the opium of the masses or a sedative marketed by the culture industry, true though those statements may be at times, is surely not to tell the whole story. To the extent that K-pop is, more or less, a mass-produced commodity with mass appeal, it may very well be true that critics have condemned it to the inferno of *odi profanum vulgus,* for the stench of the demotic clings to popular music. And it doesn't matter.

Postlude

"GANGNAM STYLE" WAS THE GLOBAL POP SENSATION of 2012.[1] It registered more than a billion hits on YouTube and became the most-watched music video in that medium's short but star-studded history. Psy's signature dance moves could be seen everywhere. In an oncology ward near Oxford, England, a seventy-eight-year-old British woman addled by morphine exclaimed, "That's ... that's ... 'Gangnam Style'!" every time she encountered a screen, whether it was attached to a CT scanner or belonged to a television set broadcasting *Coronation Street*.[2] From "Obama Style" to "Mitt Romney Style," the sheer number of imitations and parodies bespoke the omnipresence of "Gangnam Style." When the Chinese authorities suppressed the artist Ai Weiwei's "Grass-Mud Horse Style," Ai's fellow artist Anish Kapoor shot back with "Gangnam for Freedom."[3] So much for those who believed that K-pop would never make it in the United States, or for those who still deny that pop music has any significance, whether artistic or political.[4]

An indispensable element of popularity, when it comes to "Gangnam Style" or any other piece of popular music, is that it be catchy, as if to ride the proverbial wave. Catchiness, as an aesthetic principle, has numerous synonyms, at times embodied in literal-sounding metaphors (such as "hook") and at times expressed in more literary terms (such as "leitmotif"), but the point is that a popular-music video must have memorable and reproducible lyrical refrains and dance steps. These units of sound and movement generate a short narrative, which in turn can be elaborated and transposed to generate imitations and parodies. For non-Korean listeners, only two phrases are legible in Psy's song—"Hey, sexy lady" and "Gangnam Style"—but the dance steps (a pony-riding gallop and a lasso-twirling sway) are readily comprehensible and imitable. If I am right about the centrality of units of sound and movement to this genre of music video, then Psy's glossolalic lyrics are irrelevant. After all, given his rap articulation, I had to watch the video half a dozen times before I could make out what he was saying, and this kind of experience—musical appreciation without any linguistic comprehension—is surely more common than not. The only thing that has to be understood is the reproducible refrain; the rest is phatic (or perhaps the point is that the lyrics must be recognizable as part of the music, as evinced by many opera fans who are moved by arias sung in languages that they do not understand). In this compositional style, what the audience perceives is the broad background of conventions—the format of the music video, or a recognizable music genre, such as rap—against which interesting and imitable refrains and gestures captivate and prove irresistible. That the protagonist of "Gangnam Style" is a South Korean national may render him exotic, but common cultural references—associations ranging from the obvious (the once feared but now parodied Kim Jong-il) to Mike Myers (in his role as Austin Powers)—tame any sense of Psy as the inscrutable other. And popularity frequently begets more popularity, rendering the absence of popularity more notable than popularity's saturation of the media (mass or social) and everyday interactions. The obvious humor of "Gangnam Style," its cheekiness and even its cheesiness, merely add to the charm of Psy, the scrutable Other.

To be sure, one may wish to trace Psy's work to a long tradition of Korean performance art (*kwangdae*) or to engage in a contextual and political reading of the video's lyrics and imagery. The possibilities are as numerous as the potential theories and theorists, the eager pundits and bloggers. Yet all such readings would be supererogatory, precisely because it is the reproducibility (along with the possibility of permutation) of the sound bites and dance steps that makes "Gangnam Style" so memorable, so marvelous. The sort of joy that most people find in Psy's performance is incommensurable with the sort of delight that one may derive from a year-long immersion in Proust's *A la recherche du temps perdu* or from voluntary submission to a four-straight-night performance of Wagner's *Ring*. Just as one wouldn't use the same criteria to compare Tolstoy's long novels with Chekhov's short stories, one shouldn't seek, in the name of a category called "music," to bring one's musical judgment to bear on an aesthetic comparison between Sibelius and Psy. I will add only that if we were to impose a formal definition on the video "Gangnam Style," we would call it a specimen of *Gesamtkunstwerk*. But "Gangnam Style" is neither *Der Ring des Nibelungen* nor *Das Nibelungenlied*.

To believe otherwise is make a category mistake, a classificatory error—and, to express this in the vernacular, some people just don't get it.

POPULAR MUSIC AS A CATEGORY OF EXPERIENCE

Without sanctifying or damning popular music at the level of art, we can acknowledge an inescapable reality: that popular music in the twenty-first century has become music pure and simple for the vast majority of the music-loving public. In addition, the term "popular music" no longer represents a coherent category—the sheer diversity of styles and genres within this category is daunting in and of itself—and few people require extended commentary on popular music's legitimacy. Popular music, or music, just *is;* now the only question is whether intellectuals and academics will deal with that reality or remain ensconced in the imaginary museum of absolute music or other, putatively superior, styles and genres.

As I have suggested, the very adjective "popular" has consigned, or condemned, a vast universe of music to the realm of the demotic: the vulgar and superficial, the ignoble and ignorant. Whether popular music was pilloried as a crass product of the culture industry or lamented as an unfortunate manifestation of ill-mannered youth, the history of popular music has been coeval with the history of its opprobrium. There is, however, no urgent intellectual need to rehabilitate the honor of popular music. When the distinguished literary critic Christopher Ricks or the eminent cultural historian Sean Wilentz writes a tome on Bob Dylan, these searing lines by William Butler Yeats come to mind:

> Bald heads forgetful of their sins,
> Old, learned, respectable bald heads
> Edit and annotate the lines
> That young men, tossing on their beds,
> Rhymed out in love's despair
> To flatter beauty's ignorant ear.[5]

The world of popular music, like the world of young lovers, at once defies the moral deliberation of its elders and is enmeshed in the immediacy of worldly pleasure. The unusually reflective and the prematurely wistful have their place—as do the "old, learned, respectable" heads, hirsute or bald—but we shouldn't forget that the paucity, until recently, of writing on popular music says nothing about the value of popular music in the modern world.

The world of scholarship does what it does; the recuperation of the best and the brightest begins to redeem a vast territory of passion and experience and to transmogrify it into learning, above all as history. We should be able to articulate a history of the present as well, not only to illuminate a phenomenon (without explaining it away, however) but also to see in it, and by it, something about the way we live. An impeccable logic suggests that the only proper way for one to respond to popular music, or to any other expression of the human spirit, is to engage in the same medium or genre oneself. Yet there is considerable truth in what T. S. Eliot says: it is "not always true that a person who knows a good poem when he sees it can tell us why it is a good poem."[6] Music, in turn, good or otherwise, is not completely resistant to external accounts, descriptions, and explanations; musicians, fans, producers, and writers produce such things all the time. The pragmatic reality is that, imperfect though we are at articulating things at the abstract level, all of us can still get better at talking about things, popular music included.

Popular music in its current articulation, having eschewed the cult of listening in silence (the cult, that is, of pondering in semisacred reverence, and quasi-sacred meditation, the genius of music), has recovered sound and its connections to other senses, most obviously the visual and the tactile. People watch music videos as much as they listen to music; they may sway or dance in response to aural and visual stimuli. At the very least, popular music is a multifaceted form of entertainment that one can listen to and sing to, watch and emulate, improvise on, and in turn improve. Surely the experience of consuming popular music is not passive at all—to begin with, one must make a selection from a welter of choices—and the experience is certainly not imposed from above, whether by government authorities, teachers, parents, or corporate establishments; indeed, at least in the vast swath of the advanced industrial world, an authority figure's recommendation alone would be enough to squelch both the enjoyment and the popularity of a particular piece of music. In any case, not since the heyday of European classical music, in the nineteenth century, have listeners come so close to replicating the activity of performers, whether by lip-synching or singing, by drumming or dancing.

Popular music, far from the realm of the serious and the sober, remains, along with sex, drugs, and sports, the realm par excellence of ecstasy and emotional experience. Much as we pontificate on the supremacy of art, it is usually in the domain of popular entertainment—sentimental novels, long-form television, and popular music—that people tend to experience aesthetic rupture. Nowadays it is rare to find anyone who, like Stendhal, can be stupe-fied by a work of visual art, but many people have been moved by the banal refrain of a popular song. I am surely not alone in crying over a supposedly meaningless pop song, and what could be deeper and more authentic than my tears? Moreover, tears are not just honest and sincere (or so we have come to believe); they are also, in a sense, music materialized.[7] We cannot begin to plumb the nature and depth of contemporary senses and sensibilities without understanding the role of popular music in shaping, reflecting, and inflecting emotional life.

ENVOI

Psy's 2012 viral hit "Gangnam Style" was by no means the first East Asian or Asian American musical sensation in the United States. In 2011, Far East Movement (also known as FM), a group that includes two Korean American members, reached the top spot on the *Billboard* chart with "Like a G6." Yet what is even more remarkable is that some five decades earlier, in 1963, Sakamoto Kyū (billed as Kyu Sakamoto in the United States) had a huge hit with "Sukiyaki" (the Japanese-language title was "Ue o muite arukō"), a record that spent three weeks as the number 1 song on the US charts. (In contrast, the Beatles' first release in the United States that year—"Please Please Me," an explosive hit in Britain—barely made a ripple.) Sakamoto's wave of popularity extended beyond Japan and the United States; the song, also a number 1 hit in Norway and Israel, among other countries, was one of the most memorable melodies in the world at the time.[8] Prod a sexagenarian (or someone older) in one of the OECD countries, and she is likely to recog-nize the tune and perhaps start humming it. Sakamoto would go on to have a long and successful career in Japan, one that lasted until 1985, when he died in a plane crash; outside Japan, however, he was a one-hit wonder.[9]

Several points deserve comment.

Sakamoto's song, in the United States and elsewhere, was released in the Japanese original, with Japanese lyrics, at a time when, a mere eighteen years after the end of World War II, many people of East Asian descent in the United States were still regularly confronted with the racially tinged slogan "Remember Pearl Harbor!" The song was also composed in the Japanese pentatonic scale; it was certainly not a composition that would have been expected to resonate with American and European youths. Furthermore, neither the Japanese government nor Sakamoto's Japanese producers made any systematic efforts to export the song. Thus the song, at least as an export, faced three obstacles from the outset.

It is possible, however, to explain those obstacles away.

For one thing, eighteen years is a long time—in fact, it was more than an entire lifetime for many of the teenagers who constituted Sakamoto's principal fan base around the world. For another, despite the song's exotic scale, Sakamoto himself was steeped in contemporary American popular music, being an avid fan and imitator of Elvis Presley. Indeed, he made his initial reputation in Japan as a rockabilly performer, and his Presley-like articulation rendered his words all but incomprehensible; to some Japanese listeners, he almost sounded not Japanese at all.[10] In addition, Sakamoto's melismatic singing, replete with falsetto phrases, made the tune at once familiar and strange to Japanese and non-Japanese listeners alike. Another significant point is that his singing, though marred by uncertain pitch, is remarkably rhythmic—an unusual characteristic in Japan at the time, but very much the norm in American popular music. But the non-Japanese constitution of "Sukiyaki" goes beyond Sakamoto's rhythmic singing and his emulation of Presley. He was, to recall a popular expression of the era, "in the groove."[11] And, as mentioned earlier, African American musical genres have often employed the pentatonic scale.[12] Thus, by the early 1960s, the mainstream's acceptance of black music, however qualified, may have set the stage for "Sukiyaki" to fall within the listening competence of American music fans, and the pentatonic scale may have added a touch of exoticism, in the form of the song's perceived melancholic melody. Finally, the culture industry, powerful though its influence can be, does not dictate taste; within the broad parameters of recognizably popular music, many genres and styles have succeeded, but there are no sure-fire formulas for acclaim and fame. The fact that the lyrics of Sakamoto's song were indecipherable did little to diminish listeners' enjoyment of its upbeat yet melancholic melody.[13] A catchy tune may have its logic, of which logic knows nothing.

In the end, however, we can explain only so much without courting the risk of explaining everything, and therefore nothing. Just as Psy's 2012 hit resists simplistic explanations of its rapid dissemination and enthusiastic reception (surely no K-pop producer would have expected such a level of breakaway success in the United States for Psy, widely perceived as looking less like a K-pop star than like a *ssirŭm* [Korean sumo] wrestler), Sakamoto's global hit remains mysterious at one level, something of a secular miracle. It is easy enough to reconstruct what happened. The tune, which had at best modest expectations, was used as the theme song for a Japanese television drama and became the first television-based hit song in Japan in 1961.[14] Thereafter, an American DJ received the single from a friend, played it on his radio show, and received an enthusiastic response. Capitol Records then promoted the song, Sakamoto made a triumphant appearance on a popular variety program, *The Steve Allen Show,* and success begat more success.[15] Yet this narrative still does not explain the song's enthusiastic reception. We know that neither the lyricist nor the composer—or, for that matter, the singer himself—thought that the song would be a hit even in Japan, much less around the world.[16] As the US producer Dave Dexter Jr. has recounted, "I figured the chances [against] Sakamoto's unintelligible vocal becoming a success to be somewhat more than a jillion to one."[17]

Fame has always been thus. As Aristotle put it in *Magna Moralia,* "Good fortune ... is nature without reason."[18] Riches and fame, popularity and stardom, unlike a composer's creative conception or a singer's dynamic execution, are beyond individual or even collective control and therefore reside in the realm of *fortuna.* A global hit presupposes social and technological preconditions, but these, like a narrative, do not constitute a cogent explanation. Perhaps we can use statistical parameters and trends to show a certain frequency of megahits or videos that go viral, but in the context of complexity and other contingencies, any chain of consequences is soon likely to reach the limits of what can be predicted and is therefore unlikely to provide the basis of a concise and cogent explanation. It is interesting that Aristotle was wrong on almost everything about nature, but the same cannot be said for his astute insights into human affairs. At the same time, we will never know what he would have made of "Gangnam Style" or Girls' Generation.

Sakamoto, incidentally, was most likely Zainichi, an ethnic Korean born into an extremely impoverished family in Japan. Early on, he fell deeply in love with American popular music, through a neighboring US military camp and its entertainment annexes.[19] In spite of his disadvantaged upbringing, his singing radiates happiness; he always performed with a smile and a certain joie de vivre. It is surely not a stretch of the imagination to think that listeners far away heard in his irrepressibly upbeat, earnest, enthusiastic voice— though it harbored a dark melancholic undertone—the soothing melody of music's manifold joy.

Coda

DANIEL BARENBOIM REMARKS, "THE BEGINNING of a concert is more privileged than the beginning of a book. One could say that sound itself is more privileged than words"; whereas words are bound up in everyday life, music and sound are "ambivalent," since they are "both inside and outside the world."[1] Transposing across genres is surely more challenging than translating between languages, which is an almost impossible enterprise, and certainly so when pondered philosophically, though the existence of concrete triumphs, like the existence of secular miracles, tempers the temptation to issue an interdiction.[2] Readers are perforce judges; gnawing criticisms seem much more fortunate than neglect (that most damning critique) and therefore oblivion. Be that as it may, the moment I savor most at a concert is the moment when the music has stopped, the sound waves recede, and silence envelops the space (though listeners bludgeoned into believing that applauding between movements is a mortal sin seem ever more anxious to annihilate that beautiful moment of stillness). And thus, I suspect, is the end of composing a book, bittersweet though it may be, for most authors.

Before closing, I wish to thank the Academy of Korean Studies, the Korea Foundation, Samsung Electronics, and Choong Kun Cho for promoting Korean studies at the University of California, Berkeley. ("This work was supported by the Academy of Korean Studies [KSPS] Grant funded by the Korean Government [MOE] [AKS-2012-BAA-2102].") Thanks too to those at the Center for Korean Studies and the Institute of East Asian Studies, especially Martin Backstrom, Dianne-Enpa Cho, Dylan Davis, Wen-hsin Yeh, and Clare You. I began writing this book at the Freie Universität Berlin, where Eun-jeung Lee and her colleagues made my stay productive and enjoyable, and completed it at Kyushu University, where Matsubara Takatoshi and his crew proved to be perfect hosts. By contrast with the preparation of my previous books, I tried out my ideas and observations at various venues and received comments for which I am grateful from the audiences at Sungkyunkwan University; Yonsei University; the Freie Universität Berlin; Sophia University; Columbia University; the University of California, San Diego; the University of Hawai'i at Manoa; the University of Virginia; and the University of California, Berkeley. For encouragement, information, and feedback, I wish to thank Jinsoo An, Jessica Cussins, Thomas Cussins, Mary Yu Danico, Hilary Finchum-Sung, Caren Freeman, Grace Kim, Katherine Lee, Charlotte Lie, Nathan MacBrien, Ingyu Oh, Jay Ou, Charis Thompson, and Jun Yoo. Yunhee Roh helped me get the bibliographical material in the notes right. Xavier Callahan proved to be a superb and scrupulous editor. Emily Park meticulously polished the prose. Marcia Carlson did the index. Reed Malcolm, Stacy Eisenstark, and Chalon Emmons at the University of California Press handled the manuscript efficiently and effectively.

I would like to salute the writers, many of whom worked outside academic life, who patiently and painstakingly researched and wrote on Korean popular music. One stands perforce on the shoulders of one's predecessors, and it is humbling to benefit so much from their labor of love. By the same token, it would delight me if the reader, after perusing this book, were to explore the rich history of Korean popular music before K-pop, or reflect on Korean culture and arts as well as on contemporary South Korea in new ways. *Ŏtchŏnji.*

NOTES

PRELUDE

1. James Boswell, *The Life of Samuel Johnson,* orig. 1791, ed. David Womersley (Harmondsworth: Penguin, 2008), p. 244.

2. View the full concert at www.youtube.com/watch?v=K3EdWimaeAY&playnext =1&list=PLAB8AA2244897C9DC&feature=results_main. For an example of the French media coverage, see www.youtube.com/watch?v=n8wrWbVn-gM.

3. Jon Caramanica, "Korean Pop Machine, Running on Innocence and Hair Gel," *New York Times,* 25 October 2011. See also John Seabrook, "Factory Girls," *The New Yorker,* 8 October 2012, pp. 88–97.

4. See André Tucic, "Schön Frisiert und Wohlerzogen," *Berliner Zeitung,* 10 February 2012, available at www.berliner-zeitung.de/berlin/b-e-a-s-t—schoen-frisiert-und-wohlerzogen,10809148,11610354.html; François Bougon, "Notes d'ambassade en Corée du Sud," *Le Monde,* 16 June 2012; "K-Pop Confidential," *Bangkok Post,* 12 May 2013, available at www.bangkokpost.com/lifestyle/interview/349563/k-pop-confidential-super-fans-and-the-craze-that-consumes-them; and Franklin Briceno, "Korean Music Finds K-Pop Cult Following in Latin America," *Huffington Post,* 30 May 2013, available at www.huffingtonpost.com/2013/05/31/k-pop-latin-america_n_3366546.html. See also Ludovic Hunter-Tilney, "Is Pop Going Polyglot?," *Financial Times,* 13–14 October 2012.

5. For pioneering accounts of South Korean television shows' popularity overseas, see Mōri Yoshitaka, ed., *Nisshiki Kanryū* (Tokyo: Serika Shobō, 2004); Hirata Yukie, *Han'guk ŭl sobi hanŭn Ilbon* (Seoul: Ch'aek Sesang, 2005); Ishita Saeko, Kimura Kan, and Yamanaka Chie, eds., *Posuto Kanryū no media shakaigaku* (Kyoto: Mineruva Shobō, 2007); Yi Hyanjin [Yi Hyang-jin/Lee Hyangjin], *Kanryū no shakaigaku,* trans. Shimizu Yukiko (Tokyo: Iwanami Shoten, 2008); Pak Chang-sun, *Hallyu, Han'guk kwa Ilbon ŭi tŭrama chŏnjaeng* (Seoul: K'ŏmyunik'eishŏn Puksŭ, 2008); Chua Beng Huat and Koichi Iwabuchi, eds., *East Asian Pop Culture* (Hong Kong: Hong Kong University Press, 2008); and Mark James Russell, *Pop Goes Korea* (Berkeley: Stone Bridge Press, 2008).

6. The transcript of President Lee's eighty-fourth radio address is available at www.asiae.co.kr/news/view.htm?idxno=2012021913180511578.

7. Martin Fackler, "Trendy Spot Urges Tourists to Ride In and Spend, 'Gangnam Style,'" *New York Times*, 1 January 2013. Gangnam's mayor added, "Gangnam is a uniquely Korean brand."

8. For up-to-date information on K-pop, see MWave at http://mwave.interest.me/index.m, or the Gaon Music Chart at www.gaonchart.co.kr/. For the most comprehensive overviews in print, the bibliography in Japanese is nonpareil; see, for example, *Shin K-POP kanzen dēta jiten* (Tokyo: Kōsaidō, 2012), and *K-POP sutā korekushon* (Tokyo: Kinema Junpōsha, 2012). For anglophone readers, the most accessible sources are websites devoted to K-pop, such as www.soompi.com/ and www.allkpop.com/. *Billboard* maintains its "Korea K-Pop Hot 100" chart at www.billboard.com/charts/k-pop-hot-100. For earlier South Korean popular music, see the blog *Classic Korean Pop Music Archive* at http://kocpop.blogspot.com/. The "50 Most Influential K-Pop Artists Series Index" at the *Ask A Korean!* blog is idiosyncratic but instructive and available at http://askakorean.blogspot.com/1998/02/50-most-influential-k-pop-artists.html.

9. Roger Sessions, *Questions About Music* (Cambridge: Harvard University Press, 1970), p. 41.

10. Like many good stories, the quote resides in the realm of the apocryphal. According to John Efron, "When the distinguished Talmudist Saul Lieberman once publicly introduced . . . Gershom Scholem, he began with the quip, 'Now everybody knows that Kabbalah is *narishkayt* [foolishness], but the history of *narishkayt*—now that's scholarship!'" See Efron, "My Son the Alchemist," *Forward*, 7 October 1994, pp. 9–10, esp. p. 9. As the astute journalist in John Ford's 1962 film *The Man Who Shot Liberty Valance* put it, "When the legend becomes fact, print the legend." To be sure, the journalist prefaces this remark by saying, "This is the West"—but Hollywood has made all of us permutations of the American West.

11. See Oscar Wilde, "The Soul of Man under Socialism," orig. 1891, in Richard Ellman, ed., *The Artist as Critic* (Chicago: University of Chicago Press, 1982), pp. 255–89, esp. p. 283.

12. Stéphane Mallarmé, "Sur l'évolution littéraire," orig. 1891, in Mallarmé, *Oeuvres complètes,* vol. 2, ed. Bertrand Marchal (Paris: Gallimard, 2003), pp. 697–702, esp. p. 702.

13. William Boyd, *Nat Tate* (Cambridge: 21 Publishing, 1998).

14. See the background story in Pak Sŏng-sŏ, *Han'guk Chŏnjaeng kwa taejung kayo, kirok kwa chŭngŏn* (Seoul: Ch'aek i Inŭn P'unggyŏng, 2010), pp. 122–31.

1. HOW DID WE GET HERE?

1. The paucity of entertainment options in the 1970s is difficult to convey to contemporary South Korean youths, for whom a world without readily reproducible

movies and music, and without cell phones, computer games, or leisure sports, is simply unimaginable.

2. The concept of the soundscape was introduced by R. Murray Schafer, *The New Soundscape* (Don Mills: BMI Canada, 1969), to identify acoustic ecology or the environment of sound, but I am using the term "soundscape" to mean the music of a particular culture (at a particular time), or a musical culture.

3. On the global dimension of the Korean Wave-an overarching term referring to the spread of South Korean popular culture beyond South Korea-see Korea Herald, ed., *Korean Wave* (Seoul: Jimoondang, 2008). For early writings on what would become K-pop, see Chon Wŏlsŏn, *Kinjirareta uta* (Tokyo: Chūō Kōron Shinsha, 2008), and Mark James Russell, *Pop Goes Korea* (Berkeley: Stone Bridge Press, 2008), chaps. 5–6.

4. I am aware of the oft-repeated rumor of European classical music's decline and demise, which is itself a long-standing discourse at this point; see Charles Rosen, *Critical Entertainments* (Cambridge: Harvard University Press, 2000), pp. 295–96. Yet at least in South Korea in the early twenty-first century, European classical music is alive and well. Traditional Korean music may experience a major revival-I am not unaware of Geomungo Factory and other noteworthy contemporary performers-but it would constitute yet another revolution for traditional Korean music to supplant European art music in South Korea.

5. For overviews of Korean traditional music, see, inter alia, Chang Sa-hun, *Han'guk ŭmaksa* (Seoul: Han'guk Kugak Hakhoe, n.d.); Yi Hye-gu, *Han'guk ŭmak yŏn'gu* (Seoul: Kungmin Ŭmak Yŏn'guhoe, 1957); No Tong-ŭn, *Han'guk kŭndae ŭmaksa*, vol. 1 (Seoul: Hangilsa, 1995); Song Pang-song, *Chosŏn choŭmaksa yŏn'gu* (Seoul: Minsokwŏn, 2001); and Song Pang-song, *Chŭngbo Han'guk ŭmak t'ongsa* (Seoul: Minsokwŏn, 2007). On the development of indigenous instruments, see Chang Sa-hun, *Han'guk akki taegwan* (Seoul: Munhwa Kongobu Munhwajae Kwalliguk, 1969), and Keith Howard, *Korean Musical Instruments* (Hong Kong: Oxford University Press, 1995). See also the pioneering Western account by the curiously neglected German scholar Andreas Eckardt, *Koreanische Musik* (Tokyo: Deutsche Gesellschaft für Natur- und Völkerkunde Ostasiens, 1930). Eckardt later wrote (as Andre Eckardt) a useful overview, *Musik, Lied, Tanz in Korea* (Bonn: Bouvier, 1968). Maurice Courant's *Essai historique sur la musique classique des Chinois* (Paris: Delagrave, 1912) contains an appendix on Korean music and may have the dubious distinction of being the first European musicological analysis of Korean traditional music (and is, alas, unable to identify why traditional Korean music is distinct from its Chinese counterpart). In English, see Keith Pratt, *Korean Music* (London: Faber Music, 1987); Jonathan Condit, *Music of the Korean Renaissance* (Cambridge: Cambridge University Press, 2009), esp. pt. 1; and Donna Lee Kwon, *Music in Korea* (New York: Oxford University Press, 2012).

6. As is true of many other aspects of Korean culture, much of traditional Korean music can be traced to Chinese civilization, which in turn traces its roots to Central Asia. For an overview of Chinese music, see Liú Zàishēng, ed., *Zhōngguó yīnlè de lìshǐ xíngtài* (Shanghai: Shànghǎi Yīnlè Xuéyuàn Chūbǎnshè, 2003). On the

Silk Road antecedents, see, for example, Tsubouchi Shigeo, *Sirukurōdo to sekai no gakki* (Tokyo: Gendai Shokan, 2007). For pioneering accounts of comparative East Asian music, see Peter Gradenwitz, *Musik zwischen Orient und Okzident* (Hamburg: Heinrichshoften, 1977), and Ishida Kazushi, *Modanizumu hensōkyoku* (Tokyo: Sakuhokusha, 2005).

7. There were three major styles for state rituals: Chinese court music (*tangak*), native court music (*hyangak*), and Chinese-inflected ritual music (*aak*); see the instructive study by Yamamoto Hanako, *Riōsho kugagakubu no kenkyū* (Akita: Shoshi Furōra, 2011). In terms of vocal music, the elite performed or listened to *kagok, sijo,* and *kasa.* The first two were lyric songs with instrumental accompaniment; *kagok* featured longer lyrics, with more elaborate accompaniment (major and minor modes), by comparison with *sijo.* Both belonged squarely to the domain of *chŏngak* (orthodox vocal music), which stressed formal beauty. *Kasa,* by contrast, was an interstitial form that lacked a standard poetic-musical framework and singing style.

8. Confucius (Kongzi) himself valorized music, and his ideological heirs stressed the place of music in personal cultivation and social order; see Kongzi, *Lun yu,* 3.25 et seq. See also Erica Fox Brindley, *Music, Cosmology, and the Politics of Harmony in Early China* (Albany: SUNY Press, 2012).

9. The locus classicus of the Apollonian-Dionysian distinction remains Friedrich Nietzsche, "Die Geburt der Tragödie," orig. 1872, in Nietzsche, *Sämtliche Werke,* vol.1, ed. Giorgio Colli and Mazzino Montinari (Berlin: de Gruyter, 1967–77), pp. 9–156, esp. pp. 25–34.

10. For pioneering studies of *minyo,* see Ko Chŏng-ok, *Chosŏn minyo yŏn'gu* (Seoul: Susŏnsa, 1949), and Sŏng Kyŏng-nin, *Chosŏn ŭi minyo* (Seoul: Kukche Ŭmak Munhwasa, 1949). On *p'ungmul,* see Nathan Hesselink, *P'ungmul* (Chicago: University of Chicago Press, 2006).

11. The classic of *p'ansori* writing remains Sin Chae-hyo, *Sin Chae-hyo p'ansori chŏnjip,* orig. 1873(?), ed. Kang Han-yŏng (Seoul: Yonsei Taehakkyo Ch'ulp'anbu, 1969). Although often called "Korean opera," *p'ansori* is much closer to the oral tradition of epic songs, of the sort analyzed by Albert B. Lord, *The Singer of Tales* (Cambridge: Harvard University Press, 1960). See also Marshall Pihl, *The Korean Singer of Tales* (Cambridge: Harvard University Asia Center, 1994), and Pyŏn Ŭn-jŏn, *Katarimono no hikaku kenkyū* (Tokyo: Kanrin Shobō, 2002).

12. For *p'ansori*'s contemporary articulation, see Ch'oe I-du, *Myŏngjang Im Pang-ul* (Seoul: Hangilsa, 1998), and Chan E. Park, *Voices from the Straw Mat* (Honolulu: University of Hawai'i Press, 2003). The surprising popularity of the 1993 film *Sŏp'yŏnje,* directed by Im Kwŏn-t'aek, elicited a wave of national soul-searching that catapulted *p'ansori* to something of the status of soul music for South Koreans; see Cho Hae Joang, "*Sopyonje,*" trans. Yuh Ji-Yeon, in David E. James and Kyung Hyun Kim, eds., *Im Kwon-Taek* (Detroit: Wayne State University Press, 2001), pp. 134–56.

13. *Namsadang,* something of a premodern circus, disappeared after the 1940s; see Sim U-sŏng, *Namsadang p'ae yŏn'gu* (Seoul: Tonghwa Ch'ulp'an Kongsa, 1974),

p. 44. There were also all-female groups called *sadang*. Itinerant entertainers, usually called *kwangdae*, occupied the nadir of the Confucian social hierarchy and often doubled as sex workers. On *kwangdae*, see Ayugai Fusanoshin, *Karōkō, hakutoikō, dohikō*, orig. 1938 (Tokyo: Kokusho Kankōkai, 1973), pp. 480–88; Kawamura Minato, *Kīsen* (Tokyo: Sakuhinsha, 2001), pp. 47–48; and Hayashi Fumiki, *Kankoku sākasu no seikatsushi* (Tokyo: Fūkyosha, 2007), pp. 37–38. As *paekchŏng, kwangdae* were outcasts or untouchables, and what they did was perforce polluted. On *paekchŏng*, see Kim Yŏng-dae, *Chōsen no hisabetsu minshū*, orig. 1978, trans. Hon'yaku Henshū Iinkai (Osaka: Buraku Kaihō Kenkyūjo, 1988), and Pak Chong-sŏng, *Paekchŏng kwa kisaeng* (Seoul: Seoul Taehakkyo Ch'ulp'anbu, 2003).

14. The central place of music, both singing and the playing of instruments, is clear in Yi Nŭng-hwa's pioneering *Chosŏn haeŏhwasa*, orig. 1927 (Seoul: Tongmunsŏn, 1992). The tradition continued during the colonial period, as evinced by the curriculum of the Pyongyang Kisaeng School (the Korean Dancing Girls' School, according to a contemporary illustration); see Kawamura, *Kīsen*, pp. 147–58. Yi's work suggests the recent decline of *kisaeng* culture by emphasizing the role of *kisaeng* as sex workers laboring in *saesuga* (bars and teahouses); see also John Lie, "The Transformation of Sexual Work in 20th-Century Korea," *Gender & Society* 9 (1995), 310–27. Although there has been an element of beautification in the highlighting of courtesans' aesthetic pursuits, Chosŏn-period *kisaeng* actually did include accomplished poets and musicians.

15. Shamanist music, which probably had a deeper resonance with the larger population, has faced a degree of modern scholarly disdain and dismissal so extreme as to render shamanist music virtually inaudible in the contemporary reconstruction of traditional Korean music. On the place of shamanist music in early twentieth-century Korea, see Akamatsu Chijō and Akiba Takashi, eds., *Chōsen fuzoku no kenkyū*, 2 vols. (Tokyo: Ōsakayago Shoten, 1937–38), and Akiba Takashi, *Chōsen fuzoku no genchi kenkyū* (Tanbaichi: Yōtokusha, 1950). For musical analysis, see, for example, Mikyung Park, "Music and Shamanism in Korea," Ph.D. diss., University of California, Los Angeles, 1985, esp. pp. 148–83. A modern reincarnation of Korean shamanist music in European musical form is Isang Yun's 1978 composition *Muak*. On the nature and influence of Buddhist music, see Pak Pŏm-hun, *Han'guk pulgyo ŭmaksa yŏn'gu* (Seoul: Changgyŏnggak, 2000).

16. Regional variations on a popular folk tune such as "Arirang" remained significant well into the twentieth century. "Standards"—whether in folk music, folktales, or even speech itself—emerged and converged only with the rapid cultural integration that took place in the twentieth century.

17. The role of music in social life is emphasized, for example, by the pioneering ethnomusicologist John Blacking, *How Musical Is Man?* (Seattle: University of Washington Press, 1973), pp. 32–33.

18. By contrast with the modern European conceptualization of music, the idea of sound and soundscape that I am suggesting here is similar to the sorts of ideas advocated by John Cage, *Silences* (Middletown: Wesleyan University Press, 1961), pp. 3, 12, 71–72. See also Steven Feld, *Sound and Sentiment* (Philadelphia: University

of Pennsylvania Press, 1982), and Charles Keil and Steven Feld, *Music Grooves* (Chicago: University of Chicago Press, 1994).

19. The contemporary locus classicus of the idea of "absolute music" is the work of Theodor Adorno; see, for example, his "Spätstil Beethovens," orig. 1937, in Adorno, *Gesammelte Schriften*, vol.17 (Frankfurt: Suhrkamp, 1997), pp. 13–17. I do not mean to impose a false unity on European classical music. As Artur Schnabel recognized, "absolute music" was "comparatively very young.... This absolute, autonomous, independent music has developed into what is perhaps the most exclusive medium for the spiritual exaltation of the active individual in an intimate private sphere of personal experience"; see Schnabel, *My Life and Music*, orig. 1961 (New York: Dover, 1988), p. 5.

20. If we were to consider Biedermeier Vienna, for example, we would see that musical life hardly approached the ideal of absolute music; the experience of listening was intertwined with such extramusical activities as dancing, or wining and dining. See, inter alia, Eduard Hanslick, *Geschichte des Concertwesens in Wien* (Vienna: Braunmüller, 1869), and Alice M. Hansen, *Musical Life in Biedermeier Vienna* (Cambridge: Cambridge University Press, 1985). To be sure, it is these extramusical-and hence frivolous-accompaniments that justified the pejorative appellation "Biedermeier."

21. See the discussion in Ju Yong Ha, "The Great and Majestic," Ph.D. diss., City University of New York, 2007. It is also worth noting that (to use the language of Western music theory) tetratonic, dodecaphonic, and other scales were employed in traditional Korean music, but probably the most common was the tritonic scale, with a dominant middle tone. See the interesting discussion in Hwang Chun-yŏn, *Han'guk chŏnt'ong ŭmak ŭi nakjo* (Seoul: Seoul Taehakkyo Ch'ulp'anbu, 2005), pp. 167–78. We should also recall that European classical music often used the pentatonic scale; see Jeremy Day O'Connell, *Pentatonicism from the Eighteenth Century to Debussy* (Rochester: University of Rochester Press, 2007).

22. *Changdan,* alternating long and short beats, incorporates tempi and dynamics and is typical in both *chŏngak* and *p'ansori* musical performance; see Chang Sa-hun, *Han'guk chŏnt'ong ŭmak ŭi yŏn'gu* (Seoul: Pojinje, 1975). There are different *changdan* beats, but they are usually subdivided into three, which is the basis for thinking that the standard *kugak* rhythm is three beats. Sakurai Testuo, in *Ajia ongaku no sekai* (Kyoto: Sekai Shisōsha, 1997), suggests (pp. 39–41) that most traditional Korean musical pieces are in four beats rather than three, and that the misapprehension is born of our Eurocentric musical knowledge. An understanding of the traditional Korean rhythm as three beats would emphasize not only links to Silk Road cultures but also the differentiation of traditional Korean music from the traditional music of the Chinese mainland and that of the Japanese archipelago; see Koizumi Fumio, *Minzoku ongaku no sekai* (Tokyo: Nihon Hōsō Shuppan Kyōkai, 1985), pp. 52–53, 60–61.

23. Constantin Brailoiu's term *métabole* illuminates the linear and nonharmonic quality of traditional Korean music; see his "Un problème de tonalité," in Brailoiu, ed., *Mélanges d'histoire et d'esthétique musicales offerts à Paul-Marie Masson*, vol.1 (Paris: Masse, 1955), pp. 63–75.

24. Let me stress again that facile generalizations can be misleading; the almost fundamentalist faith in the score was surely alien to European musical performers before the nineteenth century. See Frederick Dorian, *The History of Music Performance* (New York: Norton, 1942), p. 155.

25. Consider, for instance, the valorization of organic logic and structure as the foundation of European music, as articulated by Eduard Hanslick, *Vom Musikalisch-Schönen*, orig. 1854, 10th ed. (Leipzig: J. A. Barth, 1902), pp. 280–82. There is nothing of the sort in traditional Korean music, and the very question would have struck performers and listeners as bizarre. In part, this is because of the great distance between the modern practice of performing a piece of classical music from a printed score and the practices of musicians who operated in oral, improvisatory modes. See, inter alia, Bernhard Morbach, *Die Mukikwelt des Mittelalters* (Kassel: Bärenreiter, 2004), chap. 2, and Anne Smith, *The Performance of 16th-Century Music* (Oxford: Oxford University Press, 2011), pp. 15–18.

26. Also symptomatic is the subtitle of a book by Kim Choon Mee, *Harmonia Koreana: A Short History of 20th-Century Korean Music* (Seoul: Hollym International, 2011); see esp. p. 15, where Kim describes the book as "a brief overview of how Western classical music was introduced, took root and developed in Korea." This double elision-with classical music reduced to "music," and South Korea reduced to "Korea"-highlights the prevailing mind-set in South Korea. Park Chung-hee, who increasingly turned to nationalism in order to strengthen his precarious hold on power, established the Bureau of Cultural Property Preservation in 1962 and the Korean Culture and Arts Foundation in 1974, both of which sought to promote *kugak*. Park's reliance on nationalism to prop up his regime undoubtedly played a part in his espousal of traditional Korean music. However, it would have been highly unlikely for such a policy to have been pursued by a person of elite *yangban* background in the 1960s. Slightly earlier, in 1959, Seoul National University had created its department of Korean music, but it is with the launching of academic journals such as *Han'guk ŭmak yŏn'gu* (1971–) and *Minjok ŭmakhak* (1976–) that *kugak* was established as a field of scholarship.

27. See Margaret Walker Dilling, *Stories Inside Stories* (Berkeley: Institute of East Asian Studies, University of California, 2007). In her study of the music for the 1988 Seoul Olympics, Dilling reports that "only a few of the eleven composers for the ceremonies felt secure in their knowledge of traditional Korean music theory from either study or performing" (p. 248).

28. The decline of people's music was especially noticeable during the rapid industrialization and rural exodus of the 1960s and 1970s; see, for example, Robert C. Provine Jr., *Drum Rhythms in Korean Farmers' Music* (Seoul: n.p., 1975), p. 2, and Sakurai Tetsuo, *"Sori" no kenkyū* (Tokyo: Kōbundō, 1989), pp. 265–69. It would be an exaggeration, however, and the reflection of a Seoul-centric perspective, to say that the demise of people's music occurred during the 1970s; see, for example, Nancy Abelmann, *Echoes of the Past, Epics of Dissent* (Berkeley: University of California Press, 1996), pp. 60–61. On the revival of traditional people's music by the contemporary people's (*minjung*) movement, see Namhee Lee, *The Making of*

Minjung (Ithaca: Cornell University Press, 2007), pp. 191–92. On the revival of itinerant musicians, see Nathan Hesselink, *SamulNori* (Chicago: University of Chicago Press, 2012). For an example of a contemporary reappreciation, see Yi So-ra, *Nongyo ŭi kil ŭl ttara* (Seoul: Miral, 2001).

29. A video is worth a thousand words. See the video of a "traditional" group, Miji, at www.youtube.com/watch?v=tJEg-ljdYgE. Here, too, the impact of K-pop, whether in sound or sartorial style, is undeniable. Be that as it may, *sanjo* is a belated development from the late nineteenth century, and contemporary performances of *p'ansori* tend to be resolutely modernist.

30. The Eurocentric cast recalls early European attempts to make sense of Europeanization; see, for example, Walter Wiora, *Die vier Weltalter der Musik* (Stuttgart: Kohlhammer, 1961), chap. 4. There is no point in denying the elite's embrace of European music, although the regnant soundscape proved much more robust, and the chief consequence of Europeanization was the creation of a hybrid or heterogeneous soundscape.

31. For overviews of the introduction of European music to the Korean peninsula, see Yi Yu-son (You-sun Lee), *Han'guk yangak p'alsinnyonsa* (Seoul: Chungang Taehak Ch'ulp'anbu, 1976), esp. chap. 2, and Choong-sik Ahn, *The Story of Western Music in Korea* (Morgan Hill: Bookstand Publishing, 2005).

32. To summarize briefly, Western musical hegemony overshadowed *gagaku* and other received Japanese musical styles; see Terauchi Naoko, *Gagaku no "kindai" to "gendai"* (Tokyo: Iwanami Shoten, 2010), pp. 17–20. *Gagaku* itself was institutionalized and preserved as ritual music for the imperial household; see Tsukahara Yasuko, *Meiji kokka to gagaku* (Tokyo: Yushisha, 2009), pp. 4–9. Initially, Western music meant Christian music, especially hymns, according to Teshiragi Shun'ichi, *Sanbika-seika to Nihon no kindai* (Tokyo: Ongaku no Tomosha, 1999), p. 8. But European classical music became the foundation of music itself for official Japan. As a cardinal example of this phenomenon, the nineteenth-century German composer and pianist Ferdinand Beyer ("Baieru" in Japanese), an extremely minor figure, was elevated to dominant status on the basis of his having authored a widely disseminated introductory piano textbook, which millions of Japanese schoolchildren have encountered and endured since the late nineteenth century, and as I also did as a child; see Yasuda Hiroshi, *Baieru no nazo* (Tokyo: Ongaku no Tomosha, 2012), pp. 22–23. For an overview of European classical music in Japan, see, for example, Nakamura Rihei, *Yōgaku dōnyū no kiseki* (Tokyo: Tōsui Shobō, 1993).

33. Ishida, *Modanizumu hensōkyoku*, p. 355. See also Chang Sa-hun, *Yŏmyŏng ŭi tongsŏ ŭmak* (Seoul: Pojinjae, 1974).

34. Hans-Alexander Kneider, "Franz Eckert," in Martin H. Schmidt, ed., *Franz Eckert-Li Mirok-Yun Isang* (Norderstedt: Books on Demand, 2010), pp. 44–51.

35. The exposure of the elite to Western music occurred in times of battle and during ceremonies, when the aural amplitude of the Western military band was accompanied by the visual might of steamships, cannons, and Western technology in general; see the suggestive discussion in Chiba Yūko, *Doremi o eranda Nihonjin* (Tokyo: Ongaku no Tomosha, 2007), pp. 24–27. The new Meiji regime in turn

impressed the population at ceremonies via the new, stentorian Western music performance. The impressive martial music shaped musical education itself; see Bonnie C. Wade, *Music in Japan* (New York: Oxford University Press, 2005), pp. 11–14.

36. Maeda Kōji, *Meiji no ongaku kyōiku to sono haikei* (Tokyo: Chikurinkan, 2010), pp. 72–73. Most Japanese, like most other people listening to music from different cultures, seem to have found Western music strange and even repulsive; see Naitō Takashi, *Meiji no oto* (Tokyo: Chūkō Shinsha, 2005), pp. 11–12. Yet Miyashiro Michio's 1929 composition *Haru no umi* (The sea in spring) is now regarded as representative of Japanese music, though it was considered new and Western when it was performed in the 1930s; see Chiba, *Doremi o eranda Nihonjin*, p. 6.

37. Nakayama Eiko, *Meiji shōka no tanjō* (Tokyo: Bensei Shuppan, 2010), pp. 443–45. In particular, the act of singing together (*gasshō*)-an inevitable corollary of choral singing-was considered edifying in and of itself; see Yamauchi Atsuko, "Nihon gasshō kotohajime," in Tonoshita Tatsuya and Yokoyama Takuya, eds., *Nihon no gasshōshi* (Tokyo: Seikyūsha, 2011), pp. 12–39, esp. pp. 32–33. From Kinoshita Keisuke's 1954 *Nijyūshi no hitomi* (Twenty-four eyes) to Sakamoto Junji's 2012 *Kita no kanariatachi* ("A chorus of angels"), Japanese movies about students often feature choral singing as central to school life and beyond.

38. Technically, most organs were harmoniums, which reached the height of their popularity in the late nineteenth century.

39. For Japan, see Chiba, *Doremi o eranda Nihonjin,* chap. 5. To be sure, the distinction between children's songs (*dōwa*) and choral songs (*shōka*) is hardly clear-cut, even in textbooks; see Matsumura Naoyuki, *Dōwa shōka de tadoru ongaku kyōkasho no ayumi* (Osaka: Izumi Shoin, 2011), pp. 177–78.

40. Although considered "traditional," *ch'anggŭk* emerged in the late 1900s; see Paek Hyŏn-mi, *Han'guk ch'anggŭksa yŏn'gu* (Seoul: T'aehaksa, 1997), and Andrew Killick, *In Search of Korean Traditional Opera* (Honolulu: University of Hawai'i Press, 2010).

41. For Japan, see Nakamura Kōsuke, *Seiyō no oto, Nihon no mimi* (Tokyo: Shunjūsha, 1987).

42. On the idea of musical competence, see Gino Stefani, "A Theory of Musical Competence," *Semiotica* 66 (1987), 7–22.

43. See, for example, Herbert J. Gans, *Popular Culture and High Culture* (New York: Basic Books, 1975); Stuart Hall and Tony Jefferson, eds., *Resistance through Rituals* (London: Hutchinson, 1976); and Lawrence W. Levine, *Highbrow/Lowbrow* (Cambridge: Harvard University Press, 1988).

44. The reductio ad absurdum of the notion that art or classical music requires no audience is articulated, for example, by Arnold Schoenberg in his letter to Alexander von Zemlinsky of 23 February 1918; see Alexander Zemlinsky, *Briefwechsel mit Arnold Schönberg, Anton Webern, Alban Berg und Franz Schreker,* ed. Horst Weber (Darmstadt: Wissenschaftliche Buchgesellschaft, 1995), p. 191. See also Milton Babbitt's 1958 essay "Who Cares If You Listen?," in Babbitt, *The Collected Essays of Milton Babbitt,* ed. Stephen Peles et al. (Princeton: Princeton University Press,

2003), pp. 48–54. Schoenberg's mandarin disdain for his sparse or nonexistent audience is a far cry from Mozart's desire for approval and his implicit aesthetic that valorized pleasure, as indicated, for instance, in Mozart's letter to his father of 26 September 1781; see Wolfgang Amadeus Mozart, *Briefe und Aufzeichnungen,* vol. 3, ed. Wilhelm A. Bauer, Otto Erich Deutsch, Joseph Heinz Eibl, and Ulrich Konrad (Kassel: Bärenreiter, 1963), p. 161. To state this idea differently, classical music *was* popular music; see, for example, Schnabel, *My Life and Music,* pp. 41–42. Until the emergence of popular music, the distinction between classical and popular music remained inchoate at best.

45. D. H. Lawrence, "Just Making Love to Music," in Lawrence, *Phoenix: The Posthumous Papers of D. H. Lawrence,* ed. Edward D. McDonald (New York: Viking, 1936), pp. 160–66, esp. p. 160.

46. The idea of absolute music also affected performance and consumption. Kenneth Hamilton, in *After the Golden Age* (New York: Oxford University Press, 2008), makes a compelling case (pp. 30–32) for an earlier "golden age" generation of Romantic pianists who played with more spontaneity and less seriousness than their contemporary heirs. Serious playing emerged along with the sacralization of the listening experience, one assumed to take place in silent contemplation; see James H. Johnson, *Listening in Paris* (Berkeley: University of California Press, 1995). In addition, the technological capability of reproducing musical performances escalated the demand for accuracy (and, ironically, extinguished the practice of improvisation) along with the formalization of the audience's response, as exemplified by the convention of holding applause until the end of a piece; see Hamilton, *After the Golden Age,* pp. 80, 96–100. I recall attending concerts of classical music in Seoul in the 1970s and 1980s, when scattered crowds would bring food and converse freely (but usually, and mercifully, softly). By the 2010s, "premodern" behavior had become well-nigh extinct.

47. The generic equation of music with popular music underscores the social integration of the audience. As Stanley Cavell has remarked of movies, they reveal a continuity of audience, high and low; see Cavell, *The World Viewed,* orig. 1971, enlarged ed. (Cambridge: Harvard University Press, 1979), pp. 14–15. The same can be said about popular music in the early twenty-first century, virtually around the world. On the dead end of art music, see, for example, Gert Jonke, *Schuld der Geläufigkeit* (Frankfurt: Suhrkamp, 1977).

48. The normative length of a song varies, but a Schubert lied, a Tin Pan Alley tune, or a K-pop single usually clocks in at around three minutes. In this regard, Dave Marsh's statement-"Singles are the essence of rock and roll"-can be generalized: a song is the basic unit of analysis in popular music; see Marsh, *The Heart of Rock and Soul* (New York: Plume, 1989), p. ix.

49. See Isaac Goldberg, *Tin Pan Alley* (New York: John Day, 1930). See also Sigmund Spaeth, *The Facts of Life in Popular Song* (New York: McGraw-Hill, 1934), perhaps the first serious study of popular music. Needless to say, the earlier form of popular music, the folk song, has a longer history of scholarship, which in English can be traced to William Chappell, *Old English Popular Music,* 2 vols. (London:

Henderson and Spalding, 1838–40). If we consult the Google Books Ngram Viewer, we note an increase in the frequency of references to popular music in the first two decades of the twentieth century (an increase that suggests the rise of popular as opposed to folk music), and of course we note the same increase in the post-World War II period as well. For a recent overview of the emergence of popular music as a commercial and industrial entity, see David Suisman, *Selling Sounds* (Cambridge: Harvard University Press, 2009).

50. John Storey, a leading scholar of popular culture, remarks: "Popular music is everywhere. . . . In my youth I had to seek it out. Now it seems to appear everywhere I go"; see Storey, *Cultural Studies and the Study of Popular Culture*, orig. 1996, 2nd ed. (Athens: University of Georgia Press, 2003), p. 110.

51. It is true that instrumental competence was widespread in bourgeois Western households. Roger Sessions, writing some forty years ago, recalls: "Even at a time I myself can remember well, most music lovers were people who 'made music' in their homes"; see Sessions, *Questions About Music*, p. 15. Rural farmers in Chosŏn Korea presumably also performed *nongak*, but—difficult though this would be to prove—it seems unlikely that the village air was forever alive with the sound of music.

52. There is undoubtedly a dark underside of technological progress, such as the alienation of instrumental competence. As noted earlier, if many music listeners in the early twentieth century were also music makers, then surely the proportion of competent musicians to classical music aficionados must have fallen, and technological progress in sound reproduction is surely part of the reason. For an intriguing history of sound reproduction, see Jonathan Sterne, *The Audible Past* (Durham: Duke University Press, 2003).

53. Murray Melbin discusses the after-dark hours in terms of "escape" (although he has little to say about entertainment) in *Night as Frontier* (New York: Free Press, 1987), pp. 58–60, 114–16.

54. See, for example, Lewis A. Erenberg, *Steppin' Out* (Chicago: University of Chicago Press, 1984). The usual focus of the new urban nightlife spans the late Victorian Age to the Jazz Age; see Peter C. Baldwin, *In the Watches of the Night* (Chicago: University of Chicago Press, 2012), and Judith Walkowitz, *Nights Out* (New Haven: Yale University Press, 2012). It should be noted that radio, almost from its inception, also played a significant role in expanding nocturnal activities; see Michael C. Keith, *Sounds in the Dark* (New York: Wiley-Blackwell, 2001).

55. David Nasaw, *Going Out* (New York: Basic Books, 1993), pp. 1–2.

56. The point here is that "silent" movies were usually not silent when they were screened for an audience. Toward the end of the silent era, in the late 1920s, some twenty-five thousand musicians worked for movie theaters; see James P. Kraft, "Musicians in Hollywood," *Technology and Culture* 35 (1994), 289–314, esp. pp. 291–92. In other words, Hollywood was the largest employer of professional musicians in the United States in the early twentieth century.

57. Fashion is part of social life, and the inevitability of competition and distinction dictates an endogenous tendency toward change. Consumption in turn provides a powerful means by which fashion is expressed. There is no need to talk of the

consumer revolution in eighteenth-century England, but few can seriously question that succeeding centuries have heightened the place of consumption and the acceleration of fashion trends and transformations. On the consumer revolution in eighteenth-century England, see Neil McKendrick, John Brewer, and J. H. Plumb, *The Birth of a Consumer Society* (Bloomington: Indiana University Press, 1992), pp. 9–10; compare Grant McCracken, *Culture and Consumption* (Bloomington: Indiana University Press, 1990), pp. 4–7.

58. For a pioneering statement, see David Riesman, *Individualism Reconsidered* (Glencoe: Free Press, 1954), pp. 187–90. See also Paul Willis, *Profane Culture* (London: RKP, 1978), pp. 62–86.

59. The category of "youth" or "young people" is surprisingly unstable; see, inter alia, John R. Gillis, *Youth and History* (New York: Academic Press, 1974), and Giovanni Levi and Jean-Claude Schmitt, eds., *Storia dei giovani,* 2 vols. (Roma: Laterza, 1994). A much more satisfying category, if one fraught with criticism and contention, is that of "generation." It is fair to say, however, that the category of "teenagers" begins to capture the distinctive youth subculture that appeared in the United States after World War II and later on in other areas of the affluent world; see Paul Goodman, *Growing Up Absurd* (New York: Random House, 1960). That subculture is more systematically analyzed in Mike Brake, *The Sociology of Youth Culture and Youth Subcultures* (London: Routledge & Kegan Paul, 1980), as well as in Brake's *Comparative Youth Culture* (London: Routledge, 1990).

60. Nathalie Sarraute, *Vous les entendez?* (Paris: Gallimard, 1972).

61. Andrew Kopkind, "The Dialectic of Disco," orig. 1979, in Kopkind, *The Thirty Years' War* (London: Verso, 1995), pp. 308–18, esp. pp. 309–13.

62. Sessions, *Questions About Music,* p. 38.

63. As Robert Herrick (1591–1674) rhapsodized in "To the Virgins to Make Much of Time": "Gather ye rosebuds while ye may, / Old Time is still a flying: / And this same flower that smiles today / Tomorrow will be dying." The sentiment is old, but its dominance is a recent phenomenon.

64. Consider, however, Frank Kermode's point, in another context, that opinion and knowledge may restore attention to long-forgotten figures of importance; see Kermode, *Forms of Attention* (Chicago: University of Chicago Press, 1985), p. 92.

65. The comparative case of Taiwan is instructive, but suffice it here to cite a pioneering study of popular music in colonial Taiwan: Huáng Xìnzhāng, *Chuánchàng Táiwān xīnshēng* (Taipei: Táiběi shì Zhèngfǔ Wénhuàjú, 2009). Huáng Qízhì provides a window into the music scenes in Shanghai and Hong Kong in his *Shídài qū de liúguāng suìyuè* (Hong Kong: Sānlián Shūdiàn, 2010).

66. John Rosselli, writing about nineteenth-century Italy, observes, "Italy's folk music . . . was far too locally bounded to be Italian in any clear national sense; its art music, on the other hand, fed an international market"; see Rosselli, *Music and Musicians in Nineteenth-Century Italy* (London: Batsford, 1991), p. 18. Rosselli also remarks of Calabrian folk music that it was "Arab-sounding and largely unrelated to music outside the region" (p. 14).

67. E. Taylor Atkins, *Primitive Selves* (Berkeley: University of California Press, 2010), pp. 151–52. Certainly "Arirang" stands as a symbol of the homeland for diasporic Koreans: see, inter alia, Kim San [Chang Chi-rak] and Nym Wales [Helen Foster Snow], *Song of Ariran* (New York: John Day, 1941), and Kim Tal-su, *Waga Ariran no uta* (Tokyo: Chūō Kōronsha, 1977). On the importance of folk songs for the Korean diaspora, see Kyō Nobuko, *Nore-nosutarugia* (Tokyo: Iwanami Shoten, 2003).

68. See Kim Si-ŏp et al., *Kŭndae ŭi norae wa arirang* (Seoul: Somyŏng, 2009), pp. 340–43, 381–82, 431–34.

69. Atkins, *Primitive Selves,* pp. 131–32. To be sure, Kim So-un, a longtime resident of Japan, created pioneering collections in *Chōsen min'yōshū* (Tokyo: Taibunkan, 1929) and *Chōsen dōyōshū* (Tokyo: Iwanami Shoten, 1933).

70. See, for example, Itō Yoshihide, *Origuchigaku ga yomitoku Kankoku geinō* (Tokyo: Keiō Gijuku Shuppan, 2006), pp. 131–32, and Tosa Masaki, *Kankoku shakai no shūen o mitsumete* (Tokyo: Iwanami Shoten, 2012), chap. 1. In the case of what came to be known as *kugak,* the pioneering musicologist Tanabe Hisao performed an important intervention to continue its instruction in 1921; see Tanabe, *Chūgoku Chōsen ongaku chōsa kikō* (Tokyo: Ongaku no Tomosha, 1970).

71. Yi Yŏng-mi argues that *ch'angga* is the "birth of Korean popular song"; see Yi, *Han'guk taejung kayosa* (Seoul: Signongsa, 1998), p. 31. The ambit of *ch'angga* was wider than that of Japanese *shōka.*

72. See Ko In-suk, *Kindai Chōsen no shōka kyōiku* (Fukuoka: Kyūshū Daigaku Shuppankai, 2004), pp. 16–22.

73. Pak Ch'an-ho, *Kankoku kayōshi* (Tokyo: Shōbunsha, 1987), pp. 119–120. This indispensable volume on Korean popular music is available in Korean as Pak Ch'an-ho, *Han'guk kayosa,* vol. 1 (Seoul: Miji Puksŭ, 2009).

74. The countercolonial connotations of choral songs made them especially popular among leftist intellectuals, an affinity that would continue into the post-Liberation period of *haebang kayo* (liberation songs); see Yamane Toshio, ed., *Karasu yo shikabane o mite nakuna* (Kobe: Chōseisha, 1990), pp. 150–51, 163–87.

75. On the early history of Korean national anthems, see Kim Yŏn-gap, *"Aegukga" chaksaja yŏn'gu* (Seoul: Chipmundang, 1998), pp. 178–85. See also Tonoshita Tatsuya, *Ongaku o dōinseyo* (Tokyo: Seikyūsha, 2008), p. 182. Franz Eckert's composition-the first Korean national anthem-fell into disuse especially after the Japanese annexation of Korea. In any case, its association with the bygone Chosŏn dynasty, not to mention with the same composer as the Japanese national anthem, rendered it problematic for pro-independence Koreans who were at once anti-Japanese and pro-American around this time. As noted earlier, it is not that *kugak* compositions actually employed the European pentatonic scale; rather, when they were written down according to Western musical notation or performed on Western instruments, they were transposed to the pentatonic scale.

76. In any book on music in modern Korea, the influential teacher Eli M. Mowry deserves a footnote. Kim In-sik was one of Mowry's first students; see Ishida, *Modanizumu hensōkyoku,* pp. 350–53.

77. In 1947, the first release by Koryo Records featured An's national anthem on the A side and the older, Scottish version on the B side. See also Nakane Takayuki, *"Chōsen" hyōzō no bunkashi* (Tokyo: Seidosha, 2004), pp. 295–97, 363. On An, see Paek Suk-gi, *An Ik-t'ae* (Seoul: Ungjin Ch'ulp'ansa, 1987). On An and the national anthem, see Kim Kyŏng-nae, *Tonghaemul kwa Paektusan i marŭgo talt'orok* (Seoul: Hyŏnamsa, 1991). Gotō Meisei's novel *Hasamiuchi* (Attacked from both sides), about the end of the Pacific War, depicts the scene in colonial Seoul on 15 August 1945, when ethnic Koreans began singing their national anthem to the tune of "Auld Lang Syne"-a song that, fittingly for Japanese ears, is sung at times of farewell, as on New Year's Eve; see Gotō, *Hasamiuchi* (Tokyo: Kawade Shobō Shinsha, 1973), pp. 136–39.

78. See, e.g., Fumitaka Yamauchi, "Policing the Sounds of Colony," *Musica Humana* 3 (2011), 83–120.

79. Pak, *Kankoku kayōshi*, pp. 39–49. See also Yasuda Hiroshi, *Nikkan shōka no genryū* (Tokyo: Ongaku no Tomosha 1999).

80. On traditional *kagok*, see Coralie Rockwell, *Kagok* (Providence: Asian Music Publications, 1972).

81. For a recent study of Hong's music, see Kim Ch'ang-uk, *Hong Nan-p'a ŭmak yŏn'gu* (Seoul: Minsogwŏn, 2010).

82. See Yi Sang-gŭm, *Sarang ŭi sŏnmul* (Seoul: Hallim Ch'ulp'ansa, 2005). The Japanese precedent is the influential journal *Akai tori,* which began publication in 1918. See Hatanaka Keiichi, *Bungei to shite no dōyō* (Kyoto: Sekai Shisōsha, 1997), pp. 3–4.

83. Han Yong-hŭi, *Han'guk ŭi tongyo* (Seoul: Segang Ŭmak Ch'ulp'ansa, 1994), pp. 66–93.

84. Into the 1980s, elite university students and their elder counterparts, especially women, would show preference for *ch'angga, kagok, tongyo,* and hymns over what they derisively called "mass music" (*taejung ŭmak*). For a representative anecdote, see Takizawa Hideki, *Seoul sanka* (Tokyo: Shūeisha, 1984), pp. 140–42.

85. Hong Nan-p'a was deeply influenced by the Japanese rendition of European art music; see Ko, *Kindai Chōsen no shōka kyōiku*, pp. 230–31. Because Japanese policy made it almost impossible for ethnic Koreans to study abroad except in Japan, the impact of Japanese music education became all the more indelible as the colonial period wore on.

86. It seems most reasonable to say that South Korean popular music emerged in the 1920s, coeval with the very term *yuhaengga*. There is no reason, however, to anoint any one genre, composer, singer, or song as representing the birth of *yuhaengga.* Yi, in *Han'guk taejung kayosa* (pp. 43–56), plausibly suggests the 1925 song "Ch'ŏngnyŏn kyŏnggyega" (Anthem to youth) as the first *yuhaengga* but also rightly points to the historical priority of *yuhaeng ch'angga*. Other writers, such as Hwang Mun-p'yong, have a tendency to go even further back, a common South Korean historiographical quirk that implicitly equates longevity with prestige; see Hwang, *Kayo paengnyŏnsa* (Seoul: Yeŭmsa, 1981). Consider, in this regard, that Jason Toynbee dates the origin of popular music as a genre to the beginnings of

radio broadcasting and to the year 1921, when more than 100 million records were sold in the United States; see Toynbee, *Making Popular Music* (London: Arnold, 2000), p. xix. In the realm of popular music, even chauvinistic Korean nationalists would find it difficult to claim priority for South (or North) Korea over the United States.

87. The word *shingeki* refers to "new theater," or Western-style theater. The genealogy of Japanese popular music is sometimes traced to *hayari uta* (popular songs) of the middle of the nineteenth century, but the establishment of Japanese popular music, in which even twenty-first-century listeners can detect a family resemblance to the popular music of today, occurred around the turn of the twentieth century, especially with the explosive popularity of "Kachūsha no uta," also know as "Fukkatsu shōka" (Kachūsha's song; "Kachūsha" is the Japanese rendering of the familiar form of the Russian name "Ekaterina"). The song was first performed in Tokyo in connection with the production of a play based on Leo Tolstoy's novel *Resurrection;* see Kurata Yoshihiro, *"Hayari uta" no kōkogaku* (Tokyo: Bungei Shunjū, 2001). The song's composer apparently sought to create something between a Japanese folk tune and a German lied; see Komota Nobuo, Shimada Yoshibumi, Yazawa Tamotsu, and Yokozawa Chiaki, *Nihon ryūkōkashi* (Tokyo: Shakai Hyōronsha, 1970), p. 36. The origin of popular song in *shingeki* is interesting, given that *shingeki* was defined, in contradistinction to *kabuki*, as theater without dancing or singing; see Shimomura Masao, *Shingeki* (Tokyo: Iwanami Shoten, 1956), p. 2.

88. Nagamine Shigetoshi, *Ryūkōka no tanjō* (Tokyo: Yoshikawa Kōbunkan, 2010), pp. 45–53.

89. Kim Chin-sŏng, *Seoul e tansŭhol ŭl hŏhara* (Seoul: Hyŏnsul Munhwa Yŏn'gu Yŏn'gusil, 1999), pp. 169–81.

90. Yi Sŏk-hun, "Seoul kugyŏng," *Tonga Ilbo*, 30 March 1932 (the poem was serialized between 29 March and 1 April). The word "pavement" is the English word transposed into *han'gŭl.*

91. An interesting peek into "the modern," including song and dance, can be found in the article "Modŏn sajŏn" (Dictionary of the modern), published in the journal *Sinmin* in September 1930. Kim, *Seoul e tansŭhol ŭl hŏhara,* chap. 4, provides a good overview of *yuhaengga* as part and parcel of the fashionable and the modern in the colonial Seoul of the 1920s.

92. The 1910s in Japan marked the popularity not only of *shingeki* but also of a Western style of opera called the Asakusa Opera, named for the district in Tokyo where it arose; its fans or groupies were known as *peragoia,* presumably a contraction of "operagoer." See Komota et al., *Nihon ryūkōkashi,* pp. 38–39.

93. Song An-jong [Sŏng An-jong], *Zainichi ongaku no 100-nen* (Tokyo: Seidosha, 2009), pp. 78–79.

94. See, for example, Kawamura, *Kisen,* pp. 48–51. For the post–World War II United States, see Frederic Dannen, *Hit Men* (New York: Crown, 1990), and William Knoedelseder, *Stiffed* (New York: HarperCollins, 1993).

95. For an overview, see Chang Yu-jŏng, *Oppa nŭn p'unggakchaengi ya* (Seoul: Minŭm, 2006), pp. 40–59.

96. The 1907 record was released by the US firm Victor. After 1910, however, Japanese businesses replaced French and American ventures and lessened their dependence on French and American technology. Colonial Korea had recording studios but no record-manufacturing plants. See Kishi Toshihiko, "Higashi Ajia ni okeru 'ryūkōka' no sōshutsu," in Wada Haruki et al., eds., *Iwanami kōza Higashi Ajia kingendai tsūshi* (Tokyo: Iwanami Shoten, 2011), pp. 313–36, esp. pp. 314–16. The SP designation-something of an afterthought-came into being to distinguish records that revolved at a speed of seventy-eight revolutions per minute (78 rpm) from the 33 rpm LP (long play) records, or LPs, that were introduced into South Korea in 1958.

97. Kim, *Seoul e tansühol ŭl hŏhara,* pp. 152–55. See also Yongwoo Lee, "Embedded Voices In Between Empires," Ph.D. diss., McGill University, 2010, chap. 2. Here it should be stressed that colonial Korea quickly followed in the footsteps of Japan, with the introduction of Japanese-made phonographs, radio broadcasts, and other infrastructure for the dissemination of popular music; see Kurata Yoshihiro, *Nihon rekōdo bunkashi* (Tokyo: Tokyo Shoseki, 1992), pp. 129–34. Nevertheless, we should not assume that modern technology necessarily transmitted modern music; for example, Japanese radio broadcasts of the 1930s aired a great number of traditional tunes, such as *naniwabushi* (traditional-sounding, often sentimental, narrated songs). See Hyōdō Hiromi, *"Koe" no kokumin kokka* (Tokyo: Nihon Hōsō Shuppan Kyōkai, 2000), pp. 244–46.

98. On the establishment of technological and social infrastructure for popular music in colonial Korea, see Kwŏn To-hŭi, *Han'guk kŭndae ŭmak sahoesa* (Seoul: Minsogwŏn, 2004), pp. 251–57. See also Kishi Toshihiko, "Higashi Ajia ni okeru 'denpa sensō' no shosō," in Kishi Toshihiko, Kawashima Shin, and Son An-sŏk, eds., *Sensō-rajio-kikoku* (Tokyo: Bensei Shuppan, 2006), and Pak Yong-gyu, "Ilcheha radio pangsong ŭi ŭmak p'urogŭraem p'yŏnsŏng kwa suyong," in Han'guk Pangsong Hakhoe, ed., *Han'guk pangsong ŭi sahoemunhwasa* (P'aju: Han'ul, 2011), pp. 90–128. For a pioneering study of radio's impact, see Aladár Alfred Szendrei, *Rundfunk und Musikpflege* (Leipzig: Kistner und Siegel, 1931).

99. Kurata, *Nihon rekōdo bunkashi* (pp. 137–38), suggests that popular participation in singing was coeval with the rise of popular music. To be sure, farmers and workers almost certainly sang on occasion, but the general point is that musical education initiated, and popular music disseminated, the very ubiquity of singing.

100. An instructive case is the highly influential Japanese lyricist Saijō Yaso, whose work spanned Western-style music from children's song (*dōyō*) to the new folk song (*min'yō*) to military music (*gunka*) to *enka* and virtually every other recognizable genre of twentieth-century Japanese popular music, including two megahits of the post-World War II period, "Aoi sanmyaku" and "Ōshō"; see Tsutsui Kiyotada, *Saijō Yaso* (Tokyo: Chūō Kōronsha, 2005). Similarly, Koga Masao, often considered the quintessential *enka* composer, was initially regarded as "Latin," largely because of his use of guitars; see Wajima Yūsuke, *Tsukurareta "Nihon no kokoro" shinwa* (Tokyo: Kōbunsha, 2010), pp. 23–24.

101. The first recording of "Nakhwayusu" was released in 1928; the version sung by Yi Kyŏng-suk was released in 1929 and is available at www.youtube.com

/watch?v=igKznWO24vk. See Ch'oe Ch'ang-ho, *Minjok sunan'gi ŭi taejung kayosa* (Seoul: Irwŏl Sŏgak, 2000), pp. 86–89.

102. Yi Ch'ŏl was the creative force behind Okeh Records, although the company was largely owned by Japanese capital. Corea Record, established in 1935, is probably the first ethnic Korean-owned company; see Yi Chun-hŭi, "Kankoku taishū ongaku ni oyonda Nihon no eikyō," trans. Kukhee Choo, in Tanikawa Tekashi, Ou Kouka, and Go Eibai, eds, *Ekkyōsuru Popyurā karuchā* (Tokyo: Seikyūsha, 2009), pp. 171–98, esp. pp. 175–77. For the tendency to amalgamate distinct genres, see Pak, *Kankoku kayōshi*, pp. 122–25, 135. Consider also the academic tendency to gather these distinct genres under the same conceptual umbrella; see Yi Chung-yŏn, *Sin Taehan'guk tong-nipkun ŭi paengman yonsa ya* (Seoul: Hyean, 1998), pt. 3.

103. Yi, "Kankoku taishū ongaku ni oyonda Nihon no eikyō," p. 178, estimates that of 4,500 songs released in colonial Korea, at least 5 percent were Japanese imports, although the total is likely much higher. We should also not forget the qualitative impact of Japanese imports, such as Fujiyama Ichirō's two megahits, both composed by Koga Masao, "Sake wa namida ka tameiki ka" (1931) and "Kage o shitaite" (1932). Both were recorded by Ch'oe Kyu-yŏp (Hasegawa Ichirō) in Korea in 1932.

104. Hwang Mun-p'yŏng, *Han'guk taejung yŏnyesa* (Seoul: Puruk'anmoro, 1989), p. 207.

105. Koga's *Heimat* (*kokyō*) was colonial Korea, where he grew up; Korea was even more important for Miyashiro Michio, the composer of the aforementioned quintessential "Japanese" song "Haru no umi" (The sea in spring). See Kikuchi Kiyomaro, *Hyōden Koga Masao* (Tokyo: Atene Shobō, 2004), pp. 52–53, 55.

106. Pae Ku-ja, known in Japan as Hai Kameko, may own the dubious distinction of having been the first ethnic Korean star in Japan in the modern period. From 1918 on, she sang and danced in an itinerant performing troupe in Japan; see Song, *Zainichi ongaku no 100-nen*, pp. 42–44. This trend would continue in the post–World War II period, when ethnic Koreans, passing as ethnic Japanese, became some of the greatest singing stars; see John Lie, *Multiethnic Japan* (Cambridge: Harvard University Press, 2001), chap. 3. Ethnic Korean artistic successes ranged widely from dance to film; see Ko U-i, *Kanryū būmu no genryū* (Tokyo: Shakai Hyōronsha, 2012).

107. "Yuranin ŭi norae," his 1930 debut song, was a hit in Japan in 1932 as "Hōrō no uta." Apparently a Japanese producer heard Ch'oe sing Japanese-style *naniwa-bushi* songs and decided to promote him in Japan; see Ishida, *Modanizumu hensōkyoku*, p. 362. Ch'oe became rabidly pro-Japanese and died in North Korea; see Pak, *Kankoku kayōshi*, pp. 149–52.

108. Thus there is a beguiling temptation to write the history of popular music as a chronicle of stars' lives; see, for example, Im Chin-mo, *Uri taejung ŭmak ŭi k'un pyŏldŭl* (Seoul: Min Midŏ, 2004).

109. The recording is available at www.youtube.com/watch?v=lG4LolklcbQ. See O Chae-ho, *Sa ŭi ch'anmi* (Seoul: Myŏngsŏwŏn, 1978); Yu Min-yŏng, *Yun Sim-dŏk* (Seoul: Minsŏngsa, 1987); and Yu Min-yŏng, *Piun ŭi sŏn'guja Yun Sim-dŏk kwa Kim U-jin* (Seoul: Saemunsa, 2009).

110. *Tonga Ilbo,* 5 August 1926, p. 2. See also articles published in *Tonga Ilbo* on 6–9 August, 11 August, and 13–14 August of that year.

111. On Yun's reluctance, see Hwang Mun-p'yŏng, *Ton to myŏngye to sarang to* (Seoul: Musumak, 1994), pp. 15–16.

112. The song is also known as "Hwangsŏng ŭi chŏk." Some commentators trace the birth of trot music to Yi's memorable song, although the term "trot" emerged only in the post-Liberation period; see Yi, *Han'guk taejung kayosa,* p. 59–62. Yi Aerisu's performance is available at www.youtube.com/watch?v=7TbZVQG2kNc. See also Ch'oe, *Minjok,* pp. 69–73.

113. At the time, popular music was sometimes called *makkan kayo* (entr'acte music), and theatrical performances were one of the two major modes by which popular songs were disseminated in the 1920s, the other being musical accompaniment to silent films. A new breed of singers, performing as actresses, slowly shed the disreputable association with lowly entertainers. Theater, like film, needless to say, was a Western import, one that began in 1908 and rapidly became popular in the 1910s and 1920s. To be sure, singers and songs often became more popular than the plays themselves; see Pak, *Kankoku kayōshi,* pp. 152–57.

114. See the discussion of social backgrounds in Pak, *Kankoku kayōshi,* pp. 126, 143–44. Unlike Yun, Yi Aerisu eventually married her lover, gave up her singing career, and died forgotten in 2009.

115. The Japanese genre of *enka* has its origins in Western choral songs and became popular during the early Meiji period among liberal political activists and the urban lower classes; see Soeda Tomomichi, *Enka no Meiji Taishō shi* (Tokyo: Tōsui Shobō, 1982), pp. 6–9. In the late 1970s and 1980s, with the success of South Korean trot singers in Japan, the relationship between Japanese *enka* and Korean trot would become the topic of a major debate; see Okano Ben, *Enka genryū, kō* (Tokyo: Gakugei Shorin, 1988). It is important to recall, however, that *enka* and trot are both diverse genres that changed over time. For arguments on the colonial-period antecedents of the post-Liberation genre of trot, see Yi Un-yong, *Uri taejung ŭmak ilki* (Seoul: Ch'anggongsa, 1996), and Son Min-jŏng, *T'ŭrot'ŭ ŭi chŏngch'ihak* (Seoul: Ŭmak Segye, 2009).

116. Koizumi Fumio argues that because eight beats constitute the usual rhythm of traditional Japanese music, the transition to the modern Western four-beat rhythm was relatively easy; see Koizumi, "Nihon no rizumu," in Geinōshi Kenkyūkai, ed., *Nihon no koten geinō,* vol. 1 (Tokyo: Heibonsha, 1969), pp. 49–50. Koizumi, *Minzoku ongaku no sekai,* also emphasizes the striking difference in rhythm between the traditional music of the Korean peninsula and that of the Japanese archipelago, as Kusano Taeko does with respect to children's songs; see Kusano, *Ariran no uta* (Tokyo: Hakubunsha, 1984), pp. 24–27. In this light, it is interesting that Yun Sim-dŏk sang in four beats in her 1926 song "Sa ŭi ch'anmi."

117. See the interesting recollection by Yi, *Uri,* chap. 9.

118. The term *yonanuki* is based on the early Japanese rendition of the diatonic scale (*do, re, mi,* and so on) as *hi, fu, mi, yo, na, mu.* Rendering that scale pentatonic meant the elimination of *yo* and *na;* hence *yonanuki* ("taking out *yo* and *na*").

Although early Japanese choral songs (*shōka*) were occasionally composed in a major key, most were in a minor key. *Yonanuki* compositions, then, are Westernized, but with a Japanese inflection in the pervasive use of the pentatonic minor.

119. In spite of the popularity of neotraditionalist themes, such as nature and the hometown (*kohyang*), romantic love (*sarang*) was already the most popular theme in *yuhaengga* of the 1930s; see Kim Kwang-hae, Yun Yŏk-t'ak, and Kim Man-su, *Ilche kangjŏmgi taejung kayo yŏn'gu* (Seoul: Pag'ijŏng, 1999), pp. 5, 31. An interesting counterpoint is Mita Munesuke's content analysis of Japanese "fashionable songs," in which "tears" and "dreams" were, respectively, the first and second most popular themes, but "love" emerged in the 1920s as a powerful motif; see Mita, *Kindai Nihon shinjō no rekishi* (Tokyo: Kōdansha, 1978), pp. 47, 80–81.

120. The recording is available at www.youtube.com/watch?v=FT_FsjZvkDQ&feature=related. For an extended narrative account, see O Chae-ho, *Mokp'o ŭi nunmul* (Seoul: Myŏngsŏwŏn, 1978).

121. Pak, *Kankoku kayōshi*, pp. 208, 236–37, 243–45.

122. On *sin minyo*, see Kwon, *Music in Korea*, pp. 127–29. On *kisaeng* singers, see Pak, *Kankoku kayōshi*, pp. 164–67, and Chang, *Oppa nŭn p'unggakchaengi ya*, pp. 130–35.

123. The only trace of Yi's song on the Internet is the image on the record's jacket; see http://nekonote.jp/toko/fal/02.html. Kim's song is available at http://belectricground.com/2011/11/05/beautiful-lyrics-series-kim-jung-gus-tumen-river-soaked-in-tears/. *Shin min'yō* (same Chinese characters) became popular in Japan in the 1920s; see Komota et al., *Nihon ryūkōkashi*, pp. 70–74. The movement was inspired in part by the similar movement in Japan (*shin min'yō undō*) that began in the mid-1920s, led by (among others) the noted poet Kitahara Hakushū; see Pak, *Kankoku kayōshi*, pp. 161–64. The Korean movement was more notable for its popular songs than for its poetic achievements, and Japanese *shin min'yō* generally hewed closer to traditional, rural Japanese music in comparison to its Korean counterparts.

124. Yi So-yŏng, "Ilche kangjŏmgi sin minyo ŭi honjongsŏng yŏn'gu," Ph.D. diss., Han'gukhak Chungang Yŏn'guwŏn, 2007, pp. 287–90. Kim Chi-p'yŏng suggests a more nationalist interpretation and anti-colonial resonance of *sin minyo*; see Kim, *Han'guk kayo chŏngsinsa* (Seoul: Arŭm Ch'ulp'ansa, 2000), pp. 90–91. See also Chang Yu-jŏng, "Sin minyo wa taejung kayo," in Kim Si-ŏp et al., *Kŭndae ŭi norae wa arirang*, pp. 268–88, esp. pp. 287–88, and Hilary Finchum-Sung, "New Folksongs," in Keith Howard, ed., *Korean Pop Music* (Folkestone: Global Oriental, 2006), pp. 10–20, esp. p. 18. Ch'oe Ch'ang-ho's *Minjoksunangi ŭi sin min'yo wa taejung kayodŭl ŭl tŏdŭmŏ* (Pyongyang: Pyŏngyang Ch'ulp'ansa, 1995) comes with a collection of photographs and musical scores. All these works tend to minimize the impact of the preceding revival of and interest in Japanese folk music (*min'yō*) in Japan.

125. The recording is available at http://upload.wikimedia.org/wikipedia/commons/5/54/Park_Hyang-rim_-_Oppaneun_punggakjaeng-i.ogg. See Chang, *Oppa nŭn p'unggakchaengi ya*, pp. 217–21.

126. Chang, *Oppa nŭn p'unggakchaengi ya*, p. 219.

127. Pak, *Kankoku kayōshi*, pp. 157–61. For instructive studies on jazz in pre–World War II China and Japan, see, respectively, Andrew F. Jones, *Yellow Music* (Durham: Duke University Press, 2001), and E. Taylor Atkins, *Blue Nippon* (Durham: Duke University Press, 2001).

128. Compare Kurata, *Nihon rekōdo bunkashi*, pp. 139–40.

129. Chang, *Oppa nŭn p'unggakchaengi ya*, p. 151. As *American Idol* demonstrates, democratic passion still seems to burn brightest when it comes to voting for singers.

130. Pak, *Kankoku kayōshi*, pp. 290–95.

131. Song, *Zainichi ongaku no 100-nen*, pp. 147–49.

132. On censorship, see Pak, *Kankoku kayōshi*, pp. 330–38.

133. Tonoshita, *Ongaku*, pp. 118–24.

134. See Mita, *Kindai Nihon shinjō no rekishi*, pp. 8–9. See also Baba Makoto, *Jūgun kayō imondan* (Tokyo: Hakusuisha, 2012).

135. Curiously, Kim, like any number of other pro-Japanese collaborators, fled to North Korea after the partition; see Pak, *Kankoku kayōshi*, pp. 302–3.

136. North Korea is beyond the ambit of this book, but let me offer a brief conspectus. In the 1950s, North Korea-buoyed by gains from land reform and an initial industrial spurt, which in turn was bolstered by Soviet and Chinese aid-had a relatively dynamic and cosmopolitan culture. The Kim Il-sung regime, notwithstanding its revolutionary rhetoric, pursued a curiously conservative cultural policy. European art music was thriving, given the sponsorship of the Soviet Union. The North Korean authorities westernized traditional Korean instruments and arranged folk tunes to sound more Western. On North Korean music policy, see Han Chŭng-mo and Chŏng Sŏng-mu, *Chuch'e ŭi munye iron yŏn'gu* (Pyongyang: Sahoekwahak Ch'ulp'anbu, 1983), which builds on Kim Il-sung (Kim Il-sŏng), *Hyŏngmyŏngjŏk munhak yesullon* (Tokyo: Miraisha, 1971); see also Song, *Chŭngbo Han'guk ŭmak t'ongsa*, pp. 861–71. Official music veered between socialist-realist anthems (a revised form of *ch'angga*) and modernized folk songs. We can often hear the distinct influence of Soviet martial music in North Korean *ch'angga*, as in the 1946 composition "Kim Il-sŏng changgun ŭi norae" (Song of General Kim Il-sung), available at www.youtube.com/watch?v = pwE10Uo_kgs. Apart from preventing the penetration of reactionary and decadent music from the United States, the authorities allowed a considerable amount of foreign popular music, especially Russian and Soviet tunes, to be aired in urban areas; see Wada Haruki, *Kita Chōsen* (Tokyo: Iwanami Shoten, 1998), pp. 137–40. In addition, *yuhaengga* persisted as numerous colonial-era popular musicians ended up in North Korea (I have already mentioned Kim Yŏng-gil and Kim Hae-song). A few prospered, some were purged, and others disappeared; on the fate of Kim Yŏng-gil (Nagata Genjirō), the eminent opera singer, see Kita Yoshihiro, *Kita Chōsen ni kieta utagoe* (Tokyo: Shinchōsha, 2011). From the second half of Kim Il-sung's regime to the reign of his heir, Kim Jong-il, popular music was trapped in the 1960s by North Korea's isolationist tendency and was a mixture of patriotic socialist-nationalist tunes, traditional and contemporary folk songs, and postcolo-

nial permutations of colonial-era Japanese and South Korean songs. Particularly when the South Korean government would proscribe a song, such as Kim Min-gi's "Ach'im isŭl," it gained official approbation; see Takaki Kei, "'Chittommo poppu de nai Kita Chōsen poppu' hihan," in Bessatsu Takarajima Henshūbu, ed., *Ketteiban! Kita Chōsen wārudo* (Tokyo: Takarajimasha, 2004), pp. 155–67, esp. pp. 161–63. At the time of Kim Jong-il's death, there was very little music-classical or popular, Korean or Western-that was even remotely appealing to people outside that involuted country. Most striking was the government's regimentation of performing organizations (and its proscription against nongovernmental groups); see Kwon, *Music in Korea*, pp. 158–68. Even so, musical creativity was not completely suppressed; "Rimjingang" (Imjin River), a contemporary folk song, was a hit in Japan in the late 1960s. According to the Japanese rock musician Fankī (Funky) Sueyoshi, who was teaching rock music in Pyongyang in the early 2010s, North Korea remains more than the sum of its governmental propaganda and its Western caricatures; see his *Pyonyan 6-gatsu 9-nichi kōtō chūgakkō-keiongakubu* (Tokyo: Shūeisha, 2012). See also Sonia Ryang, *Reading North Korea* (Cambridge: Harvard University Asia Center, 2012), pp. 207–10.

137. The best source on Yi Nan-yŏng is Chŏng T'ae-yŏng, *Pak Hwa-sŏng kwa Yi Nan-yŏng* (Mokp'o: Nyusŭ T'udei, 2009). See also Roald Maliangkay, "Koreans Performing for Foreign Troops," *East Asian History* 37 (2011), 59–72, esp. pp. 66–67.

138. On K.P.K., see Pak, *Han'guk kayosa*, vol. 2 (Seoul: Miji Puksŭ, 2009), pp. 23–26, and Maliangkay, "Koreans Performing for Foreign Troops," pp. 66–68.

139. See the fascinating oral-history interview with the eldest of the Kim Sisters, available at www.library.unlv.edu/oral_histories/pdf%20files/kim_sisters.pdf. For the number of the Kim Sisters' appearances on *The Ed Sullivan Show*, see www .edsullivan.com/most-frequent-ed-sullivan-show-guests.

140. The contrast with Japan, as noted earlier, is instructive. For many Japanese people, bourgeois respectability entailed lessons in koto and other Japanese instruments well into the post-World War II period. Exceptions exist, but few elite Koreans promoted traditional music over European music in the post-Liberation period.

141. On Isang Yun, see Jeongmee Kim, "The Diasporic Composer: The Fusion of Korean and German Musical Culture in the Works of Isang Yun," Ph.D. diss., University of California, Los Angeles, 1999.

142. See John Lie, *Han Unbound* (Stanford: Stanford University Press, 1998), chap. 2, on the destruction of *yangban* dominance in South Korea.

143. The rejection of Japanese cultural imports appears to have been the outcome of informal practices rather than the result of an official edict. It was not so much that a ban was explicitly articulated as that the cultural restrictions imposed by colonial rule were lifted.

144. On sexual entertainment, see Lie, "The Transformation of Sexual Work in 20th-Century Korea," and Katharine H.S. Moon, *Sex Among Allies* (New York: Columbia University Press, 1997). To be sure, American GIs often craved the "real thing," whether in sexual partners or musical performers; see Sherrie Tucker, *Swing Shift* (Durham: Duke University Press, 2000), p. 229.

145. See Sŏn Sŏng-wŏn, *P'alkun sho esŏ raep kkaji* (Seoul: Arŭm Ch'ulp'ansa, 1993), p. 25.

146. See, for example, Kyō Nobuko, *Nikkan ongaku nōto* (Tokyo: Iwanami Shoten, 1998), p. 153. If we were to add all the income derived from GI-related entertainment, including sex work, there is little doubt that total income from the camp towns would have easily exceeded the official revenue figures for South Korean exports in the 1950s and possibly even in the 1960s.

147. Chŏng Sun-il and Chang Han-sŏng, *Han'guk TV 40-nyŏn ŭi paljachwi* (Seoul: Hanul, 2000), pp. 314–15. Televised South Korean music shows often mimicked their Japanese counterparts, but the quintessential Japanese music program *Lotte uta no arubamu,* which began airing in 1958, not only emulated American musical variety shows but was also sponsored by a Zainichi-owned business corporation.

148. For an overview, see Sin Hyŏn-jun, Yi Yong-u, and Ch'oe Chi-sŏn, *Han'guk p'ap ŭi kogohak 1960* (Seoul: Han'gil'at'ŭ, 2005), chap. 1.

149. See, for example, Pak Sŏng-sŏ, *Han'guk Chŏnjaeng kwa taejung kayo, kirok kwa chŭngŏn* (Seoul: Ch'aek i innŭn P'unggyŏng, 2010), pp. 42, 58–59, 67.

150. Song, *Zainichi ongaku no 100-nen,* pp. 168–70. The South Korean involvement in Vietnam was profound. To take only the most obvious consequence, the dynamism of South Korean exports owed a great deal to US demand generated by the Vietnam War; see Lie, *Han Unbound,* pp. 62–67.

151. Ordinary South Koreans were banned from entering US military bases and their facilities. Most citizens could only gaze from afar at a material cornucopia that recalls those shops in the former Soviet satellites whose goods were reserved for foreigners (which is to say that these goods were off limits to people who did not have "hard" currency to spend). Coca-Cola, and chocolate in the form of Hershey bars-both emblems of otherworldly sweetness-were occasionally handed out to local youths and became objects of indescribable desire, as did more savory fare, such as the canned sausages, wieners, and Spam that became primary ingredients of *pudae chigye* (troop stew), that iconic dish of South Koreans exemplifying US military influence.

152. Yi, "Kankoku taishū ongaku ni oyonda Nihon no eikyō," pp. 186–88.

153. See, for example, Han Yong-hŭi, *Han'guk ŭi tongyo* (Seoul: Segang Ŭmak Ch'ulp'ansa, 1994), pp. 124–38. Consider such luminaries as Pak Hwa-mok, Kim Sun-ae, and Kim Yo-sŏp, who vitalized the genre in the post-Liberation decades.

154. The aural is a stubbornly conservative faculty. What does not register as music by the time a person reaches adulthood is often dismissed as bad music if not as mere noise. One reason why colonial-period Koreans belted their national anthem to the tune of "Auld Lang Syne," or why postcolonial South Koreans embraced jazz and blues, may stem from the kinship of Scottish folk songs, black American music genres, and the traditional Korean soundscape with the Western pentatonic scale. In this regard, the widespread use of the blue note in jazz and blues offers another convergence between African American and Korean styles of singing. The pentatonic scale is prevalent not just in Asia but also in western Africa, whose diaspora,

of course, includes African Americans. For a suggestive early statement of this issue, see Curt Sachs, *The Rise of Music in the Ancient World* (New York: Norton, 1943), pp. 92–95. See also M. L. West, *Ancient Greek Music* (Oxford: Clarendon Press, 1992), pp. 388–90. Whether because of the similar soundscape, the preponderance of African American GIs in post-Liberation South Korea, or the sheer influence of African Americans in US popular music, African American-inflected music, from jazz to soul to hip-hop, has long had a wide and appreciative audience in South Korea. On the popularity of soul music in South Korea in the 1970s, see Sin Hyŏn-jun, Yi Yong-u, and Ch'oe Chi-sŏn, *Han'guk p'ap ŭi kogohak 1970* (P'aju: Han'gil At'ŭ, 2005), pp. 52–57.

155. Yamane Toshirō's chronology corrects many errors and is probably the most reliable outline of South Korean popular songs from 1945 to 1949; see www.ksyc.jp /mukuge/257/yamane.pdf.

156. See, in general, Pak, *Han'guk kayosa*, vol. 2. See also Sŏn Sŏng-won, *Uri taejung kayo* (Seoul: Hyŏnamsa, 2008), pp. 63–66.

157. The suggestive comparative case is Japan. See Yasuda Tsuneo, "Amerikanizēshon no hikari to kage," in Nakamura Masanori et al., eds., *Sengo Nihon senryō to sengo kaikaku,* vol. 3 (Tokyo: Iwanami Shoten, 1995), pp. 251–85. On popular music in particular, see Tōya Mamoru, *Shinchūgun kurabu kara kayōkyoku e* (Tokyo: Misuzu Shobō, 2005); especially interesting is the fate of those who were military musicians before 1945, who would end up performing for their erstwhile enemies after 1945 (pp. 30–33) and would then proceed to have a significant impact on the evolution of Japanese popular music.

158. Yi, *Han'guk taejung kayosa*, pp. 118–33.

159. See Kishi Toshihiko, *Higashi Ajia ryūkōka awā* (Tokyo: Iwanami Shoten, 2013), pp. 210–12. See also Aoki Shin, *Meguriaumonotachi no gunzō* (Tokyo: Ōtsuki Shoten, 2013).

160. Pak, *Han'guk Chŏnjaeng kwa taejung kayo,* pp. 122–31. The song's popularity can be inferred from the proliferation of covers, including those by the noted French singer Yvette Giraud and the Japanese "jazz" singer Hamamura Michiko. It is also interesting to note the variations in the spelling of the title, especially the first two words. South Korean orthography was far from being well established in the early 1960s.

161. See, for example, Takizawa, *Seoul sanka,* pp. 145–47.

162. Chŏn, *Kinjirareta uta,* pp. 156–60. Not only was popular music considered to be of ephemeral interest, South Koreans in the post-Korean War period also tended to eschew hoarding and collecting, in anticipation of another war. Probably the most important reason for the disappearance of Han's record was the introduction, in 1958, of the 33 rpm LP, which rendered Han's original 78 rpm SP recording obsolete.

163. The film was based on Chŏng Pi-sŏk's wildly popular serialized novel *Chayu puin* (Seoul: Chongumsa, 1954). The tragedy of the Korean War and the turbulence of the post-Korean War years found sensational expression in the form of a liberated, and ultimately fallen, woman.

164. The contrast with Japan is interesting: female *enka* singers often wear kimonos, even today in the 2010s, but their South Korean counterparts rarely appear in *hanbok*. In both countries, male singers mostly wear Western-style suits. To be sure, there is considerable variation, and there are distinct trends. On *enka,* see Christine R. Yano, *Tears of Longing* (Cambridge: Harvard University Asia Center), 2002.

165. See, for example, Song, *Zainichi ongaku no 100-nen,* pp. 168–70. Son Mog-in, who composed "Mokp'o ŭi nunmul," grew up singing Christian hymns and majored in piano at the Tokyo Imperial University of Music; see Chŏn, *Kinjirareta uta,* pp. 136–37.

166. The film *Sŏp'yŏnje,* mentioned earlier, depicts the fate of a family of *p'ansori* performers. Particularly poignant is the scene in which Westernized circuslike musicians-*t'in tomaesang,* the modern permutation of *kwangdae*-outplay (at least in volume) and outdraw the *p'ansori* performance. Interestingly, *t'in tomaesang* became a ubiquitous urban presence in post-World War II Japan as *chindonya,* and many of the performers were said to be ethnic Koreans or Burakumin (descendants of traditional outcasts).

167. An SP disc had a capacity of perhaps four minutes and thirty seconds. Although LPs did not officially appear in South Korea until 1958, in Japan they had been introduced as early as 1951.

168. On Yi Mi-ja, see her autobiography, *Insaeng* (Seoul: Hwanggŭm, 1999).

169. Kyō, *Nikkan,* p. 134.

170. There is a similar and oft-repeated claim in Japan that *enka* supposedly captured the Japanese soul, at least among a significant segment of the population in the post-World War II decades. Yet this claim contradicts the long-standing denigration of the genre; see Wajima, *Tsukurareta "Nihon no kokoro" shinwa,* pp. 11–13. Similarly, it was the heirs of *yangban* culture-intellectuals and other purported leaders of the South Korean nation-who dismissed trot music in the post-Liberation period.

171. Chon, *Kinjirareta uta,* pp. 52–59.

172. Yi, "Kankoku taishū ongaku ni oyonda Nihon no eikyō," pp. 192–93.

173. The long legacy of colonial rule affected the tastes and mind-sets of postcolonial leaders. Although Kim Il-sung became known for his *chuch'e* ideology of national autonomy and autarchy, Park Chung-hee's early political expression did not deviate from his adversary's line; see Lie, *Han Unbound,* pp. 81–82. A Japanese journalist (and eminent Korea hand) told me that both Kim and Park loved the Japanese film series *Tora-san,* directed by Yamada Yōji. On Park's indulgence in women as well as in song (Japanese *enka,* although some of the songs were performed in Japan by Zainichi singers), see Im Sang-su's 2006 film *Kuttae kusaramdŭl* ("The president's last bang"). Park was a fan of the South Korean singer Sim Subong, who sang the Zainichi singer Miyako Harumi's song for him before he was killed. Although Sim, who was present at the assassination, has denied that Park even liked *enka,* it remains unclear why she, a college student at the time, would have chosen to perform a song whose appeal was presumably limited to older men. Whatever Park's personal tastes, collective awareness of the impact that Japanese culture

had on him seems to have disappeared from South Korea, along with the ubiquitous practice of uttering Japanese phrases (also portrayed in Im's period-sensitive movie). Cho Kap-che's *Yugo!* (Seoul: Han'gilsa, 1987) is insightful with respect to Park's background, including his three wives.

174. Nakamura Tomoko, "Kankoku ni okeru Nihon taishūbunka tōsei ni tsuite no hōteki kōsatsu," *Ritsumeikan Kokusai Chiiki Kenkyū* 22 (2004), 259–76. Jinsoo An discusses the problem of *waesaek* in South Korean films of the 1960s in "The Ambivalence of the Nationalist Struggle in Deterritorialized Space," *China Review* 10 (2010), 37–61, esp. pp. 45–47. The Rhee regime also sought to eliminate "Japanese" influences in popular music, most notably in 1956 by initiating movements (*undong*) to promote "healthy" music (*kŏnjŏn kayo*) and extirpate *waesaek* music. Like many of the flailing regime's other efforts, these two movements achieved little.

175. It is probably no accident that many of the *enka* singers best known for *kobushi* and *unari* (wailing), such as the extraordinary vocalist Miyako Harumi, were ethnic Koreans; see the 1966 video at www.youtube.com/watch?v=ZKAnwCjFANs. The southern school of *p'ansori* performance stressed melismatic, emotive singing, and so it makes sense that most diasporic Koreans in Japan, who hailed from the southern part of the Korean peninsula, had an *enka* singing style that was typically melismatic and emotional.

176. The association of Yi Mi-ja and *han* was widely acknowledged; see the article on her fortieth-anniversary concert in *Han'guk Ilbo,* 10 September 1999.

177. For example, compare the singing styles of Yi Nan-yŏng and Yi Mi-ja in "Mokp'o ŭi nunmul" (Tears of Mokp'o). The original Yi Nan-yŏng recording is available at www.youtube.com/watch?v=1bIl-LFofBs, and Yi Mi-ja's cover is available at www.youtube.com/watch?v=VFK10_4IcjM. Contrast Yi Nan-yŏng singing an American-style song in 1963 at www.youtube.com/watch?v=OZ7YfZtdbjM.

178. Chon, *Kinjirareta uta,* p. 132.

179. Kyō, *Nikkan ongaku nōto,* p. 138; Chon, *Kinjirareta uta,* p. 130.

180. Kyō, *Nikkan ongaku nōto,* p. 135.

181. John Lie, *Zainichi (Koreans in Japan)* (Berkeley: University of California Press, 2008), pp. 129–39, 147–48.

182. Pak, *Kankoku kayōshi,* pp. 247–48. The South Korean government banned many of Chang's songs in the early 1970s, a move that prompted her to emigrate to the United States. She performed for the last time at a "retirement" concert in Los Angeles in 1978 and died in that city.

183. The Korean version had appeared in 1975 and became a stupendous hit, establishing Cho's reputation in South Korea.

184. Lie, *Multiethnic Japan,* pp. 58–67.

185. Son Mog-in's autobiographical account is illuminating; for his discussion of the Kasuba song, see Son, *Mot ta purŭn t'ahyang sari* (Seoul: HOTWIND, 1992), esp. pp. 104–7.

186. The original 1955 version, by Eto Kunieda, attracted hardly any attention at all in Japan (see "Hayasugita ryūkōka," *Asahi Shimbun,* 9 April 2010), although more than twenty years later the setting of the song-the Algerian struggle for

independence-may have had special relevance to Japanese listeners, who largely opposed the US military's involvement in Vietnam; the situation in anticommunist South Korea was of course radically different.

187. The long *o* in Japanese rendered it *kayō,* but both Koreans and Japanese used the same two Chinese characters.

188. Sǒn, *Uri taejung kayo,* pp. 124–27.

189. In colonial Korea, *yuhaengga* spread not only geographically but also across the social hierarchy from its initial base among urbanites. Yet its dissemination was limited by technological factors: few rural households owned phonographs, radio broadcasting was limited, and nationwide tours were largely limited to cities. By the 1960s, more people owned record players and radios; however, the decisive technological shift was the spread of television in the 1970s. Furthermore, the elite derision of trot music and melodramatic cinema remained powerful enough to sustain social and cultural hierarchy and segmentation in South Korea.

190. Chǒng and Chang, *Han'guk TV 40-nyǒn ǔi paljachwi,* p. 119.

191. Song, *Zainichi ongaku no 100-nen,* p. 186.

192. In South Korea, by contrast with the situation in the United States-and even with the situation in Japan, where a substantial period elapsed between the widespread dissemination of radio and that of television-the late appearance of radio blunted that medium's role in shaping tastes in popular music. Nevertheless, radio station AFKN was a crucial player in the airing of American popular music. See Lee, "Embedded Voices," chap. 5. Not only was AFKN on the air almost continuously, the vast majority of its programs broadcast American popular music.

193. See Kim Yǒng-ch'an, "1970-nyǒndae t'ellebijǒn oehwasirijǔ suyong ǔi munhwajǒk ǔimi," in Han'guk Pangsong Hakhoe, *Han'guk pangsong ǔi sahoemunhwasa,* pp. 333–72, esp. pp. 356–58.

194. In the late 1980s, Yi Paksa (Epaksa) would accelerate the tempo to the point where this type of music was called *ppongtchak disco.*

195. See the brief overview in Yi Hye-suk and Son U-sǒk, *Han'guk taejung ǔmaksa* (Seoul: Rijǔ aen Puk, 2003), pp. 92–119.

196. It is important to emphasize that television broadcasting began only in 1961, and that well under 5 percent of South Korean households, mainly in major cities, owned television sets at that time.

197. There was something distinctive about South Korean teahouses and watering holes, characterized by dark interior hues and low, plush seating as well as by scandalously loud conversations among irreparably inebriated men. It was also difficult to escape the whiff of sex work. Alcohol consumption was strictly functional: I recall trying to order a martini, shaken or stirred, at a high-end bar in the late 1970s and having to explain how it might be concocted.

198. See Pak, *Han'guk kayosa,* vol.2, pt. 6.

199. Ishida Ayumi's 1968 hit "Blue Light Yokohama" was widely aired in South Korean cities in the early 1970s. The song gained attention outside Northeast Asia after it was featured in Kore-eda Hirokazu's 2008 film *Aruitemo, aruitemo* (Still walking), and it found new listeners when it was covered by Yuki Saori in her 2011

collaboration with Pink Martini. For background on the song, see Kō Mamoru, *Kayōkyoku* (Tokyo: Iwanami Shoten, 2011), pp. 67–71. Similarly, Itsuwa Ayumi's 1980 folk song "Koibito yo" (Lover) was played again and again, relentlessly, in many Seoul coffee shops in the 1980s. See Chon, *Kinjirareta uta,* pp. 162–73, 232–35.

200. Song, *Zainichi ongaku no 100-nen,* pp. 179–85.

201. Ibid., pp. 131–44.

202. See the video at www.youtube.com/watch?v=zclXIyAwIVY.

203. Reported, for example, on the *KBS World* website at http://world.kbs .co.kr/french/program/program_artist_detail.htm?No=106307#sel_lang_open. In fact, Yun Pok-hŭi often wore miniskirts. In the mid-1990s, the image in the photograph would be used by the department store Shinsegae in conjunction with an advertising campaign.

204. See Sin, Yi, and Ch'oe, *Han'guk p'ap ŭi kogohak 1960,* pp. 115–22, and Pil Ho Kim and Hyunjoon Shin, "The Birth of 'Rok,'" *positions* 18 (2010), 199–230.

205. See his autobiographical reflections in Sin Chung-hyŏn, *Nae kit'a nŭn chamdŭlji annŭnda* (Seoul: Haet'o, 2006).

206. See, for example, Sin, Yi, and Ch'oe, *Han'guk p'ap ŭi kogohak 1960,* pp. 216–20, 230. The Pearl Sisters bore an uncanny resemblance to the extremely popular Peanuts (Za Pīnattsu), singing twins who debuted in Japan in 1959.

207. From the standpoint of the early 2010s, with hardly a block in Seoul lacking a Starbucks or a Caffe Bene (the ubiquitous South Korean coffee chain), it is difficult to conjure up a time when coffee was a truly exotic American drink. See, in this regard, Jee Eun Song, "Building an Empire One Cup at a Time," Ph.D. diss., University of California, Davis, 2012.

208. Reported in Kan Myonsoku, "Mega hanasenai kanojotachi," *Asiana,* May 2012, pp. 86–88, esp. p. 86. The paranoid fantasy relating the external threat of North Korea to the internal danger of rock music finds no better exemplar. I first heard of this rumor in the early 1970s from someone who claimed firsthand knowledge of this overreach by the Korean Central Intelligence Agency (KCIA). Although the story smacks of urban legend, history should not cleanse the deeper reality it signifies-that of a paranoid-obsessive intelligence agency.

209. Sin, Yi, and Ch'oe, *Han'guk p'ap ŭi kogohak 1960,* pp. 123, 264.

210. For an interesting backward glance, see the 2008 film *Kogo 70* (Go-go 70s), featuring the rock band Tebŭlsŭ (Devils), which made its reputation playing in camp towns and released its first album in 1971.

211. On the political suppression of rock and popular music in the mid-1970s, see Yi and Son, *Han'guk taejung ŭmaksa,* pp. 82–91, and Sin, Yi, and Ch'oe, *Han'guk p'ap ŭi kogohak 1970,* pp. 185–215.

212. The culture of rock included not only rock music but also associated hairstyles (long) and clothing (jeans) as well as sex and drugs; see, for example, Ronald Fraser, ed., *1968* (New York: Pantheon, 1988), pp. 77–89. Yet the centrality of music, and rock music in particular, to the contemporary experience of the 1960s is something of an indisputable truth. According to John Adams, "more than any other social phenomenon of a socially phenomenal era, rock music was the fulcrum of

culture. Young people communicated to each other through the medium of its lyrics"; see Adams, *Hallelujah Junction* (New York: Farrar, Straus and Giroux, 2000), p. 40. Or, as Jenny Diski recalls of the 1960s, "In truth, the only thing that is absolutely certain is that the music then was better"; see Diski, *The Sixties* (New York: Picador, 2009), p. 3. The trend in South Korea stands in stark contrast to the general trend elsewhere of shifting from folk to rock music as the student movement escalated in the 1960s and 1970s; see David Caute, *The Year of the Barricades* (New York: Harper & Row, 1988), pp. 51–59. In this sense, the 1960s never happened in South Korea.

213. It is curious that radio broadcasting never became as popular in South Korea as it was in the United States, Japan, and elsewhere. A partial explanation is that the diffusion of radio occurred only shortly before that of television. In other words, the technologically advanced medium of television superseded radio before the latter could become an established mass medium. It would be remiss, however, to ignore radio's role in disseminating nonmainstream music, principally via AFKN radio broadcast.

214. The relatively low level of dissemination of radio and television in South Korea until the 1970s stunted the prospering of youth-oriented popular music; for a brief overview, see Kim, *Han'guk kayo chŏngsinsa,* pp. 114–17. What is more significant, the 1960s in South Korea were the era of the *yuk-sam* ("6–3") generation, named for and denoting those who were active in the struggle against the Normalization Treaty with Japan (the first major demonstration against the treaty took place on 3 June 1964); see Lie, *Han Unbound,* p. 59. But the 1960s were also steeped in the culture of sincerity and seriousness. Political radicalism (or at least anti-government politics) and a measure of cultural liberalism could be found in the so-called 386 generation, a reverse-chronological label denoting those who were born in the 1960s (6), came of age in the 1980s (8), and were in their thirties (3) in the 1990s (as far as I can tell, the term "386 generation" became widely current around 1999, more than a decade after the climax of the pro-democracy struggles of 1987 and 1988).

215. Yi and Son, *Han'guk taejung ŭmaksa,* pp. 19–20, begin their history of mass music with folk music. See also Pak, *Han'guk kayosa,* vol.2, pp. 542–65.

216. "Achi'm isŭl" would become something of a resistance anthem, reaching its apotheosis at the height of the anti-government, pro-democracy movement in 1987, when a million demonstrators reportedly sang it in chorus at the City Hall Plaza; see Chŏn, *Kinjirareta uta,* pp. 174–75. Not surprisingly, the North Korean regime embraced the song, and it became a standard of sorts. See the bizarre music video at www.youtube.com/watch?v=r5ekfvAmP9I&feature=related.

217. The recording, with an English translation, is available at www.youtube .com/watch?v=VwXBHPGrlKo.

218. As noted, the similarity extended to the shared predilection of Park Chung-hee and Kim Il-sung for the products of Japanese popular culture.

219. As we have seen, both the Japanese colonial government and the Rhee regime sought to promote "healthy" music.

220. Sŏn, *Uri taejung kayo,* pp. 196–98.

221. Roald Maliangkay, "Pop for Progress," in Howard, *Korean Pop Music,* pp. 48–61, esp. pp. 53–55.

222. See Cho Yonpiru [Cho Yong-p'il], *Fuzankō e kaere* (Tokyo: Sanshūsha, 1984).

223. See the performance, with Ch'oe/Yoshiya playing the clarinet, at www.youtube.com/watch?v=wA_Z-CH2NSQ.

224. Song, *Zainichi ongaku no 100-nen,* pp. 192–97.

225. In her early professional performances of the late 1970s, Hye at times displayed a remarkable resemblance to the contemporaneous Japanese superstar Yamaguchi Momoe. Hye was a bundle of contradictions; see, for example, her transvestite performance, available at www.youtube.com/watch?v=6st-rVVUBeI.

226. On the Fifth Republic, see Lie, *Han Unbound,* pp. 120–24.

227. Classical music appeared to be above the fray, but in fact that was far from being the case. Isang Yun, a committed political progressive, had lived in West Germany since 1959. Suspected of being a North Korean operative-he had visited North Korea in 1963-Yun was abducted by South Korean agents in West Berlin in 1967. After an international petition campaign, he was eventually released and settled in Germany. Although he never visited South Korea again, he sought to promote classical music in North Korea. See his interesting reflections in conversation with Luise Rinser, *Der verwundete Drache* (Frankfurt: Fischer, 1977).

228. Asakura Kyōji, "Chō Yonpiru," in Satō Kunio, ed., *Kankoku kayō taizen* (Tokyo: Sōfūkan, 1985), pp. 6–14, esp. p. 13.

229. On music shows of the 1980s, see Kim Sŏl-a, "1980-nyŏndae t'ellebijŏn orak p'urogŭraem ŭi palchŏn kwa munhwajŏk yŏnghyang," in Han'guk Pangsong Hakhoe, *Han'guk pangsong ŭi sahoemunhwasa,* pp. 411–66, esp. pp. 433–35, 441–43.

230. See Chang Nam Kim, *K-POP* (Seoul: Hollym International, 2012), pp. 60–64.

231. See Sin, Yi, and Ch'oe, *Han'guk p'ap ŭi kogohak 1970,* pp. 100–105, and Okson Hwang, "The Ascent and Politicization of Pop Music in Korea," in Howard, *Korean Pop Music,* pp. 3–47, esp. pp. 43–44.

232. "Kankoku no minshū kayō," in Henshū Kaigi, ed., *Uta yo, habatake!* (Tokyo: Tsuge Shobō Shinsha, 2005).

233. Sim Su-bong, who counted Park Chung-hee among her fans and was present at his assassination, won the 1978 contest with "Kuttae kusaram" (Then, that person).

234. See the original broadcast at www.youtube.com/watch?v=nK8EnxOSfxo.

235. See Craig Marks and Rob Tannenbaum, *I Want My MTV* (New York: Plume, 2011), pp. 143–58.

236. See Michael Jackson's original 1982 music video at www.youtube.com /watch?v=Zi_XLOBDo_Y. Some three decades later, what is most remarkable is how closely it hews to the prevailing convention of music videos in presenting a more or less sustained narrative; the dancing begins only at 1:52. On the impact of Michael Jackson and Madonna, among others, and the birth of dance pop on South Korea, see Yi and Son, *Han'guk taejung ŭmaksa,* pp. 191–211.

237. Kan, "Mega hanasenai kanojotachi," p. 87.

238. Later reports suggest that Kim was thoroughly molded and exploited. See, for example, Hangyŏre Nyusŭ at www.hani.co.kr/arti/culture/music/192788.html, and the South Korean Wikipedia article on her at http://ko.wikipedia.org/wiki/% EA%B9%80%EC%99%84%EC%84%A0.

239. For an overview, see Yi Tong-yŏn, *Aidŭl* (Seoul: Imaejin, 2011).

240. Some observers would insist on the continuity before and after Sŏ T'ae-ji wa Aidŭl; for example, Kwon, *Music in Korea,* stresses "cultural continuity" (pp. 168–71). Indeed, most songs from the first album were very much in concert with mainstream South Korean popular music of the early 1990s. However, the impact of the group's debut song is undeniable and it ushered in a new soundscape. On the group, see Kang Myŏng-sŏk, *Sŏ T'ae-ji rŭl ilgŭmyŏn munhwa ka poinda?!* (Seoul: Hansol Midiŏ, 1995).

241. See the original MBC broadcast, the group's first exposure to a national audience, at www.youtube.com/watch?v=EC7ySokpHWM.

242. It would not have been possible to directly compare the musical tastes of fans in the United States and fans in South Korea with respect to the early 1980s, because the age-related demographics of popular music were not the same in the two countries. But even if it had been possible in the early 1980s to ask only younger South Koreans about their musical tastes, they probably would have anointed Yi Sŏn-hŭi or Yi Mun-se, not anyone who sounded like Michael Jackson or Madonna.

243. Yi Tong-yŏn, *Sŏ T'ae-ji nŭn uriege muŏtsiŏtna* (Seoul: Munhwa Kwahaksa, 1999), pp. 48–51.

244. In Furuya Masayuki, *K Generation* (Tokyo: DHC, 2005), p. 16.

245. Given the absorption of American developments into Japanese popular music, it is slightly misleading to say that Japan had disappeared from the life of South Korean music. In fact, as I elaborate later in this chapter and in chapter 2, J-pop was a formative influence on K-pop.

246. Break dancing became a distinct style in the late 1970s and is usually understood to have descended from James Brown's "Get on the Good Foot," a track from his 1972 album of the same name. Break dancing actually entered South Korea in the 1980s, though often as a showpiece.

247. Diasporic returns may have denoted a form of homecoming for some Korean Americans, but a surprising number worked in South Korea because of blocked opportunities in the United States. Whatever the reasons, few, if any, Koreans Americans found success in U.S. popular music until very recently. See, in this regard, Nancy Abelmann and John Lie, *Blue Dreams* (Cambridge: Harvard University Press, 1995), pp.167–69.

248. Lee Soo-man of SM Entertainment sought a South Korean performer who could replicate Bobby Brown's "Every Little Step" (1988), and in particular the Roger Rabbit dance steps. He reportedly spotted Hyŏn at the It'aewŏn club Moon Night. See Hyŏn's performance at www.dailymotion.com/video/xsxgrd_hyun-jin-young-sad-mannequin_shortfilms#.UU4rVRxJN8E.

249. Furuya, *K Generation,* pp. 96–99.

250. See Yi Yŏn et al., *Ilbon taejung munhwa pekkigi* (Seoul: Namu wa Sup, 1998), and Eun-Young Jung, "Transnational Cultural Traffic in Northeast Asia," Ph.D. diss., University of Pittsburgh, 2007.

251. On Kim, see Craig Harris, "Kim Soo-chul," at www.allmusic.com/artist /kim-soo-chul-mn0001367463. Yi Sang-ŭn had been a popular singer in the late 1980s but disappeared for a while after a plagiarism scandal in 1989; see Jung, "Transnational Cultural Traffic," pp. 116–18.

252. On the origin of punk music in South Korea, see Stephen Epstein, "We Are the Punx," in Howard, *Korean Pop Music,* pp. 190–207, esp. p. 191.

253. Furuya, *K Generation,* p. 4.

254. See the video at www.youtube.com/watch?v=dqRv2Md6Slg.

255. The hoopla is well captured in the television drama series *Ŭmtaphara 1997* (2012). See also Sakai Mieko, *K-POP bakku stēji episōdo* (Tokyo: Kawade Shobō Shinsha, 2011), pp. 88–93.

256. See T'ae Chin-a's "Tongbanja" (Companion), available at www.youtube .com/watch?v=3ti_VSfxoyM, or Chang Yun-jŏng's "Saranga" (Love), available at www.youtube.com/watch?v=NbYoFJaMtzk. Morton Feldman is cited in Alex Ross, "American Sublime," *New Yorker,* 19 June 2006, available at www.newyorker .com/archive/2006/06/19/060619crat_atlarge.

INTERLUDE

1. In Mira Nair's 2007 film *The Namesake,* her rendition of Jhumpa Lahiri's 2003 novel of the same title, there is a visually striking and narratively significant scene in which the American girlfriend of the young protagonist (the son of Indian-born immigrants) arrives at a funeral wearing a black dress, only to find herself surrounded by white-robed mourners. The predominance of white on the Korean peninsula is general and generic; see Nozaki Mitsuhiko, *Koria no fushigi sekai* (Tokyo: Heibonsha, 2003), pp. 18–20, as well as entries beginning with *paek* (white) in Kim Yŏng-suk, ed., *Han'guk poksiksa sajŏn* (Seoul: Minmun'go, 1988). To be sure, the choice of funerary color has varied across status groups and certainly over time, but Murakami Chijun's colonial-period photographs leave little doubt as to the primacy of white; see www.flet.keio.ac.jp/~shnomura/mura/contents/album_4 .htm. In the case of contemporary South Korea, the impact of the United States and Christian practice seems dominant; see, for example, Min-Sun Hwang, "Contemporary Hemp Weaving in Korea," *Textile Society of America Symposium Proceedings Paper 347* (2006), available at http://digitalcommons.unl.edu/tsaconf/347/. See also Roger L. Janelli and Dawnhee Yim Janelli, *Ancestor Worship and Korean Society* (Stanford: Stanford University Press, 1982).

2. There are significant historical, regional, and status variations on sartorial colors; see Yi Yŏ-sŏng, *Chosŏn poksikko,* orig. 1947 (Seoul: Minsogwŏn, 1985), chap. 5.

3. Compare John B. Duncan, *The Origins of the Chosŏn Dynasty* (Seattle: University of Washington Press, 2000), and Martina Deuchler, *The Confucian*

Transformation of Korea (Cambridge: Harvard University Asia Center, 1992), both of which provide a sense of continuities and discontinuities in "premodern" Korea.

4. It is problematic, however, to emphasize Korean autonomy vis-à-vis the Qing empire; see, for example, the salience of Korean autonomy in the very late phase of Chosŏn rule, as documented by Kirk W. Larsen, *Tradition, Treaties, and Trade* (Cambridge: Harvard University Asia Center, 2011).

5. Akiba Takashi, *Chōsen fuzoku no genchi kenkyū* (Tanbaichi: Yōtokusha, 1950), was the first to stress the dual social organization of Korea.

6. Hierarchical and ascriptive status distinctions permeated the polity, rendering Chosŏn Korea exceedingly inegalitarian. On the social structure of Chosŏn Korea, see, for example, Kim Hong-sik, *Chosŏn sidae ponggŏn sahoe ŭi kibon kujo* (Seoul: Pagyŏngsa, 1981).

7. On the underdevelopment of the Chosŏn state, see James Palais, *Politics and Policy in Traditional Korea* (Cambridge: Harvard University Press, 1975).

8. For a discussion of Confucianism's growing impact on nonelite Koreans, see Deuchler, *Confucian Transformation of Korea*. On the emergence of patriarchal family and village structures, see Yi Hae-jun, *Chosŏn sigi ch'ollak sahoesa* (Seoul: Minjok Munhwasa, 1996), chap. 1.

9. Eugene Y. Park, *Between Dreams and Reality* (Cambridge: Harvard University Asia Center, 2007), argues for the inefficacy of the military examination system in achieving meritocracy. However, Kyung Moon Hwang suggests that meritocracy was alive and well by the late Chosŏn period; see Hwang, *Beyond Birth* (Cambridge: Harvard University Asia Center, 2005). See also Yi Sŏng-mu, *Han'guk ŭi kwagŏ chedo* (Seoul: Chinmundang, 1994), chap. 4.

10. See John Lie, *Han Unbound* (Stanford: Stanford University Press, 1998), p. 178, and Yun Kyŏng-hun, *Kankoku no kyōiku kakusa to kyōiku seisaku* (Okayama: Okayama Daigaku Kyōiku Shuppan, 2010), pp. 56–57.

11. Here we see the influence of contemporary Japan, where *juku*—the proximate source of *hagwŏn*—are considerable in number. The modern university was instituted during the colonial period, and so the overt impact of Japan was initially profound, although that influence had become a rapidly fading memory by the 1980s. (A secondary source of initial influence had been Germany, more than the United States, owing to the prewar Japanese veneration of German culture.)

12. Cornelius Osgood, *The Koreans and Their Culture* (New York: Ronald Press, 1951), p. 44. For an interesting ethnography of Korean village life, see Zenshō Eisuke, *Chōsen no shūraku*, 3 vols. (Seoul: Chōsen Sōtokufu, 1933–35). As far as I know, no one has found a Protestant or Confucian work ethic in traditional Korea.

13. On some signs of the new work ethic, see Cho Kyŏng-dal, *Shokuminchiki Chōsen no chishikijin to minshū* (Tokyo: Yūshisha, 2007), pp. 61–67.

14. See Hŏ Kyun, *Hong Kil-dong chŏn*, orig. 1607 (Seoul: Hanyang Ch'ulp'ansa, 1995), and Pak Chi-wŏn, *Yangbanjŏn*, orig. 1780 (Seoul: Chosŏn Kŭmyung Yŏnhaphoe, 1947).

15. Sin Ch'ae-ho, "Toksa sillon," orig. 1908, in Sin, *Sin Ch'ae-ho yŏksa nonsŏlchip* (Seoul: Hyŏndae Sirhaksa, 1995). See also Henry H. Em, *The Great Enterprise* (Durham: Duke University Press, 2013), pp. 97–99.

16. Lie, *Han Unbound,* pp. 45–52. See also Sheila Miyoshi Jager, *Narratives of Nation Building in Korea* (Armonk: M. E. Sharpe, 2003), pp. 86–96.

17. *Xiào jīng* [The book of filial piety] is explicit on the need to value and preserve the body that the parents gave you, which led, among other bizarre manifestations, some *yangban* not to clip their nails; see *Xiào jīng,* orig. 400 B.C.E.?, ed. Wāng Shòukuān (Shànghǎi: Shànghǎi gǔjí chūbǎn shè, 2007), p. 3. *Xiào jīng* was surely one of the most widely read Confucian tracts in Chosŏn Korea.

18. On the rise of romantic love in colonial Korea, see Kwŏn Podǔrae, *Yŏnae ǔi sidae* (Seoul: Hyŏnsil Munhwa Yŏn'gu, 2003). The phenomenon is part of the larger assertion of female subjectivity and individuality, as exemplified by the rise of the "new woman" (*sin yŏja*); in this connection, see Inoue Kazue, *Shokuminchi Chōsen no shin josei* (Tokyo: Akashi Shoten, 2013). On the Japanese antecedent, see Koyano Atsushi, *Nihon ren'ai shisōshi* (Tokyo: Chūō Kōronshinsha, 2012).

19. See, for example, Boudewijn Walraven, "Popular Religion in a Confucianized Society," in JaHyun Kim Haboush and Martina Deuchler, eds., *Culture and the State in Late Chosŏn Korea* (Cambridge: Harvard University Asia Center, 1999), pp. 160–98, esp. pp. 160–61.

20. John Lie, "'What Makes Us Great,'" in Yun-shik Chang and Steven Hugh Lee, eds., *Transformations in Twentieth-Century Korea* (London: Routledge, 2006), pp. 138–52.

21. If the Chosŏn dynasty had collapsed earlier, wouldn't it have been easier to detect the existing sprouts of capitalist industrialization on the Korean peninsula? And wouldn't the Westernizing regime have sought to emulate the ways of capitalist industrialization and colonial expansion, à la Meiji Japan? After all, the 1894–96 Kabo Reforms had ended official status hierarchy, and the beginnings of the nation-state were detectable by 1880; see Tsukiashi Tatsuhiko, *Chōsen kaika shisō to nashonarizumu* (Tokyo: Tokyo Daigaku Shuppankai, 2009), pp. 11–12, 365–66. Furthermore, local and long-distance markets were thriving in Chosŏn Korea, so much so that ceramics, ginseng, and paper, among other products, achieved regional and even global renown; see Cho, *Shokuminchiki Chōsen no chishikijin to minshū,* pp. 61–67. Yet no amount of counterfactual reasoning, however useful as a heuristic, can annul the reality of Japanese rule over, and Japanese influence on, colonized Korea. On Korean modernity as colonial, see Pak Chi-hyang, *Ilgǔrŏjin kǔndae* (Seoul: P'urǔn Yŏksa, 2003), chap. 1.

22. Korean popular music would have taken a different direction had it been colonized by Russia or the United States—but, as noted in chapter 1, both the hardware and the software of Korean popular music came largely by way of Japan during the colonial period.

23. Consider the preponderance of Japanese-derived vocabulary for philosophical and theoretical discourse; see Kang Yŏng-an, *Uri ege ch'ŏlhak ǔn muŏt in'ga*

(Seoul: Kungni, 2002), chap. 4. See, in general, Serk-Bae Suh, *Treacherous Transla-tion* (Berkeley: University of California Press, 2013).

24. John Lie, *Zainichi (Koreans in Japan)* (Berkeley: University of California Press, 2008), pp. 9–11. See also John Whittier Treat, "Choosing to Collaborate," *Journal of Asian Studies* 71 (2012), 81–102.

25. Kim Yunsik, for example, stresses the coeval character of modernity and (national) literature, a character that is in turn related to the modern nation-state; see Kim, *Han'guk kŭndae munhak yŏn'gu pangbŏp immun* (Seoul: Seoul Taehakkyo Ch'ulp'anbu, 1999), pp. 138–39.

26. Attempts to exculpate Yi Kwang-su usually cite his imprisonment and tor-ture at the hands of the Japanese authorities. Another possibility is the underdevel-opment of standard literary Korean, a deficiency born of the dominance of Chinese literary culture and of the lack of cultural integration during the Chosŏn dynasty. Kim Tong-in—perhaps the greatest modern Korean writer after Yi's disgrace—is remembered for his castigating account of his senior (*sŏnbae*) Yi Kwang-su in his 1946 story "Panyŏnja" [Traitor] (*Paengmin*, October 1946), but we should not forget Kim's obsession with and admiration for Yi, articulated in his 1934 study *Ch'unwŏn yŏn'gu* (Seoul: Sin'gu Munhwasa, 1956). More to the point, Kim admits to the dif-ficulties of modern literary Korean by comparison with his native Pyongyang dialect and even with modern literary Japanese; see Kim, *Chosŏn kŭndae sosŏl*, orig. 1929 (Seoul: Chosŏn Ilbosa, 1988). That is, even as early as the late 1920s, some modern Korean intellectuals found it easier to write in literary Japanese than in literary Korean, which in turn was far from being standardized.

27. See the preface to "Japanese Children" in Kim So-un [Tetsu Jinpei], *Sankan mukashigatari*, orig. 1941 (Tokyo: Kōdansha, 1985), p. 3.

28. Like a good autodidact, Im Chong-guk monomaniacally captures a moment of truth in his devastating portrayal of pro-Japanese Koreans; see Im, *Ilche ha ŭi sasang t'anap* (Seoul: P'yonghwa Ch'ulp'ansa, 1985).

29. Murakami Chijun's string of studies on Korean folk beliefs and practices remains a towering achievement; see www.flet.keio.ac.jp/~shnomura/mura /contents/murayama.htm. It is easy to chide Murakami for his ethnocentrism and his inability to engage deeply with the Korean people, but I don't know of any other anthropologist of the time who fared any better. On Japan's Orientalism, see Stefan Tanaka, *Japan's Orient* (Berkeley: University of California Press, 1993).

30. Yi Kwang-su, "Munhak iran hao?," orig. 1916, in Yi, *Yi Kwang-su chŏnjip*, vol. 1 (Seoul: Yusinsa, 1979), p. 551. See also Ch'oe Nam-sŏn, *Chosŏn sangsik mundap*, orig. 1946 (Seoul: Hyŏnamsa, 1973), chap. 8.

31. Hatano Setsuko, *Kindai Kankoku sakka no Nihon ryūgaku* (Tokyo: Hakutei-sha, 2013).

32. Yanagi Muneyoshi, *Chōsen to sono geijutsu* (Tokyo: Sōbunkaku, 1922). See also Han Yŏng-dae, *Yanagi Muneyoshi to Chōsen* (Tokyo: Akashi Shoten, 2008). The fame of the Korean vases was celebrated in what was surely one of the first appearances of Korea in European fiction—namely, Octave Mirbeau's *Le Jardin des supplices*, orig. 1899 (Paris: Fasquelle, 1957), chap. 8. The vases' renown sits uncom-

fortably with what has been, until recently, their neglect by most Koreans. Indeed, the neglect of traditional Korean crafts, such as *hanji* (Korean paper), is nothing short of scandalous; see Aimee Lee, *Hanji Unfurled* (Ann Arbor: Legacy Press, 2012).

33. Ko U-i, *Kanryū būmu no genryū* (Tokyo: Shakai Hyōronsha, 2012), pp. 11–15. There is an interesting passage on Ch'oe in Kawabata Yasunari's novel *Maihime* (Tokyo: Shinchōha, 1951), pp. 144–46. See also Sang-cheul Choi, "Seung-hee Choi," Ph.D. diss., New York University, 1996.

34. Quoted in Korea Foundation, *Traditional Music* (Seoul: Seoul Selection, 2011), p. 12. See also Tanabe Hisao, *Chūgoku Chōsen ongaku chōsa kikō* (Tokyo: Ongaku no Tomosha, 1970).

35. Yang Su-jŏng's fictional portrait of a soon-to-be executed Korean nationalist during Japanese rule is extremely poignant; see Yang, *Hanŭl ŭl pogo ttang ŭl pogo* (Seoul: Hwimun Ch'ulp'ansa, 1965). Asked by a sympathetic guard what he would like to have as his last meal, Yang's anti-colonial nationalist says he wants curry rice, that quintessential food of Japanese modernity. Although curry rice is South Asian in origin, its proximate source was England, and *karē raisu* was long considered the emblematic *yōshoku* (Western cuisine) in Japan. See Kosuge Keiko, *Karē raisu no tanjō* (Tokyo: Kōdansha, 2002). On North Korea's claim to political legitimacy in the anti-colonial struggles, see Wada Haruki, *Kin Nissei to Manshū kōnichi sensō* (Tokyo: Heibonsha, 1992).

36. On the early years of North Korea, see Charles K. Armstrong, *North Korean Revolution* (Ithaca: Cornell University Press, 2002).

37. Ham Sŏk-hŏn recalls that *haebang* (liberation) "arrived like a thief"; see Ham, *Ttŭt ŭro pon Han'guk yŏksa,* orig. 1962 (P'aju: Han'gilsa, 2003).

38. Lie, *Zainichi,* pp. 9–10.

39. Because of the entanglement, during the colonial period, of anti-colonial nationalism with socialist and communist revolutionaries, even those intellectuals who chose the South over the North were suspect and were often jailed and executed. One striking example is Kim Tae-jun, the author of the first history of Korean literature; see Kim, *Chungbŏ Chosŏn sosŏl sa,* orig. 1933 (Seoul: Han'gilsa, 1990). See also An U-sik, "Kaisetsu," in Kim Tae-jun, *Chōsen shōsetsushi,* trans. and ed. An U-sik (Tokyo: Heibonsha, 1975), pp. 327–404, esp. pp. 402–3. On the violent and authoritarian character of the Rhee regime, see Kimura Kan, *Kankoku ni okeru "ken'ishugiteki" taisei no seiritsu* (Kyoto: Mineruva Shobō, 2003), pp. 142–45.

40. There has yet to be an adequate scholarly biography of the "father" of South Korea. See, however, Hŏ Chŏng, *Unam Yi Sŭng-man* (Seoul: T'aegŭk Ch'ulp'ansa, 1972), and Yi Han-u, *Yi Sŭng-man 90-yŏn,* 2 vols. (Seoul: Chosŏn Ilbosa, 1995–96).

41. Even in 2013, the two main South Korean promoters of (South) Korean Studies—the Korea Foundation and the Academy of Korean Studies—refused to support scholarship on North Korea.

42. Still the best single book on the Rhee years is Gregory Henderson, *Korea* (Cambridge: Harvard University Press, 1968). On the 1950s, see also Yi Tae-gŭn, *Han'guk chŏnjaeng kwa 1950-yŏndae chabon ch'ukchŏk* (Seoul: Kkach'i, 1987), and

Kim Sŏk-chun, *Migunjŏngsidae ŭi kukka wa haengjŏng* (Seoul: Yihwa Yŏja Taehak-kyo Ch'ulp'anbu, 1996).

43. Eui Hang Shin and Kyung-Sup Chang, "Peripherization of Immigrant Professionals," *International Migration Review* 22 (1988), 609–26, esp. p. 615.

44. Henderson, *Korea,* remains the locus classicus on the wretchedness of the Rhee regime. See also Sŏ Chung-dŏk, *Han'guk hyŏndaesa 60-yŏn* (Seoul: Yŏksa Pip'yŏngsa, 2007), chap. 1.

45. Many US-oriented South Koreans seemed to believe in the radically different characteristics of the new *yangban* class; see, for example, Channing Liem's review of Osgood, *The Koreans and Their Culture,* in *American Historical Review* 56 (1951), 899–901. As I argue later in this interlude, the break with the past occurred as a result of the land reform that took place during the Korean War.

46. It is important to stress that by the last decade of colonial rule a new generation of educated ethnic Koreans was bilingual but more proficient in Japanese; see, for example, the recollection of his elder brother by Kim Pyŏng-ik, *Tu yŏllim ŭi hyanghayŏ* (Seoul: Sol, 1991).

47. Kimura Kan, *Chōsen/Kankoku nashonarizumu to "shōkoku" ishiki* (Kyoto: Mineruva Shobō, 2000), p. 71.

48. On the politics of South Korea in the 1950s and 1960s, see (in addition to Henderson, *Korea*) Sungjoo Han, *The Failure of Democracy in South Korea* (Berkeley: University of California Press, 1974), and Quee-Young Kim, *The Fall of Syngman Rhee* (Berkeley: Institute of East Asian Studies, University of California, 1974).

49. For a brief overview in English, see Bruce Cumings, *The Korean War* (New York: Modern Library, 2010). For contrasting accounts, see Wada Haruki, *Chōsen sensō zenshi* (Tokyo: Iwanami Shoten, 2002), and Sheila Miyoshi Jager, *Brothers at War* (New York: Norton, 2013).

50. The Korean War remains a rarely discussed but significant factor in the post-Liberation South Korean diaspora. Grace M. Cho points to the immediate impact of US GIs marrying South Korean women; see Cho, *Haunting the Korean Diaspora* (Minneapolis: University of Minnesota Press, 2008).

51. Yun Jeson, *Kankoku no guntai* (Tokyo: Chūō Kōronshinsha, 2004), pp. 64–66. See, in general, Seungsook Moon, *Militarized Modernity and Gendered Citizenship in South Korea* (Durham: Duke University Press, 2005).

52. The redistribution of concentrated landownership stemmed in part from the attempt to undermine the appeal of North Korea; see Lie, *Han Unbound,* pp. 9–15. See also Sin Pyŏng-sik, "Han'guk ŭi t'oji kaehyŏk e kwanhan chŏngch'i kyŏngjejŏk yŏn'gu," Ph.D. diss., Seoul National University, 1992.

53. See Kim Yŏng-mo, *Han'guk chihaech'ŭng yŏn'gu* (Seoul: Ilchogak, 1982), pp. 118–21.

54. Lie, *Han Unbound,* pp. 108–12. For a more detailed local study, see Mun Ok-p'yo and Kim Il-ch'ŏl, *Kŭngyo nongch'on ŭi haech'e kwajŏng* (Sŏngnam: Han'guk Chŏngsin Munhwa Yŏn'guwŏn, 1993).

55. At least according to the definition offered by the organization Han'guk Kosŏ Tong'uhoe; see An Ch'un-gŭn, *Kosŏ* (Seoul: Taeinsa, 1991), p. 12. Although my

holdings of Korean-language books are minimal, it is disturbing to learn that I have some books that are not to be found at www.worldcat.org.

56. Itō Abito suggests that South Koreans lack interest in things, a cultural trait that puts them in marked contrast to Japanese people; see Itō, "Kankoku de 'mono o tōshitemiru' koto," in Asakura Toshio, ed., *"Mono" kara mita Chōsen minzoku bunka* (Tokyo: Shinkansha, 2003), pp. 11–24, esp. pp. 12–15. This cultural trait was likely exacerbated by massive transformations, especially those brought by the Korean War. Given the widespread renown of Korean crafts, such as those involving pottery and paper, scholars have downplayed the salience of crafts traditions, and therefore of interest in things, on the Korean peninsula.

57. Lie, *Han Unbound*, pp. 44–52.

58. For a sympathetic take on the dictator's life, see Cho Kap-che, *Pak Chŏng-hŭi* (Seoul: Kkach'i, 1992).

59. Lie, *Han Unbound*, pp. 44–47, 101–6.

60. The best contemporary reportage can be found in T. K., *Kankoku kara no tsūshin*, 3 vols. (Tokyo: Iwanami Shoten, 1974–77).

61. See, for example, Philip J. Ivanhoe, *Confucian Moral Self Cultivation,* 2nd ed. (Indianapolis: Hackett, 2000).

62. Lie, *Han Unbound*, pp. 51–52, 178–79.

63. Ibid., chap. 3.

64. See Pak Kŭn-ho, *Kankoku no keizai hatten to Betonamu sensō* (Tokyo: Ochanomizu Shobō, 1993), pp. 65–69, 141–49.

65. Cho Se-hŭi's *Nanjangi ka ssoa ollin chagŭn kong* [The dwarf] (Seoul: Munhak kwa Chisŏngsa, 1978) remains a powerful portrait not only of the alienation of the poor but also of the dysfunctions and malfunctions of Yusin-era South Korea.

66. See John Lie, "Introduction," in Lie, ed., *Multiethnic (South) Korea?* (Berkeley: Institute of East Asian Studies, University of California, 2014).

67. Similarly, according to one articulation of Japanese colonial ideology, Japan and Korea had stemmed from the same cultural (and racial) source, and so colonial practice merely had to peel away the encrustation of "Koreanness" that had rendered Korea divergent from the joint Japanese-Korean birth and path; see John Lie, *Multiethnic Japan* (Cambridge: Harvard University Press, 2001), chap. 4.

68. The abolition of Chinese characters was mooted in the immediate post-Liberation years, but only during Park's rule did the policy against Chinese characters become institutionalized. Park also sought ethnic cleansing through the removal of ethnic Chinese people from South Korea; see Wan Enmei, *Higashi Ajia gendaishi no naka no Kankoku Kakyō* (Tokyo: Sangensha, 2008).

69. The revolution continues. Some South Korean universities, in the name of globalization, recognize and reward only English-language publications. Ironically, then, the structure of the Chosŏn era—with mandarins communicating in Chinese, a language inaccessible to the masses—has been reconfigured: the elite communicate in English, and the nonelite communicate in Korean.

70. Lie, "Introduction."

71. The figures in this paragraph are taken from Lie, *Han Unbound,* and Hattori Tamio, *Kaihatsu no keizaishakaigaku* (Tokyo: Bunshindō, 2005), chap. 3. On early statistics in South Korea, see Kyō Gozen, *Kankoku no tōkei jijō* (Tokyo: Ajia Keizai Kenkyūjo, 1965).

72. John Lie, "The Political Economy of South Korean Development," *International Sociology* 7 (1992), 285–300.

73. John Lie, "The Transformation of Sexual Work in 20th-Century Korea," *Gender & Society* 9 (1995), 310–27.

74. Lie, *Han Unbound,* pp. 74, 78.

75. Soowon Kim, Soojae Moon, and Barry M. Popkin, "The Nutrition Transition in South Korea," *American Journal of Clinical Nutrition* 71 (2000), 44–53.

76. Kim Yŏng-ju, *Han'guk ŭi ch'ŏngnyŏn taejung ŭmak munhwa* (Seoul: Han'guk Haksul Chŏngbo, 2006), pp. 137–46.

77. Among university graduates, according to Kang Hibong, the incidence of premarital sex was about 41 percent in 1978 but had climbed to 89 percent by 2011; see Kang, *Darekani oshietakunaru Kanryū no himitsu* (Tokyo: PHP Kenkyūjo, 2012), p. 103.

78. It is commonly said that Kim Dae-jung wore colorful shirts during his 1997 presidential campaign (although, as I recall, they were largely in shades of blue), in part to forestall criticisms that he was too old. Certainly when I was working in South Korea in the late 1980s, a long-sleeved white shirt with a staid tie constituted the sole accepted and acceptable uniform. I occasionally sported a bright-colored tie, leading perceptive observers to conclude that I must not really be "Korean"; this test of ethnic identification had ceased to have any effectiveness by the turn of the millennium.

79. In surveys, Buddhism often ranks above Christianity as the primary religion of South Koreans. However, whereas Christians tend to be regular churchgoers, the same cannot be said of Buddhists. In terms of religiosity and social influence, the primacy of Christianity seems incontrovertible. See, in this regard, Ch'oe Hyŏng-muk, *Han'guk Kidokkyo wa kwŏlloyk ŭi kil* (Seoul: Rok'ŭ Midiŏ, 2009).

80. Akiyama Eiichi, *Kankoku ryūtsū o kaeta otoko* (Fukuoka: Nishi Nihon Shinbunsha, 2006), pp. 72–75. The initial reaction was tepid to negative. According to Akiyama (p. 73), the mass media warned of the negative Japanese commercial influence. Lotte Department Store in South Korea was established by a Zainichi entrepreneur; see Im Chong-wŏn, *Lotte wa Sin Kyŏk-ho* (P'aju: Ch'ŏngnim Ch'ulp'ansa, 2010).

81. Seymour Martin Lipset, *The First New Nation* (New York: Basic Books, 1963).

82. On the current condition of Rhee's statue, see http://english.chosun.com /site/data/html_dir/2008/03/28/2008032861021.html. See also Todd A. Henry, *Assimilating Seoul* (Berkeley: University of California Press, 2014), pp. 207–8.

83. See Bruce Cumings, *North Korea* (New York: New Press, 2004), chap. 3.

84. *Wolgan Chosŏn,* August 1998.

85. By contrast, all three major banknotes in Japan feature major modern cultural figures: the scientist Noguchi Hideyo, the writer Higuchi Ichiyō, and the philosopher Fukuzawa Yukichi. All five banknotes in China depict Mao Zedong. Of the five banknotes in North Korea, one depicts Kim Il-sung, another depicts a

mythical winged horse (*ch'ŏllima*), and the remaining three depict anonymous North Korean workers, soldiers, women, and children.

86. Only in the latter half of the Chosŏn period did *kimch'i* begin to incorporate the recently imported chili peppers and thus become spicy (at least in most modern variants); see Yun Sŏ-sŏk, *Uri nara siksaenghwal munhwa yŏksa* (Seoul: Sin'gwang, 1999), chap. 6, and Kim Sang-bo, *Chosŏn sidae ŭi ŭmsik munhwa* (Seoul: Karam Kihoek, 2006), pp. 279–84.

87. Leo Kim, "Explaining the Hwang Scandal," *Science as Culture* 17 (2008), 397–415.

88. See Lie, "Introduction," and *Han Unbound,* appendix. See, in general, John Lie, *Modern Peoplehood* (Cambridge: Harvard University Press, 2004).

89. Kang In-hŭi, *Han'guk siksaenghwalsa*, orig. 1979, 2nd ed. (Seoul: Samyŏngsa, 1990), chap. 7.

90. Hŏ Kyun, "Tomun taejak," orig. 1611, in Son Nak-pŏm, ed., *Han'guk kodae halp'aengbŏp* (Seoul: Kukche Taehak Kugŏ Kungmunhak Yŏn'gusil, 1975), chap. 3.

91. Kang, *Han'guk siksaenghwalsa,* chap. 10.

92. Ch'oe Kil-sŏng, *Kankoku minzoku e no shōtai* (Tokyo: Fukyōsha, 1996), pp. 99, 102.

93. As the great scholar Chŏng Yag-yong (better known as Tasan) reputedly said, it is important to read the *Analects* every day. Over the past two decades I have lectured in front of hundreds of South Korean students and have yet to meet anyone who admits to having read this rather short book in its entirety. See Chŏng, *Yŏkchu nonŏ kogŭm chu* (Seoul: Sasam, 2010), p. 75.

94. See, for example, Heonik Kwon and Byung-Ho Chung, *North Korea* (Lanham: Rowman & Littlefield, 2012). Compare Sonia Ryang, *Reading North Korea* (Cambridge: Harvard University Asia Center, 2012).

95. See Kim Yŏng-dae, *Chōsen no hisabetsu minshū,* orig. 1978, trans. Hon'yaku Henshū Iinkai (Osaka: Buraku Kaihō Kenkyūjo, 1988), pp. 12–15, 26–27. As a gauge of South Koreans' lack of interest in this topic, I have not been able to locate the Korean-language original; it is nowhere to be found, for example, at www.worldcat .org. For an English-language account, see Herbert Passin, "The Paekchong of Korea," *Monumenta Nipponica* 12 (1956), 195–240.

96. The founding chairman of Hyundai is reported to have demonstrated Korean shipbuilding prowess by displaying a South Korean banknote depicting the legendary "turtle boat" of the sixteenth century; see Tamaki Tadashi, *Kankoku zaibatsu wa doko e iku* (Tokyo: Fusōsha, 2012), p. 171. This sort of chutzpah, now normative among South Koreans, has led to numerous broken promises, the most spectacular of which involved the research fraud perpetrated by Dr. Hwang.

2. SEOUL CALLING

1. In the pedantic spirit of this paragraph, I hasten to add that "South Korea" is far from being a commonsense term, since most people, inside and outside South

Korea, elide the word "South" so that "Korea" stands for both North Korea and South Korea. This habit is deeply problematic, especially in light of the trend in South Korea to resist the very idea of unification (South Korean maps sometimes leave the territory of North Korea blank).

2. For an instance of the tendency to write South Korean popular music history as the history of K-pop, see Chang Nam Kim, *K-POP* (Seoul: Hollym International, 2012).

3. The widespread practice of misreporting sales, exacerbated by the economic recession, came to light in 1999. Ever since, the South Korean industry association has compiled monthly sales figures, and from 2011 on those figures have been augmented by weekly Mnet charts; see http://mwave.interest.me/kpop/chart.m.

4. The music video is available at www.youtube.com/watch?v=BykZNO5GCfA.

5. The clip can be seen at www.youtube.com/watch?v=nQt7Mw6MhV4.

6. Chang ranked fifth in the Korean Gallup Poll's 2012 survey of the most popular singers; another trot singer, T'ae Chin-a, came in ninth. See the poll at www .allkpop.com/2012/12/korea-gallup-poll-reveals-the-most-popular-k-pop-stars-in-2012. As noted in chapter 1, trot has often stood for popular music itself, and many trot singers have performed in various genres. Chang, like Cho Yong-p'il, reportedly had hopes at first of becoming a rock singer.

7. Furuya Masayuki, *K Generation* (Tokyo: DHC, 2005), pp. 27–33.

8. The video is available at www.youtube.com/watch?v=ZPaK5sTRm6A.

9. John Lie and Ingyu Oh, "SM Entertainment and Soo Man Lee," in Tony Fu-Lai Yu and Ho-Don Yan, eds., *Handbook of East Asian Entrepreneurship* (London: Routledge, 2014).

10. See the video at www.youtube.com/watch?v=pJ27mfX_1Ew. After Tupac Shakur's death, his mother filed a lawsuit claiming that Baby V.O.X. had made unauthorized use of her son's work. The resulting notoriety probably exceeded whatever attention Baby V.O.X. had garnered in the United States at the time. Earlier, Shakur had rapped about the Korean American shopkeeper Soon Ja Du's murder of an African American girl, Latasha Harlins, and played a part in the alleged racial animosity between African Americans and Korean Americans; see Nancy Abelmann and John Lie, *Blue Dreams: Korean Americans and the Los Angeles Riots* (Cambridge: Harvard University Press, 1995), pp. 148–70.

11. See Jordan Siegel and Yi Kwan Chu, *The Globalization of East Asian Pop Music,* HBS case no. 9–708–479 (Cambridge: Harvard Business School, 2010), pp. 8–10.

12. Ugaya Hiromichi, *J poppu to wa nanika* (Tokyo: Iwanami Shoten, 2005), pp. 2–7.

13. Japanese and Korean have practically the same grammatical structure but are poles apart in terms of phonetics—that is, it is extremely difficult to sound like a native speaker in both languages. But BoA did it; see www.youtube.com/watch?v=TA8ZBCUweCY&feature=fvsr.

14. There are no reliable statistics to validate this claim.

15. The music video is available at www.youtube.com/watch?v=hxfICoV2FEg.

16. See the video at www.youtube.com/watch?v=qzgccjUBJig.

17. Available at www.youtube.com/watch?v=bWQMdvMnKSA.

18. See the video at www.youtube.com/watch?v=uqsHnxo35cg.

19. Earlier African American musicians—such as Fats Domino and, probably most influentially, Chuck Berry—introduced the backbeat to the mainstream American audience. In the case of K-pop, however, it is safe to say that the proximate influences were not those earlier musicians but rather the postdisco rhythmic cadences of disco rap and hip-hop.

20. Tsuchiya Keisuke, "Erekutoro ga Kankoku popyurā myūsikku ni ataeta eikyō," in Kubota Yasuhira and Tsuchiya Keisuke, eds., *New Korean Music Guidance* [sic] (Tokyo: Ongaku Shuppansha, 2012), pp. 54–55, esp. p. 54.

21. The synergistic K-pop hook may induce an alternative ("shamanistic") state of consciousness, as suggested by Michael Harner's concept of sonic driving; see Harner, *Cave and Cosmos* (Berkeley: North Atlantic Books, 2013), pp. 44–48. It would be nifty to view Wonder Girls and other K-pop acts as modern shamans. Nevertheless, although there may be some similarities between a shaman's and a K-pop artist's performance practices, and between the symptoms (such as hypnotic trance) exhibited by the two types of audiences, the belief systems underlying shamanism and capitalism could hardly be more different. Thanks to Xavier Callahan for the intriguing suggestion.

22. It may be possible to see in this phenomenon a modern manifestation of traditional Korean gender-based spatial differentiation. At the same time, the gender-segregated training program for aspiring pop stars accounts in large part for the absence of mixed-gender groups. In addition, preteens and even teenagers tend to be gender-segregated, even in the United States; the attempt to appeal to this age bracket also accentuates the norm of single-sex groups.

23. Sun Jung, *Korean Masculinities and Transcultural Consumption* (Hong Kong: Hong Kong University Press, 2011), pp. 35–39, describes the non-national, soft masculinity of lead actors in South Korean television dramas, but the latest articulation of K-pop masculinity seems increasingly to veer toward the harder, more American version of masculinity.

24. See www.youtube.com/watch?v=QQeRojDfFmk.

25. John Seabrook, "Factory Girls," *The New Yorker,* 8 October 2012, pp. 88–97, esp. p. 92.

26. Kitahara Minori, *Sayonara, Kanryū* (Tokyo: Kawade Shobō Shinsha, 2013), pp. 16–17.

27. Ibid., p. 17.

28. On Rain's global and transnational appeal, see Hyunjoon Shin, "Have You Ever Seen the Rain? And Who'll Stop the Rain?," *Inter-Asia Cultural Studies* 10 (2009), 507–23.

29. See again the poll cited in n. 6 to this chapter.

30. See, for example, www.itzcaribbean.com/skull.

31. John Lie, *Han Unbound* (Stanford: Stanford University Press, 1998), pp. 41–42. See also Paku Chon Hyon [Park Jong Hyun/Pak Chong-hyǒn], *KARA, Shōjo Jidai ni miru "Kankoku no tsuyosa"* (Tokyo: Kōdansha, 2011), pp. 76–79.

32. I hope I am not making a controversial point here, but the locus classicus remains Thorstein Veblen, *Theory of the Leisure Class* (New York: Huebsch, 1899).

33. To be sure, the inverse may also be true: exotic provenance and distinct appearance, behavior, and conduct may enhance appeal.

34. As Andrew Khan writes, "Although the two nations are separated by little more than 30 miles of water, the gulf between the French music industry and British hearts has seemed unbridgeable at times"; see Khan, "Sounds of France," *The Guardian,* 28 May 2012.

35. Hannes Gmelin, *Nationalität in populärer Musik* (Hamburg: LIT Verlag), chap. 5.

36. The video *Kids React to K-pop,* available at www.youtube.com /watch?v=yd6EQ4MxTWE, depicts reactions ranging from wariness and wonder to ridicule and rejection.

37. Timothy D. Taylor, *Global Pop* (London: Routledge, 1997), pp. 1–5. As Taylor observes, however, in 1991 the economic share of "world music" in the overall music industry was equal only to that of two rather small segments—jazz and classical music.

38. Ibid., pp. 199–201.

39. See Ivan Raykoff and Robert Dean Tobin, *A Song for Europe* (Aldershot: Ashgate, 2007), and Karen Fricker and Milija Gluhovic, eds., *Performing the "New" Europe* (London: Palgrave Macmillan, 2013).

40. As for the sea in question, its name, characteristically, is disputed (and not just in Japan and South Korea; see Sam Roberts, "A Debate in New York Over the Name of a Sea Between Japan and the Koreas," *New York Times,* 11 February 2014): it's called the Sea of Japan in Japanese, and the East Sea in Korean.

41. There was even an extended debate on whether *enka* was Korean in origin. See John Lie, *Multiethnic Japan* (Cambridge: Harvard University Press, 2001), chap. 3. The South Korean singers were distinguished from their Japanese counterparts not only by nationality but also by musical style; singers from both countries were creating music in what was, broadly speaking, the same genre, but the South Korean variants tended to be faster and brighter.

42. Song An-Jong [Sŏng An-jong], *Zainichi ongaku no 100-nen* (Tokyo: Seidosha, 2009), pp. 197–98.

43. It may be paradoxical but also predictable that some assimilated Koreans transmogrified into fervent anti-Japanese ideologues; Park Chung-hee's simultaneous appreciation and proscription of Japanese popular culture is symptomatic of the fundamental ambivalence.

44. Ugaya, *J poppu to wa nanika,* pp. 173–78.

45. Nevertheless, K-pop is distinct in two ways: the new markets for K-pop were consciously constructed rather than discovered and exploited; and K-pop exports are offered as Brand Korea, an innovative type of music performed by self-identified South Koreans.

46. See the interlude for a discussion of how Park's elevation of export-oriented industrialization turned South Korea into a country intensely focused on exports and economic growth. See also Lie, *Han Unbound,* pp. 54–73.

47. Only in the twenty-first century has the South Korean economy finally made the transition from emulation to innovation—and, not surprisingly, innovators and leaders, far more than adopters and followers, are inclined to worry about protecting their creative credits and copyrights.

48. The figure for China was $182 million, for Taiwan it was $172 million, and for Hong Kong it was $100 million. See PricewaterhouseCoopers, *Global Entertainment Outlook* (New York: PricewaterhouseCoopers, 2013), pp. 265, 293–94.

49. See Jonathan Sterne, *MP3* (Durham: Duke University Press, 2012).

50. The peak year for record sales in Japan was 1998, with a steady decline thereafter, in spite of rigorous copyright protection; see Mōri Yoshitaka, *Popyurā ongaku to shihonshugi* (Tokyo: Serika Shobō, 2007), p. 152.

51. Kanno Tomoko, *Suki ni natte wa ikenai kuni* (Tokyo: Bungei Shunjū, 2000), pp. 16–17.

52. John Lie, "The Asian Economic Crisis; or, What Crisis?," *CSE Newsletter* 2 (2000), 1–5, available at www.bus.umich.edu/FacultyResearch/ResearchCenters /Centers/Cse/CseSite/Newsletter/Current/Lie.pdf.

53. In spite of the efflorescence of economic sociology—for one account, see John Lie, "Sociology of Markets," *Annual Review of Sociology* 23 (1997), 341–60—it remains the case, unfortunately, that sociological accounts offer inadequate explanations of voluntaristic agency. See Frank H. Knight, *Risk, Uncertainty and Profit* (Boston: Houghton Mifflin, 1921).

54. The amount of the 2013 budget comes from a senior figure in the Ministry of Culture and Tourism. In 2010, the total amount was reported to be $95 million; see Siegel and Chu, *Globalization of East Asian Pop Music,* p. 21. The impact of this governmental support is far from clear, given its indirect nature; it ranges from enhancing the capacity for digital transmission of content to supporting academic studies of K-pop. Indeed, SM Entertainment executives in particular were skeptical about, if not alarmed by, the potential for governmental intervention and interference. Yet it would be problematic to deny the efficacy of state sponsorship. In a November 2011 meeting with Eric Schmidt, President Lee reportedly lobbied the Google CEO for a K-pop channel to be added to YouTube, and such a channel subsequently did appear.

55. Mōri, *Popyurā ongaku to shihonshugi,* p. 157.

56. Siegel and Chu, *Globalization of East Asian Pop Music,* p. 1.

57. We can see a similar transformation in the film industry. The period after the financial crisis led, paradoxically, to a time of unprecedented experimentation and innovation, which culminated in incandescent masterpieces in 2003, such as *Oldboy* (*Oldŭboi*), by Park Chan-wook (Pak Ch'an-uk), and *Memories of Murder* (*Sarin ŭi ch'uŏk*), by Bong Joon-ho (Pong Chun-ho). On the transformation of the South Korean cinema industry, see Darcy Paquet, *New Korean Cinema* (New York: Columbia University Press, 2009), and Jinhee Choi, *The South Korean Film Renaissance* (Middletown: Wesleyan University Press, 2010). Similarly, the era of new Internet-based games, such as *Starcraft* (2000) and *Lineage* (2003), arrived in South Korea early in the decade. I am grateful to Jinsoo An for this insight.

58. See Nishimori Michiyo, *K-POP ga Ajia o seihasuru* (Tokyo: Hara Shobō, 2011), pp. 43–52, and Sakai Mieko, *K-POP Bakkustēji-episōdo* (Tokyo: Kawade Shobō Shinsha, 2011), chap. 6.

59. Yang Hyŏn-sŏk, formerly a member of Sŏ T'ae-ji wa Aidŭl, created YG Entertainment after the group's disbandment, with a strong emphasis on hip-hop and R & B; Yang became famous overnight as the agent of Psy. As for Pak Chin-yŏng (Jin Yong Park) of JYP Entertainment, he had also been a successful singer and songwriter. Lee Soo-man of SM Entertainment is discussed here in more detail.

60. On Lee and SM Entertainment, see, inter alia, Mark James Russell, *Pop Goes Korea* (Berkeley: Stone Bridge Press, 2008), chap. 5; Paku, *KARA,* chap. 2; Chon Wŏl-sŏn, *K-POP* (Tokyo: Shōgakkan, 2012), chap. 7; and Lie and Oh, "SM Entertainment." On Lee's notion of "culture technology," see Miura Fumio, *Shōjo Jidai to Nihon no ongaku seitaikei* (Tokyo: Nihon Keizai Shinbun Shuppansha, 2012), pp. 91–98.

61. According to the 2006 annual report by the International Federation of the Phonographic Industry, the "physical piracy level" was estimated at 85 percent for China in the middle of the first decade of the 2000s; see *The Recording Industry 2006 Piracy Report: Protecting Creativity in Music,* p. 11, available at www.ifpi.org/content/library/piracy-report2006.pdf.

62. Kigoshi Yu, *Shōjo Jidai & KARA no himitsu* (Tokyo: Sanī Shuppan, 2011), chap. 1.

63. For everything one might wish to know (but might not think to ask) about Super Junior, see SUPER JUNIOR Kenkyūkai, *SUPER JUNIOR kenbunroku* (Tokyo: Sōryūsha, 2013).

64. An intriguing feature of K-pop's appeal in Thailand is its popularity in gay bars catering to Thai and Asian men. Not only does K-pop dominate the music that is in the air but individuals and groups vie to cover their favorite K-pop dance routines. Indeed, K-pop is sometimes called Gay Pop.

65. The length of military service varies according to its nature, but the minimum is twenty-one months for the army, and the maximum is thirty-six months for some kinds of civil service work. The public outcry against deferments and exemptions has made such accommodations less common; in the world of music, the decisive case involved the disgraced rapping sensation Yu Sŭng-jun, also known as Steve Yoo, who fled to the United States and became a naturalized US citizen in 2002, just before he was due to be drafted for military service, and was subsequently deported from South Korea and banned from reentering the country. Given allegations of abuse, including exemptions from service and shortened service for politically connected youths, recent regimes have been reluctant to grant exceptions, even for global superstars.

66. South Korean martial music in turn has come to incorporate hip-hop; see Sakai, *K-POP Bakkustēji-episōdo,* pp. 59–64.

67. The renaming and refashioning of "Negro music" as rock 'n' roll was a conscious strategy intended to make black music palatable to white audiences; see Charlie Gillett, *The Sound of the City,* orig. 1970, rev. ed. (New York: Da Capo Press, 1983), p. 13.

68. Nishimori, *K-POP ga Ajia o seihasuru*, pp. 137–44. K-pop stars are not divas.

69. See, inter alia, Paku, *KARA*, chap. 2; Sakai Mieko, *Naze K-POP sutā wa tsugikara tugini kurunoka* (Tokyo: Asahi Shimbun Shuppan, 2012), chap. 3.

70. Tiffany, at three years, spent the least time as a trainee, whereas the longest-serving member, Sunny, was a *yŏnsusaeng* for nine years, if we include her stint at another agency; see Shōjo Jidai Kenkyūkai, ed., *Shōjo Jidai kenbunroku* (Tokyo: Sōryūsha, 2010), p. 19.

71. Shōjo Jidai Kenkyūkai, *Shōjo Jidai kenbunroku*, pp. 20–22.

72. Kimizuka Futoshi, *Nikkan ongaku bizinesu hikakuron* (Tokyo: Asupekuto, 2012), pp. 85–88.

73. Takatsuki Yasushi, *Kankoku geinōkai uramonogatari* (Tokyo: Bungei Shunjū, 2011), pp. 76–81. There is a certain circulation between professional entertainers and those professional courtesans known as *t'enp'ŭro*, which means "10 percent" and denotes the top tier of hostesses. The pervasive hiring of escorts and courtesans is deeply entrenched in contemporary South Korean business culture; for background, see John Lie, "The Transformation of Sexual Work in 20th-Century Korea," *Gender & Society* 9 (1995), 310–27. Young women who resemble popular actresses or singers often command a premium in the economy of contemporary South Korean sex work.

74. The executive went on to say that this was the same practice pursued by Hyundai when it attempted to expand in the US automobile market in the 1990s.

75. The "dark" side of K-pop finds a ready parallel in J-pop; see Ugaya, *J poppu to wa nanika*, pp. 225–27. See also Kurosaki Satoshi, "Rekōdokaisha no shōhai o waketa gōwan to sono giman" *Saizō*, August 2013, pp. 30–33.

76. See, for example, Takatsuki, *Kankoku geinōkai uramonogatari*, pp. 60–64.

77. K-POP Aruaru Iinkai, *K-POP aidoru & ota aruaru* (Tokyo: Take Shobō, 2013).

78. Miura, *Shōjo Jidai to Nihon no ongaku seitaikei*, pp. 140–43.

79. Consider in this regard the extremely developed online gaming industry; see Dal Yong Jin, *Korea's Online Gaming Empire* (Cambridge: MIT Press, 2010).

80. For an account of the capricious and ultimately authoritarian decision-making process in a Hollywood film studio, see John Gregory Dunne, *The Studio* (New York: Farrar, Straus and Giroux, 1969). To extend the analogy between K-pop and Hollywood, if we were to ask why every national film industry cannot crank out B movies, the answer would be, in part, that making B movies is in fact very difficult; schlock though many Hollywood movies may be, they are nevertheless high-quality products that require a wide variety of skilled professionals, not just stars, and even a B movie relies on its producers' ability to manage and market their products.

81. In the United States, the prevailing ideology of authenticity, autonomy, and originality valorizes would-be rock stars who begin by joining garage bands and playing local gigs. Moreover, whether we think of Michael Jackson or Madonna, of Far East Movement or the Yeah Yeah Yeahs, we expect a certain stylistic consistency

from a particular artist or group (not that performers don't constantly seek to improve and innovate). A K-pop group is not entirely without identity or continuity, as any fan can explain ad nauseam, but a group's appearance and even its musical genre can change radically from one album to the next; SHINHWA, as already mentioned, began as a clean-cut, bubblegum-pop boy band, went through a brief goth phase, re-emerged as a group of urban hipsters, and recently came out as an act made up of sophisticated musclemen. Managerial authority also accounts for frequent changes of a group's members as individuals are chosen, dropped, combined, and recombined. South Korean producers do not run totalitarian institutions, however; lawsuits are filed, and individuals do change employers. SHINHWA, for example, began as an SM Entertainment act, shifted to Good Entertainment, and eventually became independent. As another example, Hyuna (Kim Hyŏn-a), the pole-dancing woman on the subway train in "Gangnam Style," started with Wonder Girls (JYP Entertainment) but later joined 4Minute (Cube Entertainment) and is now a member of Trouble Maker in addition to performing as a solo act.

82. The most popular of these audition shows, *Superstar K,* claims that fully 4 percent of South Koreans have applied for the audition process, but that figure is clearly exaggerated, since many aspirants apply more than once; see Kimizuka, *Nikkan ongaku bizinesu hikakuron,* p. 188. See also Sakai, *K-POP Bakkustēji-episōdo,* pp. 43–46.

83. Swee-Lin Ho, "Fuel for South Korea's 'Global Dreams Factory,'" *Korea Observer* 43 (2012), 471–502. Today the range of pursuits is considerably diversified, including not just academics, classical music, and K-pop but also sports—figure skating, for example, after Kim Yu-na (Kim Yŏ-na) won a gold medal at the 2010 Winter Olympics.

84. Whereas the average seventeen-year-old boy was 159 centimeters tall in 1977, the comparable figure in 1997 was 174 centimeters; see D. Schwekendiek, "Determinants of Well-Being in North Korea," *Economics and Human Biology* 6 (2008), 446–54. In other words, the average height for South Korean men increased by six inches over a period of two decades. At the same time, as noted earlier, South Korean standards for male and female pulchritude were moving away from the older, agrarian ideal of a round face and stocky body and embracing more modern (and perhaps more Western) features and frames, including, for men, a chiseled face and a more muscled body. In the late 1980s, for example, the most popular figure in Sobangch'a, the first South Korean idol boy band, was a chubby chap, someone who would be unlikely today to make the cut and become a K-pop trainee.

85. It is bracing to recall that plastic surgery emerged only after World War I, in response to the clamor for reconstructive surgery of the war-wounded; see Sheila M. Rothman and David J. Rothman, *The Pursuit of Perfection* (New York: Pantheon, 2003), pp. 103–4. It is also difficult today to believe that plastic surgery was widely condemned in South Korea as recently as thirty-five years ago and became accepted only toward the end of the twentieth century.

86. *Xiào jīng* [The book of filial piety], once the most widely read Confucian tract, is explicit on the undesirability of altering the body received from one's

parents; see *Xiào jīng*, orig. 400 B.C.E.?, ed. Wāng Shòukuān (Shànghǎi: Shànghǎi gǔjí chūbǎn shè), 2007. Sometime in the late twentieth century, however, the sentiment shifted radically, as if to say, "Why wouldn't ancestors welcome improvements in their descendants?"

87. To be sure, Internet sites showing "before" and "after" photos of famous actors and singers seem popular; see, for example, http://blog.asiantown.net/-/16060 /Makeup_and_Plastic_Surgery_do_real_wonders__Korean_Stars_Before_ and_After.

88. Sakai, *K-POP Bakkustēji-episōdo*, pp. 32–35.

89. The survey is discussed in Terawaki Ken, *Kankoku eiga besuto 100* (Tokyo: Asahi Shinbunsha, 2007), p. 103.

90. According to the International Society of Aesthetic Plastic Surgeons, South Koreans rank at the top worldwide for cosmetic procedures per capita; see *ISAPS International Survey on Aesthetic/Cosmetic Procedures Performed in 2011*, available at www.isaps.org/Media/Default/global-statistics/ISAPS-Results-Procedures-2011. pdf. On South Korea's reputation as a "plastic surgery mecca," see Violet Kim, "Welcome to the Plastic Surgery Capital of the World," *CNN Travel*, 9 August 2012, available at http://travel.cnn.com/seoul/visit/ideals-beauty-plastic-surgery-capital-world-389581. To gauge the importance of plastic surgery for K-pop, consider the significant representation of plastic surgeons in the World Association of Hallyu Studies, the academic association for the study of the Korean Wave.

91. Sugimoto Masatoshi, *Kankoku no fukushoku* (Tokyo: Bunka Shuppan-kyoku, 1983), p. 121.

92. For a pioneering effort to make sense of East Asian popular music, see Ishida Kazushi, *Modanizumu hensōkyoku* (Tokyo: Sakuhokusha, 2005).

93. Before K-pop there had been non–ethnic Korean stars, such as Chu Hyŏn-mi (Joo Hyun-mi), who debuted as a trot singer in 1985.

94. Needless to say, not only is the nation itself a modern phenomenon, the nation is also neither a homogeneous entity nor devoid of external influence; see John Lie, *Modern Peoplehood* (Cambridge: Harvard University Press, 2004).

95. For an early account, see Hirata Yukie, *Han'guk ŭl sobihanŭn Ilbon* (Seoul: Chaeksesang, 2005), p. 131.

96. John Lie, *Zainichi (Koreans in Japan)* (Berkeley: University of California Press, 2008), pp. 147–50.

97. John Lie, "Why Didn't 'Gangnam Style' Go Viral in Japan? Gender Divide and Subcultural Heterogeneity in Contemporary Japan," *CrossCurrents* 9 (2013), 44–67.

98. See, for example, Hayashi Kaori, *"Fuyusona" ni hamatta watashitachi* (Tokyo: Bungei Shunjū, 2005), and Mizunuma Keiko, *Yamato nadeshiko wa naze Kanryū ni hamarunoka?* (Tokyo: Futabasha, 2011).

99. Lie, "Why Didn't 'Gangnam Style' Go Viral in Japan?"

100. Chon Wŏl-sŏn, *Kinjirareta uta* (Tokyo: Chūō Kōron Shinsha, 2008), pp. 162–67.

101. Chon, *K-POP*, pp. 77–85, 96–100.

102. Lie, "Why Didn't 'Gangnam Style' Go Viral in Japan?"

103. See Miyadai Shinji, Ishihara Hideki, and Ōtsuka Akiko, *Sabukaruchā shinwa kaitai* (Tokyo: Paruko Shuppan, 1993), chap. 2.

104. For a general introduction, see Okada Toshio, *Otakugaku nyūmon* (Tokyo: Shinchōsha, 2000). For an interesting chronicle of the 1980s by one of its architects, see Ōtsuka Eiji, *Otaku no seishinshi* (Tokyo: Kōdansha, 2004).

105. See, for example, Neil Shah, "Japanese Collectors Face a Record Shortage of Obscure Music," *Wall Street Journal*, 22 September 2012.

106. Ugaya, *J poppu to wa nanika*, pp. 26–28, 91–95.

107. Kikuchi Kiyomaro, *Nihon ryūkōka hensenshi* (Tokyo: Ronsōsha, 2008), pp. 274–75. See also Carolyn Stevens, *Japanese Popular Music* (London: Routledge, 2007). For useful overviews of J-pop, see Ugaya, *J poppu to wa nanika,* and Michael Bourdaghs, *Sayonara Amerika, Sayonara Nippon* (New York: Columbia University Press, 2012).

108. Ugaya, *J poppu to wa nanika,* pp. 44–46.

109. See Bourdaghs, *Sayonara Amerika, Sayonara Nippon,* chap. 6.

110. Satō Yoshiaki, *J-POP* (Tokyo: Heibonsha, 1999), pp. 12–13.

111. Kikuchi, *Nihon ryūkōka hensenshi,* pp. 291–95.

112. According to Ugaya Hiromichi, "The fantasy that 'Japanese popular music has become even with [or equal to] the world' is what gave birth to the nomenclature 'J-pop'"; see Ugaya, *J poppu to wa nanika,* p. 11.

113. The AKB48 acronym stands for Akihabara, the electronic and subcultural mecca of Japan, and for the group's forty-eight members (although in November 2013 the number of the group's members was reportedly eighty-nine). Akimoto Yasushi is the impresario of both AKB48 and Onyanko Kurabu. There are many AKB48 copycat groups in Japan, such as SKE48.

114. Fortunately, readers can judge for themselves. Compare, for example, two music videos that were both big hits in Japan: www.youtube.com/watch?v=lkHln WFnAoc&feature=list_related&playnext=1&list=AL94UKMTqg-9CrZ-P_ rw1paPmSQwmrVBvo and www.youtube.com/watch?v=fhseD2tRLUY.

115. See Hamano Satoshi, *Maeda Atsuko wa Kirisuto o koeta* (Tokyo: Chikuma Shobō, 2012). Notwithstanding John Lennon's famous remark that the Beatles were "more popular than Jesus," it is curious that a singer who is virtually all but unknown outside the Japanese archipelago should be compared to a world-historical figure.

116. On marketing AKB48, see Murayama Ryōichi, *AKB48 ga hittoshita itsutsu no himitsu* (Tokyo: Kadokawa Shoten, 2012).

117. See, in this regard, Christine R. Yano, *Pink Globalization* (Durham: Duke University Press, 2013).

118. For a debate on the source of AKB48's popularity, see Kobayashi Yoshinori, Nakamori Akio, Uno Tsunehiro, and Hamano Satoshi, *AKB48 hakunetsu ronsō* (Tokyo: Gentōsha, 2012).

119. The budget for "culture" has increased dramatically since the late 1980s, and so have corporate-sponsored events, but the target audience has been almost entirely domestic; see Ugaya, *J poppu to wa nanika,* pp. 13–15.

120. For BIGBANG's impact in Japan, see Nishimori, *K-POP ga Ajia o seiha-suru,* pp. 20–26.

121. Lionel Trilling vaguely but nevertheless brilliantly depicts the shift from sincerity as a form of moral responsibility to authenticity as an instance of inwardness; see Trilling, *Sincerity and Authenticity* (Cambridge: Harvard University Press, 1972). This idea is developed in turn by Charles Taylor, *The Ethics of Authenticity* (Cambridge: Harvard University Press, 1992). An interesting articulation of the notion of authenticity in popular music can be found in Hugh Barker and Yuval Taylor, *Faking It* (New York: Norton, 2007).

122. Wilhelm H. Wackenroder and Ludwig Tieck, *Herzensergießungen eines kunstliebenden Klosterbruders,* orig. 1797 (Leipzig: Reclam, 2005). See also Rüdiger Safranski, *Romantik* (Munich: Fischer, 2008), chap. 5.

123. Kenneth Hamilton, *After the Golden Age* (New York: Oxford University Press, 2008).

124. See Susan Boyle's sensational appearance on *Britain's Got Talent* at www .youtube.com/watch?v=RxPZh4AnWyk. For Ch'oe, see www.youtube.com /watch?v=BewknNW2b8Y. Boyle's plain appearance and Ch'oe's life of hardship made for interesting story lines.

125. Both Herbert Simon and Malcolm Gladwell have pointed to the requisite amount of practice and training before someone can achieve mastery in a line of work; see Simon, *Reason in Human Affairs* (Stanford: Stanford University Press, 1983), p. 28, and Gladwell, *Outliers* (New York: Little, Brown, 2008), pp. 39–42.

126. As Howard Singerman writes, "The image of the artist that we have inherited from the nineteenth century—a driven, alienated, and silent individual—clashes directly with the idea of a university-trained professional artist"; see Singerman, *Art Subjects* (Berkeley: University of California Press, 1999), pp. 209–10.

127. Gabriel Trade posited the universality of imitation as the essence of social life; see Trade, *Les Lois de l'imitation* (Paris: Alcan, 1890), p. 181. Surely social life without imitation is unimaginable.

128. See Ian Jack, *The Poet and His Audience* (Cambridge: Cambridge University Press, 1984), pp. 170–71.

129. Thomas Hughes, describing a widespread European conception of Americans in the twentieth century, cites "foreign critics" who "saw Americans behaving like machines. They had become interchangeable in appearance, attitudes, morals, and mores. Clean-shaven American men and doll-faced, heavily made-up American girls seemed to have emerged from a Ford assembly line"; see Hughes, *Human-Built World* (Chicago: University of Chicago Press, 2004), p. 72.

130. Craig Marks and Rob Tannenbaum, *I Want My MTV* (New York: Dutton, 2011), p. xi.

131. At the beginning of the nineteenth century, the eminent composer Karl Friedrich Zelter, like many of his peers, found Beethoven's music incomprehensible; he approached it with "terror" and found it "like children whose father is a woman or whose mother is a man," and in this, Zelter reflected the first reactions of members of the enlightened listening public, who needed immersion in Beethoven's new

music before they could find it beautiful and sublime; see Charles Rosen, *Musical Entertainments* (Cambridge: Harvard University Press, 2000), pp. 117–18.

132. Ezra Pound once wrote, in connection with the poetry of Ernest Dowson, that the villanelle's "refrains are an emotional fact, which the intellect . . . tries in vain and in vain to escape"; see Pound, *The Literary Essays of Ezra Pound,* orig. 1915 (London: Faber and Faber, 1954), pp. 361–70, esp. p. 369. On the paradelle, a parodic villanelle form invented by the American poet Billy Collins, see Theresa M. Wellford, *The Paradelle* (Los Angeles: Red Hen Press, 2006).

133. For a demonstration of point dance, see the video at www.youtube.com /watch?v=fM-lbEEZ6Mc, which shows the K-pop group APink in rehearsal.

134. Simon Frith influentially argued that pop music's lyrics are not poems but instead use ordinary and banal language, although in such a way that "ordinary language" becomes "intense and vital" so that "the words then resonate" and "bring a touch of fantasy into our mundane use of them"; see Frith, *Sound Effects* (New York: Pantheon, 1983), pp. 37–38, esp. p. 38.

135. See the video at www.youtube.com/watch?v=mRIPLeNtMxs.

136. Edmund Burke, "A Philosophical Inquiry into the Origin of Our Ideas of the Sublime and Beautiful," orig. 1757, in Burke, *The Works of the Right Honourable Edmund Burke,* vol. 1 (Boston: John West, 1806), pp. 53–210, esp. p. 154.

137. According to Charles Rosen, "The essential condition of music is its proximity to nonsense, its refusal from the outset of a final meaning"; see Rosen, *The Frontiers of Meaning* (New York: Hill and Wang, 1994), p. 125. Much the same can be said about all artistic forms, and popular songs often belie their simple surfaces. One is reminded of Jean-Jacques Rousseau's claim that the first speeches were the first songs ("les premiers discours furent les premières chansons"); see Rousseau, "Essai sur l'origine de la langue," orig. 1781, in Rousseau, *Oeuvres complètes,* vol. 5 (Paris: Gallimard, 1995), pp. 371–429. One must imagine speeches and songs as a minefield of hermeneutic debate.

138. The shift occurs at about the 2:53 mark in the video at www.youtube.com /watch?v=E8ZrPFMr_nY.

139. Classical music, or art music, has long been a business in Europe—save (perhaps in a technical sense) at those times when it was primarily under ecclesiastical or aristocratic patronage. As Alex Ross puts it, "From Machaut to Beethoven, modern music was essentially the only music, bartered about in a marketplace that resembled pop culture"; see Ross, *Listen to This* (New York: Farrar, Straus and Giroux, 2010), p. 10. Opera, indisputably part of classical music today, was popular music in the 1700s and constituted the culture industry in eighteenth-century Italian cities and elsewhere. Indeed, the star system was alive and well in early modern Europe, whether we think of castrati singers or superstar performer-composers such as Mozart. And the stars' fame, in Mozart's case as in that of Jim Morrison, only increased after they died. On Mozart, see William Stafford, *The Mozart Myth* (Stanford: Stanford University Press, 1991), pp. 9–10, 251–52.

140. See, e.g., Jack Bishop, "Concentrations of Power and Property in the Music Industry" (2005), available at www.redorbit.com/news/technology/258789 /concentrations_of_power_and_property_in_the_music_industry/.

141. The Hollywood studio system looked for talent and potential, but no matter how beautiful the new discoveries' looks, or how masterly their performances, the studio system made them over, changing their names and fabricating their biographies, giving them new hair colors, cosmetic surgery, elocution practice, and dancing lessons, staging their debuts in fan magazines and circulating rumors to keep them in the public eye; see Jeanine Basinger, *The Star Machine* (New York: Knopf, 2007), pp. 38–63.

142. Maria Tatar, *The Hard Facts of the Grimms' Fairy Tales* (Princeton: Princeton University Press, 1987). See, in general, Jack Zipes, *The Irresistible Fairy Tale* (Princeton: Princeton University Press, 2012).

143. See the definition proposed in 1955 by the International Folk Music Council in *Journal of the International Folk Music Council* 7 (1955), p. 23. For the formation of distinct categories, including the transformation of "art" music into "classical" music, see Matthew Gelbart, *The Invention of "Folk Music" and "Art Music,"* rev. ed. (Cambridge: Cambridge University Press, 2007), pp. 256–62.

144. Popular music—a form of commodity produced and distributed for profit—is often associated with the culture industry and has become a global phenomenon; see, for example, David Grazian, *Mix It Up* (New York: Norton, 2010), pp. 6–8. More generally, the commercial and mercenary characteristics of popular culture work in tandem with the unserious and unchallenging characteristics of a form of music that provides light, easy entertainment and facile pleasure; hence this music's wide appeal. These characteristics—commercial and mercenary, unserious and unchallenging—constitute at once the very definition of popular music, even among its defenders, and the sources of the opprobrium directed at popular music; see, inter alia, Richard Middleton, *Studying Popular Music* (Open University Press, 1990), pp. 13–14; Simon Frith, "The Popular Music Industry," in Simon Frith, W. Straw, and J. Street, eds., *Cambridge Companion to Pop and Rock* (Cambridge: Cambridge University Press, 2001), pp. 26–52; and Chris Rojek, *Pop Music, Pop Culture* (Cambridge: Polity Press, 2011), pp. 2–3.

145. As I have stressed, much of the conceptual work took place in nineteenth-century Europe; see Bernd Sponheuer, *Musik als Kunst und Nicht-Kunst* (Kassel: Bärenreiter, 1987), and Matthew Gelbart, *Invention of "Folk Music" and "Art Music."*

146. Bruno Nettl, *Folk and Traditional Music of the Western Continents* (Englewood Cliffs: Prentice Hall, 1977), p. 9; this prejudice is widespread and deeply rooted. Cecil J. Sharp, a pioneering scholar of folk music, writes, "Folk song is essentially a communal as well as a racial product. There is no music so characteristic of the German people as German folk song"; see Sharp, *English Folk-Song* (London: Simpkin, 1907).

147. John Rosselli, *Music and Musicians in Nineteenth-Century Italy* (London: Batsford, 1991), p. 24; Béla Bartók, *Studies in Ethnomusicology,* ed. Benjamin Suchoff (Lincoln: University of Nebraska Press, 1997), pp. 29, 37.

148. Richard Wagner, *Das Judentum in der Musik,* orig. 1850/1869 (Berlin: Steegemann, 1934).

149. A brazen paraphrase of a quip by LeRoi Jones (as Amiri Baraka was formerly known)—"the more intelligent the white, the more the realization that he has

to steal from the niggers"—might be appropriate where some South Koreans are concerned; see Jones, *Black Music* (New York: Morrow, 1968), pp. 205–6. It is of course very difficult, however, to disentangle the soundscapes of western Africa from the musical genres of twentieth-century America; see Peter van der Merwe, *Origins of the Popular Style* (Oxford: Oxford University Press, 1989).

150. What John Gregory Dunne wrote about Hollywood entertainment in the 1960s is probably more salient in connection with the popular music of the 2010s: "By adolescence, children have been programmed with a set of responses and life lessons learned almost totally from motion pictures, television and the recording industry"; see Dunne, *The Studio*, p. 7.

151. On Verdi's notion of *tinta*, see Gilles de Van, "La Notion de *tinta*," *Revue de musicologie* 76 (1990), 187–98.

152. See Theodor Adorno, "On Popular Music," *Studies in Philosophy and Social Sciences* 9 (1941), 17–48. Adorno's argument echoes Max Weber's stress on rationalization. Paul Théberge makes a strong argument for the technologically driven rationalization of popular music, especially through the standardized beat; see Théberge, *Any Sound You Can Imagine* (Middletown: Wesleyan University Press, 1997).

153. Adorno, "On Popular Music." See the pioneering work by Stuart Hall and Paddy Whannel, *The Popular Arts* (London: Hutchinson Educational, 1964), pp. 61–67, 311–12. In that volume, Hall and Whannel sought to suggest a systematic disjunction between the production of the culture industry and the reception of the less than passive audience. Pointing to the now obvious identification between youth culture and popular music in consumer societies, they presciently underscored the importance of songs, magazines, concerts, movies, and other manifestations of popular music in providing authentic feelings and, indeed, a worldview for young listeners. Yet, like almost all commentators, they still could not resist injecting their own aesthetic preferences (regarding jazz, for example).

154. The European classical music that emerged in the early twentieth century for the first generations of listeners in Northeast Asia is of course another matter. In early twentieth-century Germany, as Berta Geissmar recalls the country in that era, amateur and professional performances were ubiquitous in small as well as large towns; see Geissmar, *The Baton and the Jackboot* (London: Hamish Hamilton, 1944), pp. 7–8. What was played was what we would call "classical music," but it would be remiss not to equate its role with the one that popular music plays in the contemporary United States. Ruth H. Finnegan's study of a post–World War II British town is even more instructive in demonstrating both the extent of music making and the continuity across musical genres; see Finnegan, *The Hidden Musicians* (Cambridge: Cambridge University Press, 1989).

155. Likewise, Shakespeare in his day appealed equally to royalty and to the masses, and few would deny the almost universal appeal of a Mozart or a Verdi to his contemporaries, rich and poor, powerful and powerless; see, for example, Anthony Arblaster, *Viva La Libertà!* (London: Verso, 1997). As for the aura of snobbery that now surrounds opera, an anecdote related by Chamfort is instructive: "A

fanatical social climber, observing that all round the Palace of Versailles it stank of urine, told his own tenants and servants to come and make water round his château"; see Jasper Griffin, *Snobs* (Oxford: Oxford University Press, 1982), p. vii. In other words, opera today is often prestigious because the right sort of people like it, and often it is liked simply because it is prestigious.

156. The rise of musical theater, for instance, is traced to the work of Jacques Offenbach; see John Kendrick, *Musical Theater* (New York: Continuum, 2008), pp. 12–13. John Bush Jones traces Broadway shows and musicals to the US enthusiasm for *Pinafore* in the late nineteenth century; see Jones, *Our Musicals, Ourselves* (Lebanon: Brandeis University Press, 2003), pp. 4–11.

157. Theodor Adorno, "Spätstil Beethovens," orig. 1937, in Adorno, *Gesammelte Schriften*, vol.17: *Musikalische Schriften*, ed. Rolf Tiedemann (Frankfurt am Main: Suhrkamp, 1997), pp. 13–17.

158. See the dialectic of consumption, differentiation, and conventionalization in Dick Hebidge, *Subculture* (London: Routledge, 1979), pp. 91–96, 102–3.

159. François-René, vicomte de Chateaubriand, *Le Génie du Christianisme,* orig. 1844, vol. 1 (Paris: Garnier-Flammarion, 1966), p. 309.

160. Even a cursory visit to a *noraebang* should be enough to convince an ordinary skeptic of a truth universally acknowledged: that South Korean popular music is not only diverse but also deeply entrenched in everyday life. In contemporary South Korea, there is a plethora of thriving musical genres, from European classical music to contemporary jazz, from *p'ansori* to punk rock, and however narrowly we define popular music, there is also and inevitably an archaeological accretion of historically popular genres: older (and some younger) South Koreans still listen to trot or *kayo;* others nostalgically hum 1960s light pop, whether South Korean, American, or Japanese. And it's not as if fans of popular music were not passionately engaged with many of the same questions and criteria that preoccupy aficionados of classical music. Authenticity, for example, is a significant issue among listeners to popular music, whether the focus is the nature of a song's lyrics and composition or a song's performance (for instance, as we have seen, lip-synching is widely condemned). Indeed, because many listeners insist that popular music be "real" and "authentic," perceived artificiality can constitute sufficient grounds for the damning dismissal of a song or a performer. See Dieter Helms and Thomas Phleps, eds., *Ware Inszenierungen* (Bielefeld: Transcript Verlag, 2013).

161. Kyō Nobuko, *Uta no okurimono* (Tokyo: Asahi Shinbusha, 2007), p. 9.

162. Im Ch'ŏr-u, *Kŭ sŏm e kago sipta* (Seoul: Sallim, 1991).

163. See Ronald Schleifer, *Modernism and Popular Music* (Cambridge: Cambridge University Press, 2011), pt. 2.

164. Commensurability cannot be presumed, however. It would be a category mistake to judge Girls' Generation's "Mr. Taxi" by the criteria of nineteenth-century European art music, just as Handel's *Giulio Cesare* would suffer violence in being appraised by the standards of K-pop. The litany of complaints is as predictable as it is problematic: for fans of Girls' Generation, Handel's offenses would include his mannered composition and his seemingly endless repetitions of *da capo* arias, whereas

Handel's admirers would take exception to the K-pop group's formulaic instrumentation and repetition of simple refrains. In both cases, appreciating the genre entails
inhabiting its circle of conventions, musical as well as extramusical. To hear
"Mr. Taxi" and *Giulio Cesare* discussed outside the boundaries of popular music and
Baroque opera, respectively, would be like listening to the Tiv respond to *Hamlet*—
possibly interesting in terms of cultural commentary, but certainly unedifying in
terms of aesthetic analysis; see Laura Bohannan, "Shakespeare in the Bush," *Natural
History* 75 (1966), 28–33. And so external critique often ends up neither here nor there,
the salient point being that the critical critic, beyond the proverbial hermeneutic
circle of understanding and empathy, is an idiot. Thus the assertion of aesthetic superiority usually expresses incomprehension and ethnocentrism, or the snobbish will to
superiority: monolingual music theorists or fans may heap scorn, loathing, and revul-
sion on the soundscapes of others, but it is not an edifying spectacle, and it is intel-
lectually disingenuous. Nevertheless, since the potential for incommensurability and
incomprehensibility is symptomatic of all forms, styles, and genres, the fallacy of
misplaced concreteness does rear its ubiquitous and ugly head. In fact, probably no
European classical music fans are equally fond of Baroque and Minimalism, or of
Vivaldi and Nono: as H. C. Robbins Landon writes, "For two hundred years, only
musicologists and historians knew the name of Antonio Vivaldi"; see Landon,
Vivaldi, orig. 1993 (Chicago: University of Chicago Press, 1996), p. 8. And much the
same thing can be said about popular music: as the massive proliferation of genres
suggests, listeners and fans are profoundly differentiated. It is not just that people like
different things; they also often assert the superiority of their favored styles over other
styles. If grumbling about popular music is occasionally heard among classical music
aficionados, it is also true that writings by popular music's fans frequently express the
same harsh denunciations against the wrong *sort* of popular music; for an illustrative
and all too typical example of the "upstart X wrecked my precious Y" genre, see Elijah
Wald, *How the Beatles Destroyed Rock 'n' Roll* (Oxford: Oxford University Press,
2009). Of course the bugbear of relativism bedevils the sort of argument advanced
here. The sociological version stresses the sheer amount of experience and expertise
possessed by sophisticated aesthetes, such as musicologists and music connoisseurs:
call it genius, talent, or merit, but (to put it crudely) people of the better sort have
better taste. This reductionist claim merely restates the reigning hierarchy, transposing superiority of status onto taste; and yet the naturalness and the necessity of these
taste stratifications are vitiated when we encounter distinct modalities of inequality.
For example, most contemporary Americans and South Koreans would rank the
sciences over the classics, just as most musicologists place Bach over the Beatles and
BEAST, but consider Evelyn Waugh's recollection: "In school we demonstrated our
contempt for 'stinks'. . . . Scientists were regarded as a socially inferior race and we
treated our masters in these subjects superciliously"; see Waugh, *A Little Learning,*
orig. 1964 (London: Penguin, 2011), p. 186. Certitude merely cements convention,
reproducing the underlying social order, and thus sociological reality, devoid of principles and criteria, is at the mercy of the vicissitudes of history. The reductio ad absurdum of this line of argumentation is the ne plus ultra of snobbishness.

165. See Alexander Baumgarten, *Texte zur Grundlegung der Äesthetik* (Hamburg: Felix Meiner, 1983), p. 16. The intuitivist critique of the intellectualized and rationalized discourse on beauty, as instantiated by Benedetto Croce's *Estetica come scienze dell'espressione e linguistica generale* (Bari: G. Laterza, 1902), usually and ironically retains the same sort of hierarchy. In Croce's case, the more intellectualist endeavor of literature, or of the visual art of painting, becomes an appropriate object of inquiry, by contrast with the presumably more emotive and nonvisual discipline of music. The great social theorists expounded on aesthetics; with the major exception of Adorno, however, and the minor exception of Weber, they rarely ventured into the realm of music. Here, I am thinking of Marx, Durkheim, Freud, and Simmel, among others. Max Weber's foray into rationalization and music is largely about the piano; see Weber, *Die rationale und soziologischen Grundlagen der Musik* (Munich: Drei Masken Verlag, 1921). It is curious indeed, given the general German cultural proclivity for music, that aesthetic discourse should rarely stray beyond literature and visual art—a striking contrast with an earlier generation of philosopher-scientists, such as Descartes, Gassendi, and Galileo, who wrote on music; see Albert Cohen, *Music in the French Royal Academy of Sciences* (Princeton: Princeton University Press, 1981), pp. 4–6. Although there have been occasional champions of music—Schopenhauer is the most ardent—what was among the highest of the arts in classical Greece and classical China has largely been marginalized or ignored in modern Europe. On the primacy of music in ancient Greece, see M. L. West, *Ancient Greek Music* (Oxford: Clarendon Press, 1992), p. 1, where West goes on to note that "the subject is practically ignored by nearly all who study that culture or teach about it." The invocation here of ancient Greek music, with its indubitable impact on European classical music, is not altogether irrelevant, given the plausibility of the major-third trichord that was disseminated across Asia, and of course on the Korean peninsula as well; see Curt Sachs, *The Rise of Music in the Ancient World* (New York: Norton, 1943), pp. 125–30. To return, however, to modern discussions of aesthetics, the marginalization of music is all the more remarkable in light of the recent spate of books lamenting the "decline" or "eclipse" of the visual and of visual culture; see, for example, Barbara Maria Stafford, *Artful Science* (Cambridge: MIT Press, 1996), whose subtitle includes the phrase "the eclipse of visual education." Few aesthetic theorists, certainly, would argue for music's centrality. Some might be able to say, "I write, therefore I am" or even "I paint, therefore I am," but it would just seem bizarre for an intellectual to declare, "I sing, therefore I am." Some composers do play with the battle between poetry and music (as Strauss does, for example, in his *Capriccio*), but aesthetic discourse and ideology have systematically valorized the more intellectual, the more rational, and the more visual over other faculties and genres, including the aural. Look at any number of general studies of art and aesthetics, creativity and culture, and it is remarkable how frequently music is given short shrift, if it is not neglected altogether. See, inter alia, R. G. Collingwood, *The Principles of Art* (Oxford: Clarendon Press, 1938); the trilogy by Erich Neumann, *Art and the Creative Unconscious,* trans. Ralph Manheim (Princeton: Princeton University Press, 1959); Giorgio Agamben, *L'uomo senza contenuto* (Milan: Rizzoli, 1970); and

Jean-Marie Schaeffer, *L'art de l'âge moderne* (Paris: Gallimard, 1992). Needless to say, music and dance are difficult to write about, but it is still remarkable that so many contemporary intellectuals can discourse knowledgeably or at least knowingly about classical or contemporary art, literature, and film but have almost nothing to say about classical or contemporary music, even though music has often been a central (if unacknowledged) motif for many great novelists; see, for example, Jean-Jacques Nattiez, *Proust musicien* (Paris: Christian Bourgeois, 1984, pp. 35–37). Also symptomatic of this phenomenon is the fact that ekphrasis, with the notable exception of Mussorgsky's *Pictures at an Exhibition* (1874), almost always involves poetry about paintings. Indeed, legions of philosophical heavyweights since Plato (*Phaedrus*) have been endorsing Horace's "ut pictura poesis"; see, in general, Jean H. Hagstrum, *The Sister Arts* (Chicago: University of Chicago Press, 1987), and John Hollander, *The Gazer's Spirit* (Chicago: University of Chicago Press, 1995). It is not surprising, then, that musicologists have privileged the very same criteria that relegate their own art to such a questionable status, nor is it surprising that musicologists ignore (when they don't condemn) music's less intellectualized and less rationalized manifestations, such as popular music.

166. Luciano Berio is surely right to remark that "until Beethoven, any acknowledged musical form was a quotation and a commentary, hence a form of transcription"; see Berio, *Remembering the Future* (Cambridge: Harvard University Press, 2006), p. 34. Indeed, until Beethoven, most musical compositions, which were simultaneously performances, were *pièces d'occasion,* where the second term of that phrase denotes not just "occasional" but also "secondhand." The great nineteenth-century composers—the architects of absolute music—struggled against music's seeming frivolity and ephemerality, seeking to establish music as equal in gravity to philosophy and literature, at once serious and eternal. Mark Evan Bonds has noted "the elevation of instrumental music . . . beyond the sphere of the merely sensuous into the realm of the metaphysical, [which] thereby [made] music equal if not actually superior in power to the arts of literature and painting"; see Bonds, *After Beethoven* (Cambridge: Harvard University Press, 1996), p. 15. As Bonds also argues (pp. 24–27), historical self-consciousness entrenched the imperative of originality and established the projection of one's place in history as a critical criterion. And, not surprisingly, the heirs of the nineteenth-century greats valorize musical innovation as if it were the same sort of endeavor as research in quantum mechanics or synthetic biology, but the ideology of innovation—like its backdrop, the broad belief in progress—stands uneasily with many human endeavors.

167. Gunther Schuller, *Musings* (New York: Oxford University Press, 1986), p. 264.

168. Kenneth Rexroth, *More Classics Revisited,* ed. Bradford Morrow (New York: New Directions, 1989), p. 29.

169. Would that were it so. George Steiner, among others, has repeatedly invoked the Third Reich to challenge the putative association between leading a moral life and having a taste for classical music: "We know now that a man can read Goethe or Rilke in the evening, that he can play Bach and Schubert, and go to his day's work

at Auschwitz in the morning"; see Steiner, *Language and Silence* (New York: Atheneum, 1967), p. 9. And, indeed, the inmates of the death camps appear to have experienced little benefit from the allegedly redemptive power of classical music, finding instead that it was used in the camps as an instrument of discipline and torture; see Szymon Laks, *Mélodies d'Auschwitz* (Paris: Cerf, 1991), p. 131. The principal exceptions to this rule appear to have been the inmates of the model camp at Theresienstadt/Terezín, but their fate gives pause; see Joža Karas, *Music in Terezín* (Hillsdale: Pendragon Press, 2008). It is of course difficult to deny Shirli Gilbert's claim that music did not have a singular and homogeneous impact on the prisoners; see Gilbert, *Music in the Holocaust* (Oxford: Oxford University Press, 2007), p. 17. Incidentally, despite contemporary condemnations of Richard Wagner as an anti-Semite and proto-Nazi, it was Beethoven who was the master musician of the Reich: it is no accident that Beethoven's Seventh Symphony was aired over Nazi radio on Hitler's final birthday, or that the news of his suicide was preceded by the funeral march from the composer's Third (Eroica) Symphony; see David B. Dennis, *Beethoven in Germany* (New Haven: Yale University Press, 1996), p. 74, and, in general, Michael H. Kater, *The Twisted Muse* (Oxford: Oxford University Press, 1997). In any event, the Third Reich certainly struck a terrible blow to facile assumptions about the life-affirming character of European classical music. It is not that classical music's entanglement with a murderous totalitarian regime necessarily condemns classical music, but its deployment in the service of a barbaric politics does tend to erode unreflective belief in beautiful music's edifying powers. At the same time, the "lower" sort of music—decadent music, even—has sometimes been a source of resistance to totalitarian rule. For example, Michael H. Kater's work on jazz in the Third Reich delineates a much more complex picture; see Kater, *Different Drummers* (Oxford: Oxford University Press, 1992). For more on music and resistance, see Ray Pratt, *Rhythm and Resistance* (New York: Praeger, 1990); Ray Sakolsky and Fred Wei-Han Ho, eds., *Sounding Off!* (Brooklyn: Autonomedia, 1995); and Mark LeVine, *Heavy Metal Islam* (New York: Three Rivers Press, 2008). To be sure, chapter 1 of this volume suggests that European classical music has also had its place in resisting unjust political rule, but in this regard colonial Korea seems to have been an extremely rare instance. See, however, the politically progressive role claimed for opera by Arblaster, *Viva la Libertà!* I would hasten to add, though, that this claim is made in connection with a time when opera still functioned as popular music.

170. As we have seen, music in whatever form is now readily reproducible for almost everyone in much of the world, a situation that until recently existed only for the privileged and the wealthy. Some contemporary novelist or filmmaker will surely depict this remarkable situation—the now nearly universal access to and appreciation of music—as Ludwig Tieck, among others, depicted the same situation with respect to the European bourgeoisie; see the last pages of Tieck, "Phantasus," pt. 1, orig. 1812–16, in Tieck, *Schriften*, vol. 6 (Berlin: Deutscher Klassiker Verlag, 1985).

171. According to Charles Rosen, "Understanding music simply means not being irritated or puzzled by it. . . . More positively, taking pleasure in music is in the

most obvious sign of comprehension, the proof that we understand it"; see Rosen, *Frontiers of Meaning,* p. 3.

POSTLUDE

1. John Lie, "Why Didn't 'Gangnam Style' Go Viral in Japan? Gender Divide and Subcultural Heterogeneity in Contemporary Japan," *CrossCurrents* 9 (2013), 44–67.

2. Psy's address at Oxford Union may have been fresh in her memory; see www.youtube.com/watch?v=2f99cTgT5mg.

3. Roslyn Sulcas, "One Parody Away from China's Censors," *New York Times,* 26 November 2012.

4. Among many interesting riffs on the viral video, the one by Eric Spitznagel pitted Tolkien's wizard against Psy and pronounced "Gangnam Style" the winner; see "Gandalf vs. 'Gangnam Style,'" *New York Times Sunday Magazine,* 9 December 2012, p. 17.

5. William Butler Yeats, "The Scholars," orig. 1919, in Yeats, *The Collected Works of W. B. Yeats,* vol. 1, 2nd ed., ed. Richard J. Finneran (New York: Scribner, 1997), p. 141. See Christopher Ricks, *Dylan's Vision of Sin* (Harmondsworth: Penguin, 2003), and Sean Wilentz, *Bob Dylan's America* (New York: Doubleday, 2010). Both books are by intelligent, erudite scholars, and both are very long.

6. T. S. Eliot, *The Use of Poetry and the Use of Criticism* (London: Faber & Faber, 1933), p. 17.

7. So suggests E. M. Cioran: "Tears are music in material form"; see Cioran, "Des larmes et des saints," orig. 1972, trans. Sanda Stolojan, in Cioran, *Oeuvres* (Paris: Gallimard, 1995), p. 290.

8. Satō Gō, *Ue o muite arukō* (Tokyo: Iwanami Shoten, 2011), pp. 12–13, 278–84.

9. I hasten to add that pop-music memory lives on. For example, the news of Sakamoto's death made the headlines of a Norwegian newspaper; see Kashiwagi Yukiko, *Ue o muite arukō* (Tokyo: Fuji Terebi Shuppan), 1986, p. 11.

10. Sakamoto Kyū, *"Ue o muite arukō"* (Tokyo: Nihon Tosho Sentā, 2001), pp. 23–29. On Sakamoto's strange articulation, see the impressions of the song's composer in Ei Rokusuke, *Roku-hachi-kyū no kyū* (Tokyo: Chūō Kōronsha, 1986), pp. 51, 191–93.

11. See Satō, *Ue o muite arukō,* pp. 182–83. The song's composer, Nakamura Hachidai, had a remarkably cosmopolitan course of musical training. After studying classical music with a German instructor in colonial Qingdao, he made the transition to jazz in the post–World War II period and then, after the decline of jazz (due to the dwindling population of US GIs in Japan), he switched to composing popular songs and was influenced by a spell in New York, where he was exposed to early rock 'n' roll. See Satō, *Ue o muite arukō,* pp. 23–33, 68–69, 78–81, 112–18.

12. See chapter 1, n. 154 in this book. A case in point is "The Twist," the wildly popular 1960 hit by Chubby Checker. Moreover, in the Hollywood movie music of the first half of the twentieth century, the pentatonic scale is frequently used when a scene features the native, the primitive, or the exotic.

13. The song appealed mainly to teenagers, who found the singer and the song "cute," exotic, and mysterious, and the tune itself ultimately hummable and likable. See Sakamoto, *"Ue o muite arukō,"* pp. 58–64, and Satō, *Ue o muite arukō,* pp. 135–41.

14. Satō, *Ue o muite arukō,* pp. 10–11.

15. Dave Dexter Jr., *Playback* (New York: Billboard Publications, 1976), pp. 168–69. See also the 1998 Japanese documentary on Sakamoto's appearance on *The Steve Allen Show,* available at www.youtube.com/watch?v=iW3efimtboo.

16. Ei, *Roku-hachi-kyū no kyū,* p. 194.

17. Dexter, *Playback,* p. 169.

18. Aristotle, "Magna Moralia," in Aristotle, *The Complete Works of Aristotle,* ed. Jonathan Barnes (Princeton: Princeton University Press, 1984), pp. 1868–1921, esp. p. 1910. For an idiosyncratic account of fame, see Leo Braudy, *The Frenzy of Renown* (New York: Oxford University Press, 1986).

19. I have never consulted Sakamoto's birth certificate, and so I cannot be sure, but the rumor of his Korean ancestry has been rife since he shot to fame in the early 1960s. See http://zainichi.sblo.jp/, and Ei, *Roku-hachi-kyū no kyū,* p. 42. See, in general, John Lie, *Zainichi (Koreans in Japan)* (Berkeley: University of California Press, 2008).

CODA

1. Daniel Barenboim, *Music Quickens Time* (London: Verso, 2008), p. 3.

2. On the paradox—the theoretical impossibility or implausibility of translation and the practical possibility of translation—see, for instance, the discussions in Barbara Cassin, ed., *Vocabulaire européen des philosophies* (Paris: Seuil, 2004).

GLOSSARY OF KOREAN TERMS

AAK Chinese-inflected ritual music

CHAEBŎL big business

CHANGDAN traditional Korean rhythm

CH'ANGGA choral song

CH'ANGGŬK choral theater

CHESA ancestor worship

CHIBANG SIN MINYO rural new folk song

CHIMSŬNG beast

CHO (musical) mode

CHŎNGAK orthodox music

CHŎNGGANBO musical notation

CH'ŎNGNYŎN youth

CHŎNMIN outcast

CHUNBISAENG preparatory student

HAEBANG KAYO liberation song

HAGWŎN cram school

HAN ressentiment

HANBOK Korean clothing

HAN'GŬL Korean script

HANJI Korean paper

HANOK Korean traditional roof

HYANGAK native court music

ICH'A second stage

KAGOK lieder/song

KAGYO meritocratic examination system

KASA vocal music genre

KAYAGŬM zitherlike instrument

KIJICH'ON camp village

KISAENG courtesan

KOHYANG hometown

KŎMUN'GO zitherlike instrument

KŎNJŎN KAYO "healthy" popular music

KUGAK national music

KUKSU national essence

KWANGDAE itinerant entertainer

KYŎNG ŬMAK light music

MAKKAN KAYO entr'acte music

MINJUNG the people

MINJUNG KAYO the people's song

MINSOK ŬMAK the people's music

MINYO folk tune

MODŎN modern

NAMSADANG Korean circus

NONGAK farmers' music

NORAEBANG karaoke establishment

NORAE UNDONG song movement

ŎTCHŎNJI somehow

PAEKCHŎNG outcast

P'ANSORI traditional genre of narrative music

PPALLI fast

PPONG, PPONGTCHAK two-beat rhythm associated with trot

P'UNGMUL drumming music

RAMYŎN Korean ramen

ROKKU PPONG rock-infused trot (see *t'ŭrot'ŭ ko-ko*)

SADAEJUŬI ideology of "serving the greater power"

SADANG all-female itinerant troupe

SAESUGA bars and teahouses

SAMUL NORI stylized genre of *nongak*

SANGMIN ordinary people

SANJO scattered melody

TABANG tearoom

TAEJUNG ŬMAK mass music

TANGAK Chinese court music

T'ONG KIT'A barrel guitar; a moniker for folk music

TONGYO children's song

TTANTTARA jangling, or loud noise

T'ŬROT'Ŭ "trot"

T'ŬROT'Ŭ KO-KO "trot go-go" (see *rokku ppong*)

ŬMAK music

UNDONGGA movement music

URI our

WAESAEK Japanese style

YANGBAN traditional elite

YANGAK Western music

YANGMIN good or ordinary people

YŎNSUSAENG practicing student

YUHAENGGA popular song

Chu Hyŏn-mi (Joo Hyun-mi), 52, 211n93
chunbisaeng (preparatory students), 124
Chun Doo-h Hwan regime, 11, 51, 89
classical music. *See* European classical music
Clazziquai Project, 99
clothing: body exposure and, 133–134; color of, 66, 195n1, 202n78; in contemporary South Korea, 87–88; of Korean and Japanese singers, 188n164; 1970s performers and, 45–46; traditional culture and, 35, 66, 87, 197n17; Western, and colonial era, 25. *See also* fashion; *hanbok*
coffee, 46, 191n207
colonial period, 18–29, 71–73
commercialization of music: rise of popular music and, 15–18; *yuhaengga* and, 21–22. *See also* culture industry; export of Korean music; popular music; technological progress
communal singing. *See* choral songs; *noraebang*
communism, 73. *See also* anticommunist nationalism
Confucian-Chinese tradition, 210n86; capitalist industrialization and, 80, 85–86; careers in K-pop and, 131, 132; contemporary South Korea and, 67–70, 93, 131; Japanese modernity and, 72–73; Korean War and, 77–78
Confucius (Kongzi), 168n8
conscription, universal male, 77, 123, 208n65
consumption of popular music, 15–16, 55, 108, 135. *See also* export of Korean music; technological progress; young people
contemporary South Korea: absence of heroes in, 88–90; anti-Japanese sentiment in, 136–137; Confucian culture and, 67–70, 93, 131; genre diversity in, 217n160; *kugak* and, 11–12; nationalism in, 66, 70, 90–95; status differences in, 85–86. *See also* cultural amnesia
"Cool Japan," 139
copycat videos, 8, 105
copyright protection, 116, 134
Corea Record, 181n102
Counter-Korean Wave (Ken-Kanryū), 135
"cram schools." See *hagwŏn*

Croce, Benedetto, 219n165
cultural amnesia, 91–94; colonial period and, 71–73; Korean War and, 76–78; Park regime and, 81–82; youth culture and, 17
culture industry: cultural amnesia and, 93–95; K-pop as, 140, 142, 145, 155; long history of, 21, 22, 214n139; national boundaries and, 111–114; popular music and, 22, 118, 148–149, 152, 155, 161, 215n144. *See also* commercialization of music; export of Korean music; film industry

dance: fusion of music with, 56–57; moves in K-pop and, 105–106, 122, 145; Sŏ T'aeji and, 62; signature moves in, 105–106, 122, 145. *See also* break dancing; "point dance"
democratization, 59–61. *See also* capitalist industrialization; post-Liberation period
digitalized music. *See* music reproduction technology
"diploma disease," 68, 131–132
Diski, Jenny, 192n212
domestic market: colonial period and, 23–24; export and, 114; in Japan, 137; K-pop conquest of, 108–109
DR Music label, 101

Eak Tai Ahn. *See* Ik-t'ae
echt (precise and authentic). *See* authenticity
Eckardt, Andreas, 167n5
Eckert, Franz, 13, 177n75
economic growth: focus on, in Park regime, 79–81, 114–115; in Japan, 139; in 1970s South Korea, 42–43; worker exploitation and, 84–85. *See also* capitalist industrialization; export of Korean music; IMF crisis
Ed Sullivan Show, 30
education in South Korea: careers in K-pop and, 131–132; Chosŏn era and, 68; in colonial period, 18; Japanese influence on, 13–14, 72, 196n11; shift to Korean script and, 81–82. *See also* examination system; *hagwŏn;* music education

emotion, 9, 37–38, 152. See also *enka; p'ansori;* trot music

enka (Japanese genre): characteristics of, 37, 40, 189n174; ethnic Korean singers and, 41, 113; Park and, 188n173; trot and, 182n115

ensemble effects, 104–105, 122, 147–148. See also *ch'angga*

entrepreneurs, 22, 117–119, 129. *See also* K-pop agencies

ethnic Koreans, 30; in colonial period, 22, 28, 200n46; in Japan, 41–42, 101, 113, 135, 162, 178n85, 181n106; Korean culture and, 72–73; transnational movements of, 19, 23, 28, 52; trot and, 37, 135; unity of, 81

Eto Kunieda, 189n186

Europe, as market, 136

European classical music: as category, 15; commensurability and, 10–12, 217n164; decline of, 167n4; ethnic Koreans and, 37, 152–153; introduction into Korea, 12–14; listening context for, 15–16; as popular music, 151, 216n154; popular music critiques and, 217n164; in post-Liberation Korea, 30–31; virtue and, 154, 220n169

Eurovision, 112–113

"Every Little Step" (Bobby Brown), 194n248

examination system: Chosŏn period and, 68, 196n9; K-pop and, 125, 131–132; lifestyle and, 70, 84, 132

EXO, 123. *See also* education; hagwŏn

export of Korean music: entrepreneurs and, 28, 117–120; as foundational myth, 114–115; idol groups and, 63–64; as industrial imperative, 109–120; motivations for, 110–111, 114–115. *See also* culture industry; capitalist industrialization

fame, explanation of, 161–162

Fankī (Funky) Sueyoshi, 185n136

fans: J-pop acts and, 102; K-pop and, 124, 146–147. *See also* audience

Far East Movement (FM), 160

fashion, 133–134, 175n57. *See also* clothing

film industry, 207n57, 209n80. *See also* Hollywood

Fin.K.L (P'ingk'ŭl), 63, 107

Finnegan, Ruth H., 216n154

Fly to the Sky (duo), 121

FM. *See* Far East Movement

folk music: authenticity and, 47–48, 149–150; in colonial period, 18–19; compared with popular music, 152; European instruments and, 19, 27, 150; preservation of, 19. *See also* minsok ŭmak; people's music

foodways, 91–92

formulaic, as term, 145. *See also* K-pop formula

French electronic dance music, 105

Frith, Simon, 214n134

Fujiyama Ichirō, 181n103

"Fukuchi manri" (movie theme), 28

funerary color, 66, 195n1

"Fuzankō e kaere" (Return to Pusan Harbor), 41

f(x) (group), 147

"Gangnam Style" (Psy video), 3, 8, 83, 136, 156–158, 210n81. *See also* Psy

Gay Pop, 208n64

"Gee" (Girls' Generation hit), 105

Geissmar, Berta, 216n154

gender archetypes, 106

gender dimorphism, 98, 106

"Genie" (Girls' Generation hit), 147

genre diversity: in colonial period, 22–23, 27; compared with Japan, 137–138; contemporary period and, 217n160; in post-Liberation period, 33–34, 43–50; shift toward K-pop and, 99, 109; in traditional music, 11–12. See also *ch'angga;* children's music; *kagok; p'ansori; yuhaengga*

Geomungo Factory, 167n4

girl groups, 63, 123. *See also* Girls' Generation; KARA; Wonder Girls

Girls' Generation (Sonyŏ Sidae, SNSD; Shōjo Jidai), 2, 98, 105, 147, 217n164; Japanese market and, 107–108; K-pop formula and, 122–123

lyrics: Korean, with American music, 43–44; Korean, with Korean music, 24; in K-pop, 106, 145, 146–147; languages in K-pop and, 122–123; post-war trot and, 37–38. *See also* hook, in K-pop; refrain, in K-pop

"Madonna of South Korea." *See* Kim Wan-sŏn

makkan kayo (entr'acte music), 182n113

marketing of popular music: Chinese market and, 100; globalization and, 100–101, 135–136; J-pop and, 138–139; K-pop and, 123, 127–130; localization strategy and, 102. *See also* export of Korean music

Marsh, Dave, 174n48

masculine aesthetic, 59, 106–107, 123, 205n23, 210n84. *See also* bodily aesthetic

mass music. *See* popular music; *taejung ŭmak*

MBC (television station), 53

meaning in music, 152, 214n137

melismatic singing, 40; elite *vs.* people's music and, 10; Japanese music and, 138, 161, 189n175; in K-pop, 161; trot and, 27, 37, 39–40, 44. *See also* emotion; *p'ansori*

meritocracy, 86, 196n9. *See also* examination system

"Michael Jackson of South Korea." *See* Pak Chin-yŏng

middle-aged audience, 135; K-pop and, 2, 57, 107, 108

Midorikawa Ako, 42

military discipline, 79. *See also* conscription, universal male; examination system; US occupation

military musicians, 187n157

minjung kayo (people's song), 53

minsok ŭmak. demise of, 11, 172n28; elite music and, 10; in post-Liberation period, 33–34. *See also* nongak; people's music

minyo (folk tunes), 9, 27, 183n124. *See also* folk music

Mita Munesuke, 183n119

Miyako Harumi, 41, 188n173, 189n175

Miyashiro Michio, 173n36

Mnet chart, 99, 100

modes *(cho)*: and pentatonic scale, 10–11

"Mokp'o i nunmul" (Tears of Mokp'o), 24–25, 25–26, 29, 152, 188n165, 189n177

moral psychology, 154

Mowry, Eli M., 177n76

Mozart, Wolfgang Amadeus, 15, 174n44

MTV, 56, 120, 140

mūdo kayō ("mood songs"), 37, 42

"Mulbanga tonŭn naeryŏk" (The roundabout history of the waterwheel), 35

Murakami Chijun, 198n29

musical instruments: American music and, 31; competence on, 175n52; Korean folk songs and, 19, 27, 150; traditional, 9, 12, 61

musical legitimacy, 148–155

musical notation *(chŏngganbo)*, 10

musical performance: dance in, 104, 105–106, 145; for US military, 31–32

musical scales, 20, 170n21, 182n118. *See also* pentatonic scale

musical taste, 12, 36, 40, 44, 49, 153, 155; class and, 30, 218n164; in Japan and South Korea, 113, 135, 194n242; of post-colonial leaders, 188n173; in United States and South Korea, 60, 133, 194n242; youth and, 98

musical theater, 14, 217n156

music education: appeal of popular music and, 153–154; in Japan and South Korea, 113; in post-Liberation Korea, 30–31

music industry. *See* culture industry; export of Korean music; K-pop agencies

music reproduction technology: digitized music and, 119, 128–129, 134; K-pop marketing and, 128–129. *See also* record companies

music venues, 15–18, 43, 54–55

music videos, 3, 5, 8, 54, 55, 56, 63, 83, 98, 99, 100, 101, 103, 105, 106, 107, 119, 124, 133, 147, 156, 157, 159, 162, 172n29, 189n175, 193n236; "Candy" by H. O. T. and, 63, 64; critiques of, 144; dance routines in, 104. *See also individual video titles*

"My Darling Clementine," 19

people's music *(minsok minjung ǔmak)*: demise of, 11, 172n28; elite music and, 10; 1980s and, 53–54, 59; in post-Liberation period, 33–34. *See also* folk music; *kugak; minsok ǔmak*

P'ingk'ǔl. *See* Fin.K.L

piracy, 61, 100, 116, 121, 208n61

Pitsok ǔi yǒin (The Woman in the Rain) (Sin album), 45

plastic surgery, 70, 132–133, 210n85, 211n90

"point dance," 145, 214n133. *See also* dance

political music *(undongga)*, 20, 26, 34. *See also* folk music; *kokumin kayō;* social critique

"Pongsǒnhwa" (Impatiens), 20

popularity, critical devaluation of, 15, 151–155

popular music: aesthetic critique of, 148–155, 217n164, 219n165; elite preferences and, 178n84; emergence of, 174n49; legitimacy of, 148–155; listening context for, 15–16; production processes in, 117–119; rationalization of, 216n152; theater and, 14, 179n87, 182n113; youth and, 216n153. *See also* American popular music; Korean popular music

post-Liberation period: American influence and, 29–36, 46, 73–76, 112; forms of popular music in, 43–50; trot dominance and, 35, 36–42

Pound, Ezra, 214n132

ppalli, ppalli (fast, fast), 79

Ppippi Band, 61–62

ppongtchak (two-beat rhythm), 25, 43

Presley, Elvis, 161

production processes in K-pop, 117–119, 124

professionalism, and K-pop, 98, 118, 123–124, 125, 127, 142

"project group" members, 124–125

protectionism, 115, 134

Psy (performer), 3, 96, 136, 156–158, 161. *See also* "Gangnam Style"

pudae chigye (troop stew), 186n151

punk rock, 97, 99, 217n160

radio, 175n54, 192n213; American music and, 31–32, 190n192

Rain (Pi / Bigroup), 107

R & B: Sǒ T'aeji and, 11, 54, 59, 62, 96, 97, 98, 99, 108, 137, 141, 208n59

record companies: development of, 33; digitalized music and, 116; early records and, 22, 23, 180n96; sales in Korea and, 27, 64, 97. *See also* music reproduction technology; technological progress

"red-white singing contest" *(Kōhaku Utagassen),* 41

refrain, in K-pop, 98, 105–106, 122, 139, 145, 156–157

Rhee Syngman (Yi Sǔng-man) regime, 34–35, 39, 73–76, 89, 189n174

rhythm: backbeat and, 205n19; *changdan* (long-short) beats and, 11, 29, 170n22; Japanese music and, 182n116; *kugak* and, 11, 170n22; *ppongtchak* (two-beat rhythm) and, 25, 43; shift to K-pop and, 104–105, 161

Ri Arisu. *See* Yi Aerisu

ritual music, 168n7

rock music, 43, 45, 46–47, 50, 54, 191n208, 191n212

Romantic ideology of art: authenticity and, 150; critique of, 143–144; logic of K-pop and, 140–143

romantic love *(sarang):* as American theme, 109; Confucianism and, 70; as K-pop theme, 70, 146; marriage traditions and, 87; *yuhaengga* and, 183n119

Rosen, Charles, 214n137

Ross, Alex, 214n139

Rosselli, John, 176n66

Rousseau, Jean-Jacques, 214n137

rural exodus, 19, 50, 84, 85

ryūkōka, 21, 23, 29, 71. See also *yuhaengga*

sadaejuǔi (tribute system), 74

"Saemaǔl ǔi norae" (The song of the new village), 49

Saijō Yaso, 180n100, 180n101

Sakamoto Kyū, 160–162, 223n19

Sakurai Testuo, 170n22

samul nori (genre of Korean musical *nongakgenre*), 11

"Saranghae kǔrigo kiǒkhae" (Fall in love, then remember), 97

"Sa ǔi ch'anmi" (Hymn to death), 24

scandals, 49, 54. *See also* suicide
Schnabel, Artur, 170n19
Schoenberg, Arnold, 173n44
scholarly critique: authenticity of K-pop and, 150–153
Schuller, Gunther, 153–154
script: for J-pop songs, 137; Korean, 81–82, 90, 93. *See also* orthography
SE7EN, 58
Sechs Kies (Cheksŭ K'isŭ), 63
Seog Woo Sohn. *See* Son Sŏk-u
Seoul: in colonial period, 28; contemporary lifestyle in, 83–84; 1980s soundscape in, 54–55; 1990s music scene in, 62; in post-Liberation era, 31, 35, 36; sense of homeland and, 77
Seoul Olympics in 1988, 57, 83, 86
Seoul Spring of 1980, 50–51
seriousness, cult of, 55–56
S.E.S., 63, 100, 121
Sessions, Roger, 175n51
sex appeal: K-pop stars and, 106–107, 108, 124
sex work, 22, 85, 169n13, 169n14, 209n73
Sshamanismt music, 10, 67, 68, 70, 78, 169n14, 169n15; and K-pop acts, 205n21
Sharp, Cecil J., 215n146
Shin, Jacky. *See* Sin Chung-hyŏn
shingeki ("new theater"), 21, 179n87
SHINHWA, 102, 103–104, 121, 141, 210n81
shin min'yō, 183n119
Shōjo Jidai. *See* Girls' Generation
Sho Sho Sho (music show), 31, 42
signature dance moves, 105–106, 122, 145
silent movies, 175n56
Sim Su-bong, 188n173, 193n233
sincerity. *See* authenticity; seriousness, cult of
Sin Ch'ae-ho, 168n11
Sin Chung-hyŏn (Jacky Shin), 45, 46, 47
Singerman, Howard, 213n126
singing style: in 1980s Korea, 52; trot and, 37, 40, 44
single-sex groups, 106, 205n22
sin kayo (new popular songs), 21, 27. See also *yuhaengga*

sin minyo (new folk songs), 23, 27; in post-Liberation periods, 33–34, 40, 43–44
sister acts, 32
Skull (reggae singer), 109
SM Entertainment: evolution of, 141–142; export idol groups and, 99–100, 101–102; recruitment at, 124–125; strategic vision of, 126; trajectory of, 120–121. *See also* Lee Soo-man
SNSD (Sonyŏ Sidae). *See* Girls' Generation
Sobangch'a (band), 57, 63, 99, 121, 210n84
Sŏ Chae-p'il (Philip Jaisohn), 72
social critique, 146. *See also* political music
social media. *See* Internet-based technologies
socioeconomic conditions: export imperative and, 114–117; Sŏ T'aeji revolution and, 59–61; success of K-pop and, 134–136; success of trot and, 42. *See also* capitalist industrialization; economic growth; urbanization
soft-rock groups, 54, 61
SOLID, 62
song length, 174n48
sonic driving, 205n21
Son Mog-in, 41–42, 188n165. *See also* "Mokp'o ŭi nunmul"
Son Sŏk-u (Seog Woo Sohn, Sung Woo Sohn), 35–36
Sonyŏ Sidae (SNSD). *See* Girls' Generation
Sŏp'yŏnje (film), 168n12, 188n166
Soribada (website), 129
sorip'an ("sound discs"), 22
"Sorry, Sorry" (hit), 105–106
Sŏ T'ae-ji wa Aidŭl, 97; emergence of K-pop and, 96, 98–99, 140; revolution caused by, 57–65, 194n240; young people and, 86–87, 98
South Korea: absence of heroes in, 88–90; anti-Japanese sentiment in, 136–137; Confucian culture and, 67–70, 93, 131; genre diversity in, 217n160; *kugak* and, 11–12; nationalism in, 66, 70, 90–95; status differences in, 85–86. *See also* cultural amnesia
Southeast Asian market, 135–136

and, 49–50. *See also* bodily aesthetic;
fashion; sex appeal

waesaek (Japanese style), 39–40, 189n174
Waugh, Evelyn, 218n164
Weber, Max, 216n152, 219n165
West, M. L., 219n165
Western soundscape: colonial-era Korea
and, 19–23, 24–25, 71; post-Liberation
Korea and, 30–33; as reference point,
111–112, 135
Whannel, Paddy, 216n153
Winter Sonata (Korean soap opera), 135
Wolgan Chosŏn (journal), 90
Wonder Girls, 105–106, 107–108, 121, 142,
146

"Xcstasy" (Baby V.O.X.), 101
Xiào jīng (The book of filial piety), 197n17,
210n86

yakuza (ethnic Japanese gangsters), 22
yangak ("Western music"), 11
yangban (landlord class): in Chosŏn Korea,
67–68; curriculum; land reform and,
77–78, 85–86; music and, 9, 18, 32,
188n170; Park and, 79; Rhee regime
and, 74, 75, 76
Yang Hyŏn-sŏk, 208n59
Yang Su-jŏng, 199n35
Yeats, William Butler, 158
Yi Aerisu (Alice Lee, Yi Po-jŏn, Ri Arisu),
24, 182n112
Yi Ch'ŏl, 28, 181n102
Yi Hae-yŏn, 34
Yi Hwa-ja, 27
Yi Hyo-ri, 106–107
"Yi Hyo-ri Syndrome," 107
Yi In-gwŏn, 34
Yi Kwang-su, 71–72, 73, 89, 198n26
Yi Kyŏng-suk, 23
Yi Mi-ja, 38, 39–40

Yi Mun-se, 52
Yi Nan-yŏng, 24–26, 29–30, 40, 152,
188n165, 189n177
Yi Nŭng-hwa, 169n14
Yi Po-jŏn. *See* Yi Aerisu
Yi Sang-ŭn (Lee Tzsche), 61, 195n251
Yi Sŏng-ae, 41
Yi Sŏn-hŭi, 53
Yi Su-man. *See* Lee Soo-man
Yi Sŭng-man. *See* Rhee Syngman regime
Yi Tongbaek, 22
Yi Yŏng-mi, 177n71
"Yŏllaksŏn ŭn ttŏnaganda" (The ferry is
leaving), 26
yonanuki, as term, 182n118
yŏnsusaeng (practicing students), 124–125
Yoo, Steve. *See* Yu Sŭng-jun
young people: careers in K-pop and, 127–
130; as category, 176n59; discretionary
income and, 16–17, 55, 60; growth of
market and, 108; musical preferences
and, 16–17; music appreciation among,
155; in 1960s South Korea and, 47, 48
YouTube, 5, 108, 119, 128
yuhaengga (genre): birth of, 178n86; broad
appeal of, 23–24, 179n91; in colonial era,
23–29, 71, 184n136; in post-Liberation
era, 34, 52; trot music and, 25, 37, 38
Yuki Saori, 190n199
yuk-sam ("6–3") generation, 192n214
Yun Kŭk-yong, 21
Yun Pok-hŭi (Yoon Bok Hee), 44–45,
87–88, 191n203
Yun Sim-dŏk, 24
Yu Sŭng-jun (Yoo Seungjun, Steve Loo),
60, 61, 208n65
Yu Yŏng-jin (Yoo Young-jin), 147
Yun, Isang, 61, 193n227

Zainichi singers, 41, 102, 162. *See also*
ethnic Koreans
Zelter, Karl Friedrich, 213n131

CPSIA information can be obtained at www.ICGtesting.com
Printed in the USA
LVOW11s0714081215

465744LV00006B/22/P